The Atlas of American Society

THE ATLAS OF AMERICAN SOCIETY

Alice C. Andrews and James W. Fonseca

Cartography and Graphic Design by Daniel F. Van Dorn

 New York University Press • New York by London

NEW YORK UNIVERSITY PRESS
New York and London

©1995 by New York University

Library of Congress Cataloging-in-Publication Data
Andrews, Alice C.
The atlas of American society / Alice C. Andrews and James W.
Fonseca ; cartography and graphic design by Daniel F. Van Dorn.
p. cm.
Includes bibliographical references and index.
ISBN 0-8147-2626-7 (acid-free paper)
1. United States—Social conditions—1980—Statistics.
2. United States—Population—Statistics.   I. Fonseca, James W.
II. Title.
HN60.A5   1995
301'.0973'021—dc20   95-5648
                    CIP

New York University Press books are printed on acid-free paper, and their binding materials are
chosen for strength and durability.

Manufactured in the United States of America

10 9 8 7 6 5 4 3 2 1

Contents

Acknowledgments

We are grateful to Daniel Van Dorn, who compiled this volume and made all the maps and graphics using principally Atlas*GIS and Harvard Graphics computer packages. We would also like to thank Karen Pirhalla who typed the text and Heather Beach who assisted us with bibliographic work and the compilation of the index. We are also grateful to a number of others who assisted us in data collection and with comments and suggestions. These individuals include Ramala Basu of the U.S. Census Bureau; Saul Cohen, Hunter College; Marvin Gordon of George Washington University; Vance Grant of the National Center for Education Research; Barry A. Kosmin of the National Survey of Religious Identification; James Rettig, College of William and Mary; and Joseph Wood and Jeremy Crampton of George Mason University. We also thank our editor, Niko Pfund of New York University Press, for his comments and encouragement. Many other individuals at government statistical agencies assisted us in tracking down their data. The Population Reference Bureau was very helpful in securing data on women and children, and we used many of their publications as background material.

Finally, we are also grateful to Wallace Andrews and Elaine Fonseca, geographer and educator, respectively, for their many helpful comments.

The Atlas of American Society

Introduction

In presenting the many maps that show how various aspects of American society vary from state to state, we have at least three goals. The first is simply that presenting these data in map form has a value; people may see at a glance where their state stands relative to its neighbors and to its region. While the maps are of primary interest, the text that accompanies each map gives substantive information about the topic and many maps are also accompanied by graphs or tables. In many cases we have tried to add a temporal dimension through the use of graphs that show how the particular indicator has changed over the years.

A second goal is to cull from these many indicators a reasonable sample of reliable and important ones and put them together into a composite index by which the states may be ranked and mapped in terms of overall social well-being. Many such indices exist, but we believe that compiling composite indices of social well-being continues to be a fruitful exercise. Certainly it continues to be a popular research topic, and one that is used in public policy advocacy. Two of the maps in this atlas are themselves based on composite indices: the overall health index of states produced by Northwestern Mutual Life, and the Kids Count index produced by the Annie E. Casey Foundation.

A third goal, very important to us as geographers, is to contribute to the continual examination of regional patterns in the United States. The maps in the atlas should be useful in examining the persistence of traditional cultural regions or the emergence of new ones. The United States is very large and very diverse in its physical geography and resource endowment, yet it is closely knit through economic ties, rapid transportation, and instantaneous communication. When these ties are combined with the trademark mobility of the American people, a logical assumption might be that the old regional identities must weaken in the face of these forces for homogeneity. Many researchers, however, have demonstrated that this is not the case. The research most related to this atlas is the recent endeavor by geographer Richard L. Morrill to demonstrate the persistence of *demographic* regions. Morrill concluded that the country could be divided into distinctive demographic regions using such variables as age structure/mortality; fertility/abortion, and lifestyle. He concluded that the "regional convergence that might be expected on the basis of the gradual convergence of income, education and urbanization levels does not appear to have occurred yet" (Morrill, 1990, p. 52).

DATA RESOURCES

A large number of public and private organizations compile and distribute data relating to American society. The primary organization, of course, is the U.S. Census Bureau on which we relied for data for a number of maps, although where reliable data more recent than 1990 were available, we used those sources. To ensure reliability of data and standardized definitions and categories of data, in many sections we relied primarily on a single source. The National Center for Education Statistics provided data for most of the maps in the two sections related to education. Data from the Centers for Disease Control and Prevention in Atlanta and the National Center for Health Statistics in Bethesda, Maryland, were used for many of the maps in the sections related to health, disease, medical care and lifestyle risks. Many other organizations also granted us permission to use their data: Alan Guttmacher Institute, American Association of Retired Persons, American Correctional Association, American Medical Association, Congressional Quarterly, Glenmary Research Center, Group Health Association of America, Inc., HCIA, Inc., National Survey of Religious Identification, Northwestern National Life Insurance Company, Population Reference Bureau, Inc., Tufts University Center on Hunger, Poverty and Nutrition Policy, *USA TODAY* and Western Interstate Commission for Higher Education. Abbreviated citations of sources are given on the maps and on the graphics and tables; full citations are found on the tables in the Appendix and in the list of sources at the end of the volume.

The reader should be aware that most maps show data for a single year; a few maps show averages over a longer period or give projections into the future. In many cases we have tried to supplement these one-year "snapshots" of data with historical trends shown on tables and line graphs.

MAPPING OF DATA

The data are displayed on maps designed in Atlas*GIS computer mapping package. Harvard Graphics was used for graphs and charts. Aldus PageMaker was used as the desktop publisher. Aldus FreeHand was used to design some maps and graphics including the cartogram. Lotus 123 was used for data compilation. The text was entered in WordPerfect.

The majority of the maps show quantities and ratios in choropleth patterns. We have tried to keep these maps clear and simple by dividing the data into three categories in most cases, thus giving high, medium and low ranges. We chose intervals that emphasize regional differences and, in many cases, intervals that place roughly equal numbers of states in each category. A map identifying the states is included at the end of this Introduction.

The maps portray the fifty states. Alaska and Hawaii are shown, but not in their real locations or in correct scale. The District of Columbia is not shown on the maps but is cited in the text where warranted, and data for it are included in the Appendix.

CHAPTER ORGANIZATION

1. City and Countryside

Five maps depicting different aspects of population distribution in America are presented. They provide background for the many other maps that portray various characteristics of the population. The first map is a cartogram on which the states are drawn in proportion to the size

2

of their populations. This is followed by a map that shows metropolitan statistical areas, where four-fifths of the American population live. Other maps show how the proportion of metropolitan population and the proportion of rural population vary from state to state. A final map by region draws attention to the division of the rural population into farm and non-farm.

2. Demographics

In this section on demographics, choropleth maps present some basic vital statistics—rates of birth, death, infant mortality, marriage, and divorce. One of the most significant population characteristics, the sex ratio (number of men per 100 women) is also mapped. Another basic characteristic, age, is not mapped because a map of young population (percent under 18) appears as Map 13.1, and a map showing the elderly (percent over 65) appears as Map 14.1. These demographic rates and characteristics are useful in understanding other maps.

3. Population Migration, Mobility and Change

American society is not only known worldwide for change and mobility, but it prides itself on these characteristics. This section will examine population change over recent years and examine how domestic and international movements contribute to this change. Within the United States the focus is on in-migration and out-migration among states. From abroad, the foreign-born population and their destinations are examined as well as in what states certain groups of new arrivals become U.S. citizens.

4. Poverty versus Affluence

A number of indicators are examined for a glimpse of America's economic engine. Household income and unemployment are two standard indicators of how well states and their respective regions are faring in providing a living for their inhabitants. An examination of life insurance shows how well individuals are insuring the continuance of that way of life through life insurance. As the importance of the role of the federal government in economic activity grows, the net flow of federal funds per capita gives us important indicators of the distribution and redistribution of wealth in American society. For those who are not faring as well, the proportion of Americans below the poverty line, and recent change for better or for worse in that indicator of poverty, provides a sketch of the need for an economic "safety net." A calculation of major types of welfare benefits examines the strength of that safety net for many Americans who are not making it on their own.

5. Racial-Ethnic Diversity

The racial and ethnic diversity of the population is related to many other variables; therefore the distribution of the major minority groups forms a pattern that underlies many of the maps. The first map presented is a map of racial-ethnic diversity based on data originally published in *USA TODAY* and used with permission. Other maps show the proportion in the population of each state of the groups used by the U.S. Census Bureau in its categorization of the population

3

"by race and Hispanic origin." Maps are presented for African Americans, Asians and Pacific Islanders, Native Americans, and Hispanics (the last being a linguistic, not a racial group).

6. Health and Disease

To examine overall patterns of health and disease, an introductory map compiled by Northwestern National Life Insurance shows the distribution of a number of diseases and measures of health as well as some key socioeconomic factors. The three major diseases responsible for most deaths among Americans are then examined: cardiovascular disease, cancer and stroke. Two sex-specific forms of cancer, breast cancer and prostate cancer, are looked at in more detail. Of all the additional diseases that could be examined, we choose to focus on tuberculosis and AIDS because of the importance of these diseases to society and because (unlike the three major diseases listed above) of their spread by contagion, giving a particularly geographical dimension to their distribution. Suicide is also examined and shown to have a relatively distinct regional pattern.

7. Medical Care and Costs

In a time of great national debate over the adequacy and cost of the American health care system, we have tried to include indicators that will throw light on different aspects of these issues. A commonly used indicator is the ratio of physicians to population, and such a map is included. It is followed by a map on Health Maintenance Organizations (HMOs), which have become very important on the health care scene. Two aspects of access to health care are then mapped: persons not covered by health insurance and the proportion of the population underserved by primary medical practitioners. The immunization status of children is mapped for those states for which data are available. The last four indicators all attempt to describe the spatial distribution of medical costs. They are hospital expenditures, Medicare payments, Medicaid eligibility, and Medicaid costs.

8. Lifestyle Risks

An important aspect of studying American society is understanding lifestyle characteristics that affect among other things, health care costs and disease. Americans make choices in their lifestyles and in use of leisure time that impact their personal health and, in turn, the overall societal costs of health care. In this section, lifestyle risks are examined including leisure-time physical activity, smoking, the overweight population, motor vehicle traffic deaths, drug use, and homelessness. Most of the maps are based on sample survey data from the Centers for Disease Control and Prevention.

9. Education K-12

Another much-discussed topic in America today is the quality of our public education system; many critics are questioning whether it is equipping young people to compete in a global economy. Our selected series of indicators begins with enrollment in Head Start, a program dating back

4

to the War on Poverty; its aim was to help poor children prepare for first grade. Fourth-grade math and reading proficiency are mapped by region. Then the rate of high school dropouts is examined, followed by a map showing the proportion of the adult population that has completed high school. The projected change in high school graduates gives a look at the future; it is important to both the labor force and to higher education. Finally, as a finance measure, the average cost per pupil is mapped by state.

10. Higher Education

American higher education is increasingly under the spotlight as children of the baby boomers push college enrollment to record highs during a time of budget crises. This section examines total college enrollment and the proportion of that enrollment in two-year colleges. Minority education is a special concern that is mapped as the proportion of enrollment made up of minority students. The proportion of college graduates by state is examined as well as accessibility of a college education as indicated by the cost of in-state tuition in public schools.

11. Crime

Crime is an issue in the forefront of national attention with many efforts underway to reduce crime, lengthen prison sentences, reduce or eliminate parole, and institute "three strikes and you're out" legislation. This section portrays the spatial dimension of crime by mapping the crime index, the FBI's measure of violent and property crime per capita. Two other dimensions of the battle against crime are mapped: police officers per capita and the incarceration rate. Because of concern about drunk driving, data compiled by Mothers Against Drunk Driving (MADD) are mapped. As firearms deaths rise and auto fatalities drop, a special map compares the rates of deaths from these two types of tragedies.

12. Status of Women

The status and condition of American women is examined through six indicators. The first two are economic—the percentage of women in poverty and the income disparity in professional occupations. The third, percentage of women in state legislatures, looks at their increasing political participation. The other three indicators comprise a group related to the reproductive health of women. They are the teen birth rate, the percentage of non-marital births to teenage women, and the abortion rate.

13. Children

The future of American society lies with its children. The maps in this series examine states by the proportion of population under age eighteen and by growth or decline in the proportion of children in the population. Both of these indicators have important implications for local schools and higher education budgets, health care, police needs, etc. Three important measures of child well-being are examined: the proportion of hungry children; children in mother-headed households; and children who do not speak English at home. A composite measure of child

5

well-being based on data compiled by the Annie E. Casey Foundation is mapped.

14. Senior Citizens

The 1990 census showed that one in eight citizens falls into the over-65 category, designated as "the elderly." To use the term they prefer, this group of senior citizens is growing and has increasing political clout. Indicators examined include the percentage of the population over 65, the projected growth in the population of senior citizens, membership in the American Association of Retired Persons, the distribution of retirement facilities, and nursing home residents.

15. Politics and Religion

Politics and religion are two important aspects of American society. Supposedly separate, the interrelation between the two is attracting more attention in the 1990s than at any time since the presidential election of 1960 when the nation's first Catholic president was elected. To examine these variables, two maps relating to religion are shown: leading religious denominations by region and a map of percentages of people reporting no religious affiliation. To examine political patterns, we looked first at political affiliation by major party, focusing on a composite measure of voting in presidential elections from 1960 to 1992. Second, political participation by state was mapped by looking at the proportion of the voting age population who actually voted in the 1992 election.

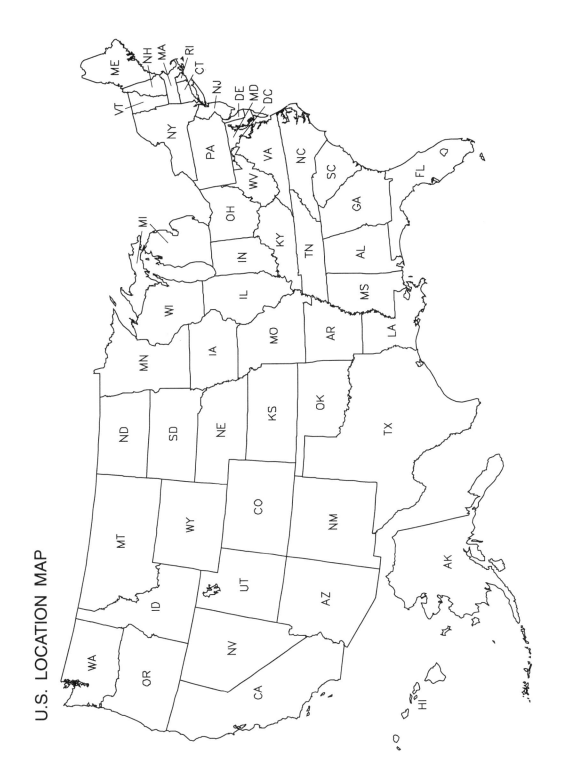

U.S. LOCATION MAP

1

City and Countryside

1.1 POPULATION DISTRIBUTION

In this atlas of American society, the primary focus is on people. Population distribution is the background against which all of the other maps in this atlas must be analyzed. The other maps attempt to show many aspects of American society, and particularly to show how measures of social well-being vary from state to state. The population size of the states, as well as their territorial size, varies greatly, depending both on the physical geography of the state and on the course of history, particularly the period in which the state was settled. What does it mean, for example, if Wyoming, huge in area, falls into the same category on a map as Rhode Island, small in area, but settled early and now almost totally urbanized? Rhode Island's population is considerably more than twice the size of that of Wyoming. In most maps in this volume, we are comparing states and so are concerned with rates, ratios, or percentages; they are shown on choropleth maps, where different shades represent different categories of data. If actual numbers were used, California and New York would be at the top of almost every list, and Alaska and Wyoming would probably be at the bottom.

This map is a cartogram, in which each state is drawn in proportion to the size of the population, while maintaining the approximate shape and the relationship to surrounding states as well as possible. It is one of many ways in which population distribution can be depicted. As this atlas stresses the state level, a cartogram by state is a good way to represent population distribution. Readers may refer back to this map (and to the actual population numbers for each state in Table 1.1) to refresh their memory on the relative population size of the states.

There are two major generalizations about population distribution in the United States, no matter what kind of population distribution map is being used. First, the eastern half of the country is more densely populated than the western (with an important exception; the West Coast itself, especially California, is densely populated). It is the interior of the West that is sparsely populated. This is a pattern explainable in terms of the availability of water. The dividing line corresponds roughly with the 100th meridian, the line of 100 degrees west longitude, and this artificial line of the earth's grid in turn corresponds remarkably closely to a line connecting areas that receive about 20 inches of rainfall a year. It roughly divides the more densely settled agricultural areas from drier areas where extensive stock raising may be the major land use. The second generalization about population distribution is that more than half of the population of the United States lives in coasal counties, that is, in counties adjacent to the Atlantic Ocean, the Pacific Ocean, the Gulf of Mexico, and the Great Lakes. Water, in one form or another, is a dominant factor in the population pattern of the United States.

The map makes it possible to see at a glance the predominance of California's population of 30 million, followed by New York's 18 million. Texas is not far behind New York, followed by Florida, Pennsylvania, and Illinois.

1.1 POPULATION DISTRIBUTION, 1992

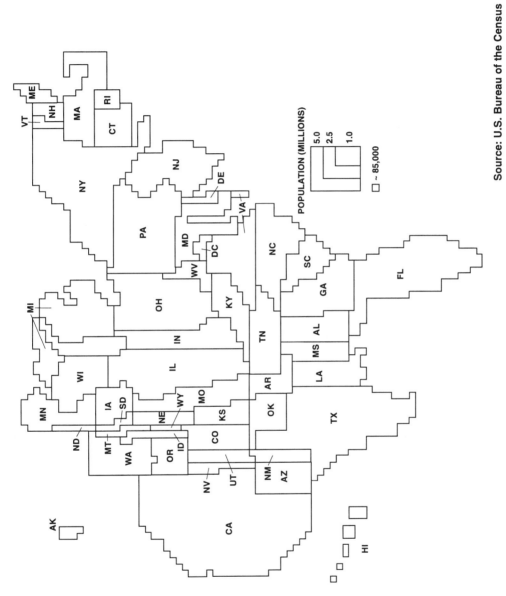

POPULATION (MILLIONS)

5.0
2.5
1.0

□ ~ 85,000

Source: U.S. Bureau of the Census

11

1.2   METROPOLITAN STATISTICAL AREAS

This map shows the outlines of some 250 metropolitan statistical areas (MSAs) and 18 consolidated metropolitan statistical areas (CMSAs) as defined by the U.S. Office of Management and Budget, with technical support from the Census Bureau. The present system of designating metropolitan areas dates from the early 1980s; it is complex but flexible, allowing for growth and change in our urban systems as patterns of employment, commuting and communications continue to evolve. In 1990 about 80 percent of the U.S. population lived in metropolitan areas. That means that four-fifths of the population live in the areas outlined on this map, which makes up slightly less than one-fifth of the land area of the country.

The map illustrates the first of the three major generalizations regarding population distribution—that the American population is concentrated in urban areas. It furthers the understanding of the other two generalizations as well. It shows that the eastern half of the country has a higher density of metropolitan areas than the western (except for the Pacific coastal strip). And this map makes it easy to comprehend that over half the population lives in the coastal counties that lie along the Atlantic Ocean, Pacific Ocean, Gulf of Mexico, and the Great Lakes. (Coastal counties are defined as being totally or in part within a coastal watershed.) Very visible on the map is the area that has come to be called Megalopolis, a string of cities and connecting urban counties stretching from Portsmouth, NH, to the Northern Virginia suburbs of metropolitan Washington, DC. Similarly, the urban strip that parallels the West Coast is prominent; the counties here are far larger than the ones on the East Coast. Metropolitan areas almost entirely outline the coast of Florida, both on the Atlantic and on the Gulf Coast. The urban strip along the Gulf of Mexico is continued into Louisiana and Texas. Along the Great Lakes there are almost continuous urban areas, notably the one that curves around Lake Michigan to include Chicago and Milwaukee.

Metropolitan statistical areas (MSAs) are defined in terms of counties or equivalents (e.g., parishes in Louisiana or independent cities in Virginia). A county or group of counties may be an MSA if it contains an officially delimited city of 50,000 or more, or if it contains an urbanized area of 50,000 or more and has a total metropolitan population of over 100,000. There is a great range from counties that barely meet the minimum requirement up to the largest MSA, Atlanta, which has a population of over three million. There is a defined hierarchy of MSAs by population size, ranging from the top Level A (one million or more) down to Level D (less than 100,000). Each census sees more small cities reaching the population size to be included on the list, as well as established urban areas moving up the ladder.

At the top of the hierarchy, MSAs have been combined into CMSAs (Consolidated Metropolitan Statistical Areas). A CMSA must have a population of one million or more (that is, be an MSA of Level A) *and* it must contain a qualifying PMSA. A PMSA (Primary Metropolitan Statistical Area) is defined in terms of an identity supported by local opinion. Either local opinion supports separate recognition for a county or group of counties that demonstrate relative independence within the metropolitan complex, or it had previously been recognized as a metro area before the changes of the 1980s and local opinion supports its continued recognition. A good example is found in the Baltimore-Washington CMSA. Created after the 1990 census, it includes three PMSAs: Baltimore, Washington, and Hagerstown, MD. Hagerstown, with a population of about 123,000, is far smaller than the two great cities, but it met the criteria for recognition as a PMSA.

12

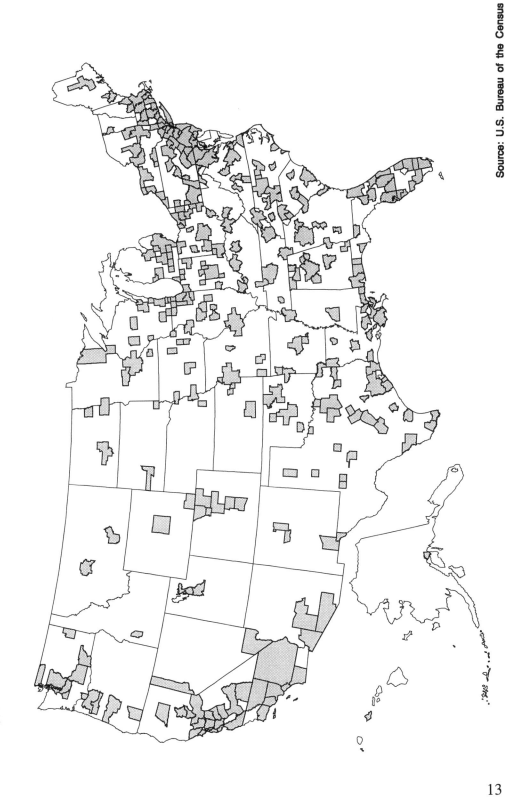

Source: U.S. Bureau of the Census

1.3   METROPOLITAN POPULATION

Building on the preceding map, this choropleth map shows how the proportion of metropolitan population varies from state to state. Metropolitan population includes the inhabitants of all the MSAs and CMSAs shown on the preceding map and is essentially all the population living in places of 50,000 or more. As indicated earlier, it includes about four-fifths of the U.S. population. The metro population grew by about 12 percent from 1980 to 1990, while the non-metro population only grew at about 3 percent. Growth has continued in the 1990s, as part of a historical continuum in which there was first rural to urban migration associated with the industrial revolution, then rapid growth in suburban areas. The current trend is for more people to be concentrated not just in towns and cities, but in larger metropolitan areas.

The percentage of population living in metro areas varies greatly from state to state, with a range from only 24 percent in Montana to 100 percent in New Jersey, a state which is totally covered by metro areas. The map shows two regions, plus three individual states, where the proportion of metro population is quite high, over 83 percent. First, there is the area from Massachusetts to Maryland; this is Megalopolis appearing on the state map, as it did on the MSA map. The state of Delaware is just below the cutoff for this category; its metro areas in the north are part of the larger Philadelphia-Wilmington-Atlantic City CMSA. In all of the states in this group except Pennsylvania, the metro percentage is over 90, perhaps a reminder that in many ways Pennsylvania really falls into two regions, Megalopolis in the East and the Midwest in the West. An even higher percentage is found in the West, where California is 97 percent metropolitan, while the two adjacent states of Nevada and Arizona are around 84 percent. The other three separate states in the high category are all big states that have grown rapidly in recent years: Florida (93% metro), Illinois (84%), and Texas (83%).

In the middle category (60–83%) are most of the Southeast, most of the Midwest, and two groups of paired states, Colorado-Utah and Washington-Oregon. In the low category some values drop to much lower levels; for example, Mississippi and Wyoming, very different, are both only about 30 percent metropolitan. The low category includes northern New England, although New Hampshire is clearly marked to become more and more metropolitan in the future. The others in the low category are all interior states except for Mississippi.

POPULATION DISTRIBUTION
AMONG METROPOLITAN AREAS BY SIZE, 1990

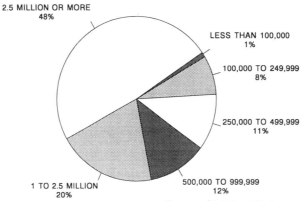

Source: *Statistical Abstract of the United States, 1993*

14

1.3 METROPOLITAN POPULATION
PERCENT IN METROPOLITAN AREAS, 1990

PERCENT

LESS THAN 60

60 TO 83

MORE THAN 83

Source: U.S. Bureau of the Census

1.4   RURAL POPULATION

Maps 1.2 and 1.3 stress urbanization, specifically the dominance of large metropolitan areas. Map 1.4 shifts the emphasis from the city-dwellers to the countryside by highlighting the more rural states. It is not simply the reverse of the preceding map showing percent in metropolitan areas. The rural/urban dichotomy differs from the metro/non-metro classification; not all urban places are in metropolitan areas, and some rural population is included in metropolitan areas. The census defines "urban" (75% of the population in 1990) as all population living in incorporated places of 2,500 or more or in "urbanized areas," which are largely defined by density of population. The "rural" category (25% of the population in 1990) is essentially whatever is not urban. It can overlap with metropolitan because metro areas are defined by county units; a county may be within a metro area yet have a significant rural population and even some farm residents. A good example is Loudoun County, Virginia, within the Washington PMSA.

The map shows three distinct regions with a high proportion (over 36%) of rural population. The first is northern New England (Maine, New Hampshire, and Vermont); these are states of villages, small towns, and cities, although New Hampshire is fast becoming more urban, as the Boston metropolitan area spills over its southern border. The second region is the Southeast, where a solid bloc of states stretches from the Carolinas to Arkansas. This region also includes the border states of West Virginia (the second most rural state with 64%) and Kentucky. The third highly rural region includes a bloc of states in the northern Great Plains and Rockies, stretching from Idaho to the Dakotas. Also attached to this group is Iowa, the premier agricultural state, where 39 percent of the population is still rural, despite the fact that the state is densely settled and contains quite a few metropolitan counties. Given the high level of urbanization and the rapid growth of big cities in the country as a whole, it seems remarkable that in 1990 the rural population was 50 percent or more in five states: Vermont (highest with 68%), West Virginia, Maine, Mississippi, and South Dakota. The dominance of rural areas in these states is an important characteristic that is helpful in understanding their position on many of the other maps in this atlas. The middle category on the map (24–36%) includes states in all parts of the country, but notably in the Midwest and Great Plains. The low category (less than 24%) *does* mirror the metropolitan map on the preceding page: it includes all of the states that were in the high category of metro population, plus several others.

California has the very lowest percentage of rural population of any state, yet it has over two million people in this category. The table below is a reminder that neither actual numbers (which depend on the size of a state's population) nor percentages tell the whole story.

STATES WITH LARGEST RURAL POPULATIONS, 1990

1.	Pennsylvania	3,693,000	6.	Michigan	2,739,000
2.	Texas	3,352,000	7.	Georgia	2,381,000
3.	North Carolina	3,291,000	8.	California	2,189,000
4.	New York	2,826,000	9.	Florida	1,971,000
5.	Ohio	2,808,000	10.	Indiana	1,946,000

Source: *Statistical Abstract of the United States, 1993*

1.4 RURAL POPULATION
PERCENT LIVING IN RURAL AREAS, 1990

PERCENT

LESS THAN 24

24 TO 36

MORE THAN 36

Source: U.S. Bureau of the Census

17

1.5   RURAL FARM AND RURAL NON-FARM POPULATION

The rural population consists of all the people living in the countryside or in towns of less than 2,500. In earlier times (as in less developed countries today), most of the residents of rural areas were engaged in the primary sectors of the economy—agriculture, forestry, fishing and mining. Most of the American population was rural until well into the twentieth century, and much of that rural population was made up of farmers and their families. The percentage of people engaged in agriculture shrinks steadily as an economy modernizes, and in the United States the percentage of farm residents is now slightly less than two percent of the total population, a percentage that has remained about the same since 1985. It is remarkable to associate the huge U.S. agricultural output with this small proportion of the population, but much of U.S. output now comes from large corporations, or agribusinesses. Furthermore, these farm residents make up only 7 percent of the total rural population. The non-farm rural population is a diverse mix, ranging from professionals and business people in small towns to commuters who may travel a hundred miles a day or more to jobs in metropolitan areas. The commuters also provide a cross section of American society, from affluent people to laborers, some of whom dwell in the many trailer settlements that now dot the rural landscape.

The map opposite shows that the farm and non-farm mix within the rural population varies considerably by region. As background to the map, it is helpful to know how the rural population is distributed in the different regions. In 1991, the largest number of rural dwellers were in the South (29.6 million people, making up about 44 percent of the total rural population of the United States). As the map shows, only about 5 percent of this rural population in the South was farm popula-tion. Next in size was the rural population of the Midwest (17.8 million making up about 26% of the U.S. total). True to its reputation, the proportion of farm residents was highest in this region—13 percent. In the Northeast, there were 11.7 million rural dwellers, making up 17 percent of the national figure. This highly urbanized region had the lowest percentage of farm residents—only 2 percent. The West had the smallest number of rural residents, 8.8 million, making up about 13 percent of the U.S. total. In this huge region, agriculture varies from the intensive agribusinesses of California to extensive stock ranches. The percentage of farmers in the rural population is second only to that of the Midwest.

The graph below shows how the rural proportion of the population has changed over time.

PERCENT RESIDING IN URBAN AREAS AND FARM AND NON-FARM PORTIONS OF RURAL AREAS: 1890–1991

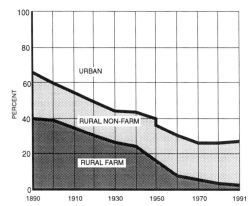

Source: *Dacquel and Dahmann*, 1993, Fig.2

18

1.5 RURAL FARM AND RURAL NON-FARM POPULATION, 1991

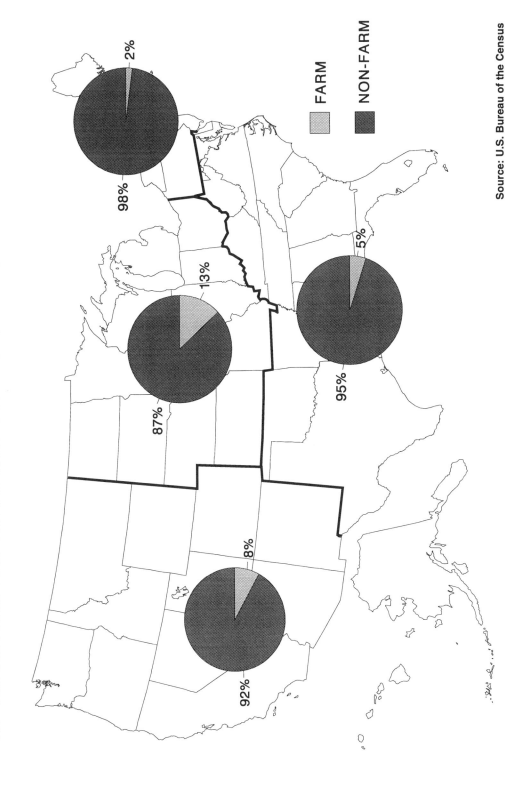

FARM

NON-FARM

Source: U.S. Bureau of the Census

19

2

Demographics

2.1 BIRTH RATE

In this section on demographics, choropleth maps using different shadings for different values present some basic vital statistics (rates of birth, death, infant mortality, marriage, and divorce) and one of the most significant population characteristics (the sex ratio). Age, another basic characteristic, is treated in more detail in later sections on children and seniors.

The most commonly used measure for comparing fertility is the birth rate—number of births per 1,000 population. It is properly called the crude birth rate, because it is not refined to account for the age and sex composition of the population. The birth rate for the United States in 1992 was 16 births per 1,000 population. The birth rate increased slightly from 1985 to 1990 and then again began to decline. This birth rate is slightly lower than that of Canada and is higher than the rates of most European countries. Worldwide, birth rates range from lows of 10 in some other industrialized countries (Germany, Japan) to highs of around 50 in some African countries (Malawi, Mali). In some advanced economies, fertility has fallen below replacement level. Although this is best demonstrated by more refined fertility measures, such as the total fertility rate, it can be seen in Germany's vital rates, where the birth rate has fallen below the death rate. Germany's population would soon be in decline if it were not for immigration.

The range of birth rates among the states is quite small; nonetheless some regional patterns are apparent. The birth rates of the states in 1992 varied from a low of 12.2 in West Virginia to a high of 20.6 in Utah. States with birth rates above the national rate of 16 are located primarily in a belt that extends from California, Nevada, and Utah around the southern rim of the country to include Mississippi and Georgia. Also in the high category are Alaska and Hawaii. The only interior state with a birth rate over the national level (other than Utah and Nevada) is Illinois. At the other extreme, the lowest birth rates in the country are found in New England and in many interior states, particularly in the northern Midwest, Great Plains, and Rockies.

Major influences on the birth rate are the age composition of the population and various cultural factors such as ethnicity, religion, and education. The age influence is seen in the lower birth rates of the northern interior states where the population is aging and there is an out-migration of young people. South Dakota, however, situated in the middle of this larger region of low fertility, shows how cultural factors, in this case a substantial Native American population, can exert an influence. Ethnicity is also seen as influencing high birth rates in the states of the Southwest, with their large Hispanic populations, and in Illinois. The best example of a religious influence is seen in Utah, the state that has had the highest birth rate for many years; in this case the great emphasis on family of the Latter-Day Saints (Mormons) plays a role, perpetuating a youthful population. Highly educated populations generally have low birth rates, as in New England. The state of the economy is yet another factor, best illustrated historically by the low birth rates that prevailed during the decade of the Great Depression. Even now, a depressed economy with an outflow of young people gives a low birth rate to West Virginia. Some states that appear to be anomalous in their region have complex explanations; for example, in analyzing fertility levels in Florida, the older population must be balanced against a sizeable population of ethnic minorities and recent young in-migrants. Also, Florida's Hispanic population is heavily made up of Cubans, who have far lower fertility rates than Mexican Americans or Puerto Ricans.

2.1 BIRTH RATE
LIVE BIRTHS PER 1,000 POPULATION, 1992

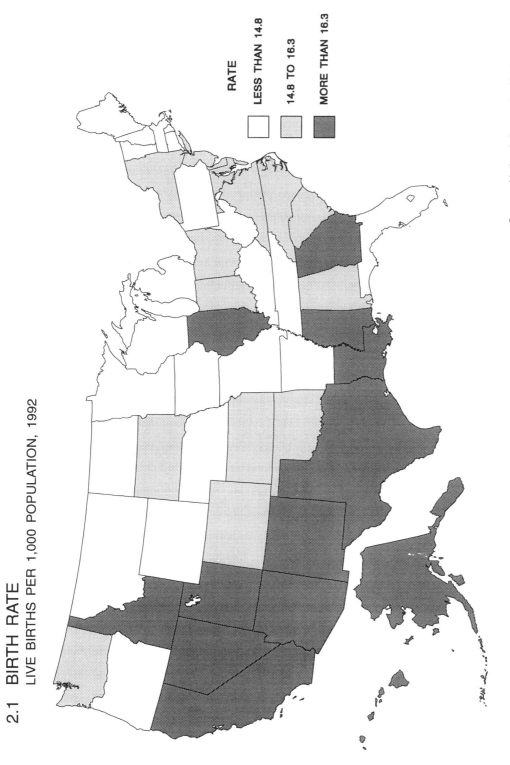

RATE

LESS THAN 14.8

14.8 TO 16.3

MORE THAN 16.3

Source: National Center for Health Statistics

23

2.2 DEATH RATE

The death rate for the United States in 1992 was 8.5 per 1,000 population, down slightly from 1991, and the lowest death rate since 1982. In recent years, the U.S. death rate has been somewhat higher than the death rate for both our North American neighbors, Canada (with a death rate of about 7) and Mexico (with a death rate of about 6). The range of death rates among the countries of the world is from about 5 to about 25 per 1,000. Quite low death rates of 5 per 1,000 or even less occur in countries with very large proportions of young people and with reasonable public health conditions (for example, Taiwan, Malaysia, Costa Rica). Among the urbanized, industrialized countries, there is a narrow range of death rates from 7 (Japan, Canada, Australia) to 11 (Germany, United Kingdom). The differences are chiefly related to the age composition of the population.

The situation within the United States is similar. Death rates vary largely due to differences in the proportions of youth versus elderly, but also to some degree to differences in accessibility to health care. This in turn is related to differences in income and education levels, which are partly related to the ethnic composition of the population. The pattern is very closely related to the map of birth rates on the preceding page, giving almost a mirror image in places. A large bloc of states in the Southwest, which had high birth rates, giving them a youthful population, also have low death rates. Higher death rates are confined largely to interior states, plus Rhode Island and Florida. The influence of the high proportion of elderly is well illustrated in Florida, and Arizona is also a major retirement state.

Demographers refine the crude death rate (number of deaths per 1,000) in many ways, chiefly by age and by cause of death. The most important age-specific death rate, the infant mortality rate, is shown on the next page. Cause-specific death rates are mapped and discussed in the section on Health and Disease. Life expectancy, or average length of life, is often used as a measure of levels of economic and social development. It varies in direct proportion to ups and downs in the death rate and is essentially another kind of measure of mortality. The graph below shows how life expectancy varies by race and sex. A dramatic difference can be noted between men and women and between whites and blacks.

AVERAGE LIFE EXPECTANCY
BY RACE AND SEX, 1992

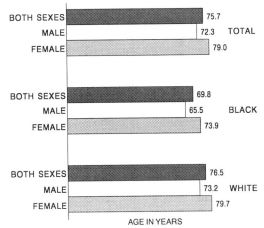

Source: *Monthly Vital Statistics Report*, Vol. 41, No. 13, 1993

2.2 DEATH RATE
DEATHS PER 1,000 PERSONS OF ALL AGES, 1992

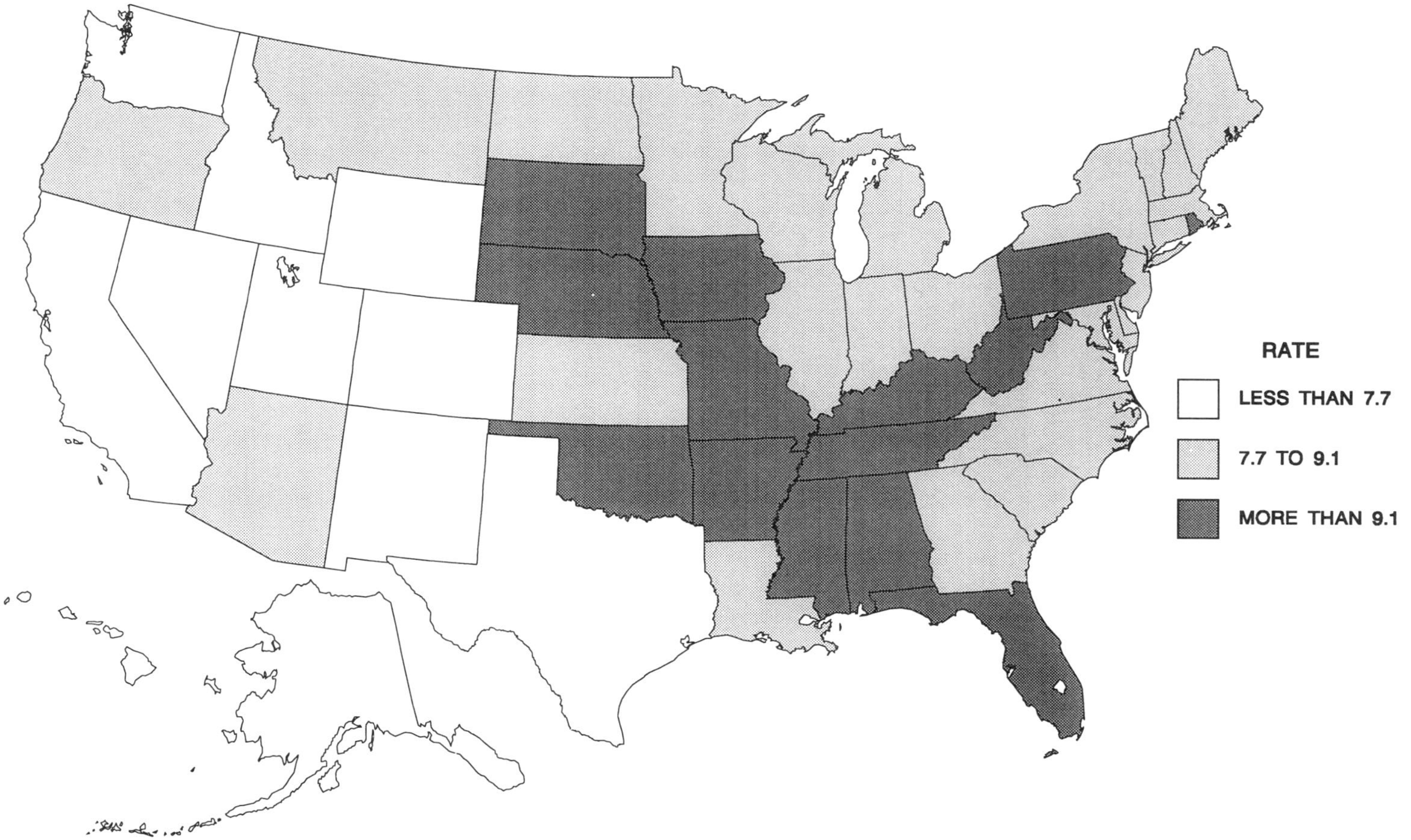

RATE

LESS THAN 7.7

7.7 TO 9.1

MORE THAN 9.1

Source: National Center for Health Statistics

25

2.3   INFANT MORTALITY

The infant mortality rate is considered to be one of the best indicators of quality of life or state of well-being in a country. At a world level, it ranges from lows of around 5 in Japan and some European countries to highs of around 150 in a few extremely underdeveloped countries. Infant mortality in the United States has fallen steadily in recent decades. It is now only about a third of what it was in 1960, having fallen from near 30 to less than 10 per 1,000.

Some generalizations stand out from the map. The rate is generally lower in the West than in the East and lower in the North than in the South. New England stands out in the East as an area of low infant mortality rates. The lower rates (less than 7.7 deaths per 1,000 live births) are associated with more affluent areas where most of the population has access to education, health care, and an adequate diet.

High infant mortality reflects lower income and lower educational attainment, which are interrelated with nutrition and accessibility to medical care, especially prenatal care. States with high rates of infant mortality are concentrated in the eastern half of the country, particularly in the South and in some states of the Midwest. The highest state rate in the country was 11.6 in Mississippi, which has a large, poor rural black population. (The District of Columbia, with its large black inner-city population, had a rate of 18.2.) States like Michigan, Illinois, and Indiana fall into the high category because of large minority urban populations. Poverty and lack of access to medical care are the major factors in this distribution. Unfortunately the racial gap in infant mortality is widening (see graph below). Rates for both whites and blacks are declining, but the black rate is not declining as rapidly. Most of the widening gap has been attributed to an increase in the number of very low birth weights among black newborns.

INFANT MORTALITY, 1960–91
DEATHS PER 1,000 LIVE BIRTHS

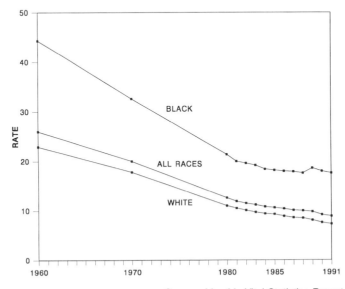

Source: *Monthly Vital Statistics Report*, Vol. 41, No. 13, 1993

2.3 INFANT MORTALITY
DEATHS OF INFANTS UNDER ONE YEAR OF AGE PER 1,000 LIVE BIRTHS, 1992

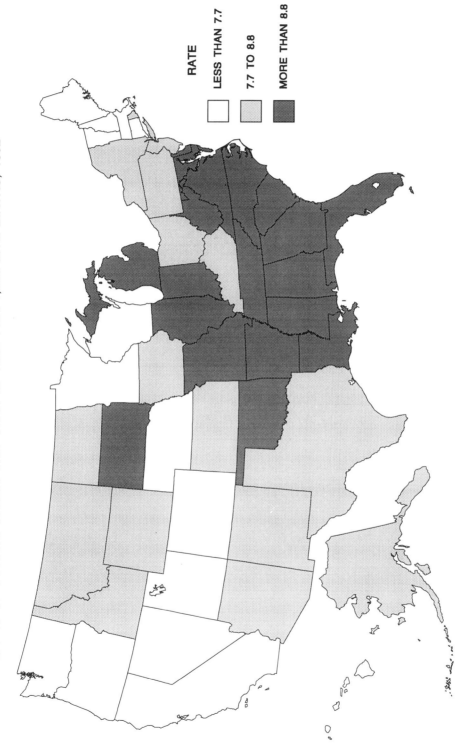

RATE

LESS THAN 7.7

7.7 TO 8.8

MORE THAN 8.8

Source: National Center for Health Statistics

2.4   MARRIAGE RATE

The pattern of marriage rates in the United States does not present a clear regional pattern, yet some relationships may be discerned on the map, which is based on rates for the latest available year, 1992. Marriage rates seem to be higher in the interior West (Utah, Idaho, Nevada, Wyoming, South Dakota), in some southern states (Virginia, Kentucky, Tennessee, South Carolina, Florida), and in Texas. Rates were also high in two remote outlying states, Vermont in the Northeast and Hawaii in the Pacific. It is difficult to see a common denominator, but a comparison with data for 1991 shows that this pattern held in the previous year as well. The highest rate has for years been in Nevada, a divorce mecca where the newly divorced may wish quickly to re-wed, which was far out of line in 1992, with a rate of over 86 per 1,000 population. This contrasts with the U.S. marriage rate of 9.3 per 1,000. Arkansas was second with 15.6, followed by Hawaii (15.2), South Carolina (14.8), and Tennessee (14.1).

The obvious influences to look for in explaining the pattern would seem to be the age structure of the population, any cultural attributes that might contribute to a higher rate of marriage, e.g. religion or ethnicity, and any legal restrictions that might promote or inhibit marriage. The last can be dealt with most simply. The legal age for marriage for both males and females is the same (18) for 48 states and the District of Columbia. Only in two states does it differ. Georgia's legal age for marriage for both sexes is 16; in Mississippi the legal age for marriage is 17 for males and 15 for females. Thus the legal age for marriage does not appear to affect the pattern. Another legal consideration might be the residence requirement for divorce, since divorce and remarriage often are close in time. In Idaho and Nevada the requirement is only six weeks, in Arkansas and Wyoming only 60 days, and Utah only three months, so there is some relationship. But in other states with high marriage rates there are much longer periods of residency required.

Age composition, so important in birth and death rates, plays a role in the marriage rate but not necessarily a major one. Its influence can be seen in the lower marriage rates in the Midwest. In Florida, however, the younger age and perhaps the religious beliefs of the large Hispanic population has produced a relatively high marriage rate, despite the significant component of senior citizens. In general, women are marrying later, a significant factor for the whole country.

The historical pattern of the marriage rate, in combination with the divorce rate, is shown on the graph accompanying the next map. In the 1950s, the marriage rate was low, as the small birth cohorts of people born during the depression decade of the 1930s reached marriageable age. This was true even though the total percentage of women who married was high, and the age at which they married was young. By the mid-1960s, the first cohorts of the baby boom began to reach the age of marriage, and the rate began to rise. It continued to rise until the early 1980s and then began to decline. By the late 1980s and early 1990s the rate had fallen and stabilized, as the women of the boomer generation married later and in many cases did not marry at all, a phenomenon associated with the increased participation of women in the labor force.

2.4 MARRIAGE RATE
MARRIAGES PER 1,000 POPULATION, 1992

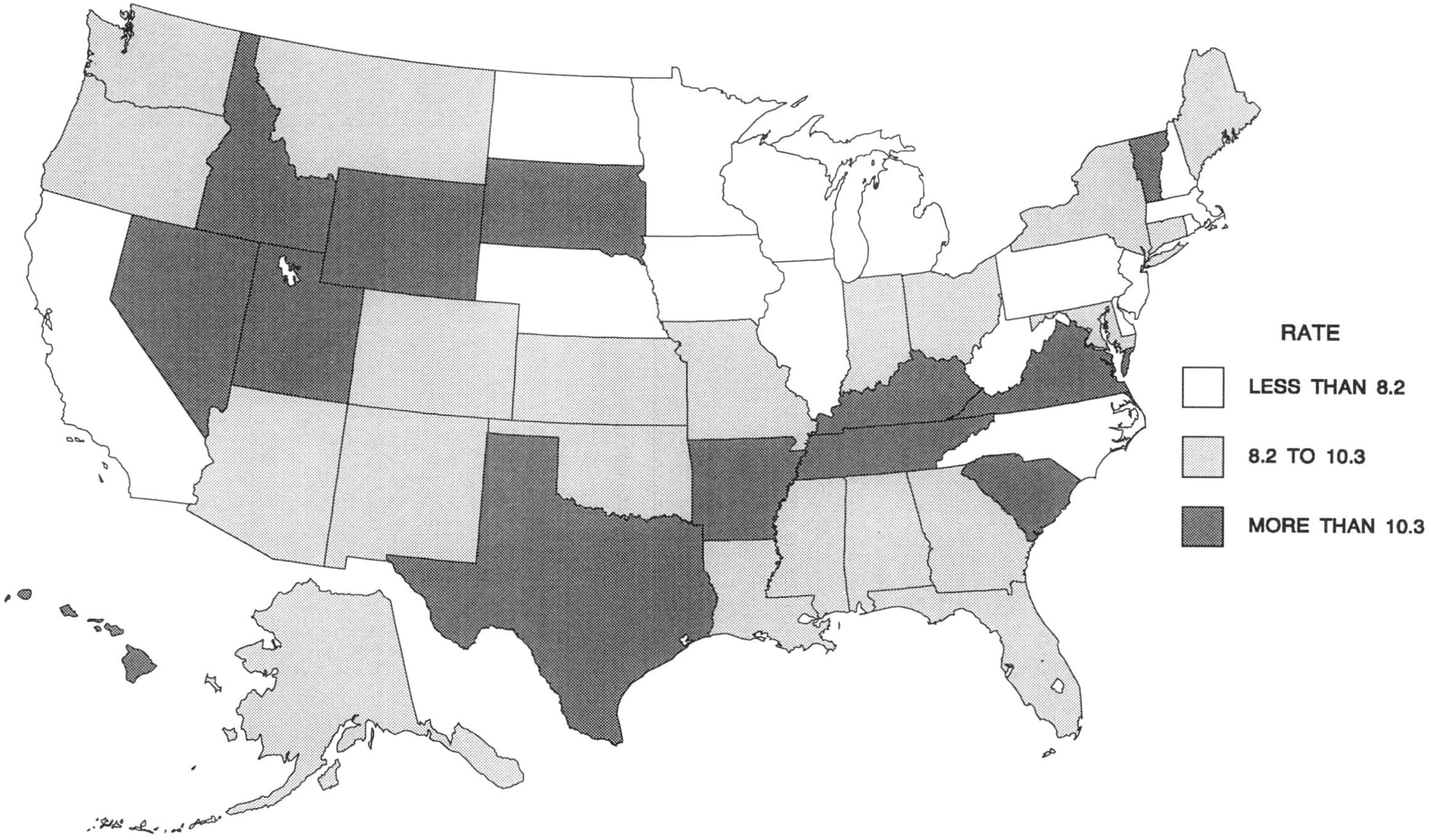

RATE

LESS THAN 8.2

8.2 TO 10.3

MORE THAN 10.3

Source: National Center for Health Statistics

29

2.5   DIVORCE RATE

For a number of years, the divorce rate in the United States has been stable at about 5 per 1,000, or just about half the marriage rate as shown on the graph below. It is commonly said that about half of all marriages will end in divorce. This has become a matter of concern; it seems to indicate that the family as an institution is changing dramatically, and some social observers declare that we are witnessing the decline of the American family. Not only divorce but remarriage after divorce has become common, so that more children grow up in families where one or both parents have been married before. Family relationships become complex. The increase in the divorce rate is connected to many other topics mapped in this atlas, such as the increase in families headed by women and the increase in the number of children who are living in poverty. These phenomena are implicated in some of the major policy debates of our day, such as the need for day care facilities and the drive to provide universal health care. Changes in the family have led to a shifting of responsibility from family members to governments at various levels. This is particularly true of responsibility for the youngest and the oldest members of our society. Thus the divorce rate is related to many other aspects of American society.

While the overall divorce rate for 1992 was 4.8, the rate varied among the states from less than 3 per 1,000 in heavily Catholic Massachusetts to a high of over 11 in Nevada, a state noted for its divorce industry, as symbolized by the city of Reno. Not all states with predominantly Catholic populations have low divorce rates, however. Except for Nevada and a few other states with rates of 7 or over (Arkansas and Oklahoma), the rates fall in a very narrow range, from 3 to 6 per 1,000. The overall pattern is one of higher rates in the Southeast and West, with lowest rates in the Northeast, North Central, and Middle Atlantic regions.

The divorce rate increased rapidly during the decades from 1960 to 1980, then declined slightly, and has stabilized in the early 1990s. A recent study by the Census Bureau showed that the younger a woman is at first marriage, the greater the chance that she will divorce. Remarriage is common, with three-fourths of remarriages occurring within five years of divorce.

MARRIAGE AND DIVORCE RATES, 1950–92

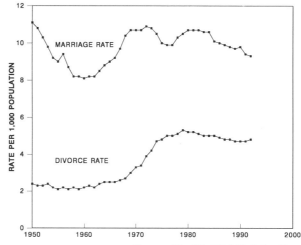

Source: *Monthly Vital Statistics Report*, Vol. 41, No.13, 1993

2.5 DIVORCE RATE
DIVORCES PER 1,000 POPULATION, 1992

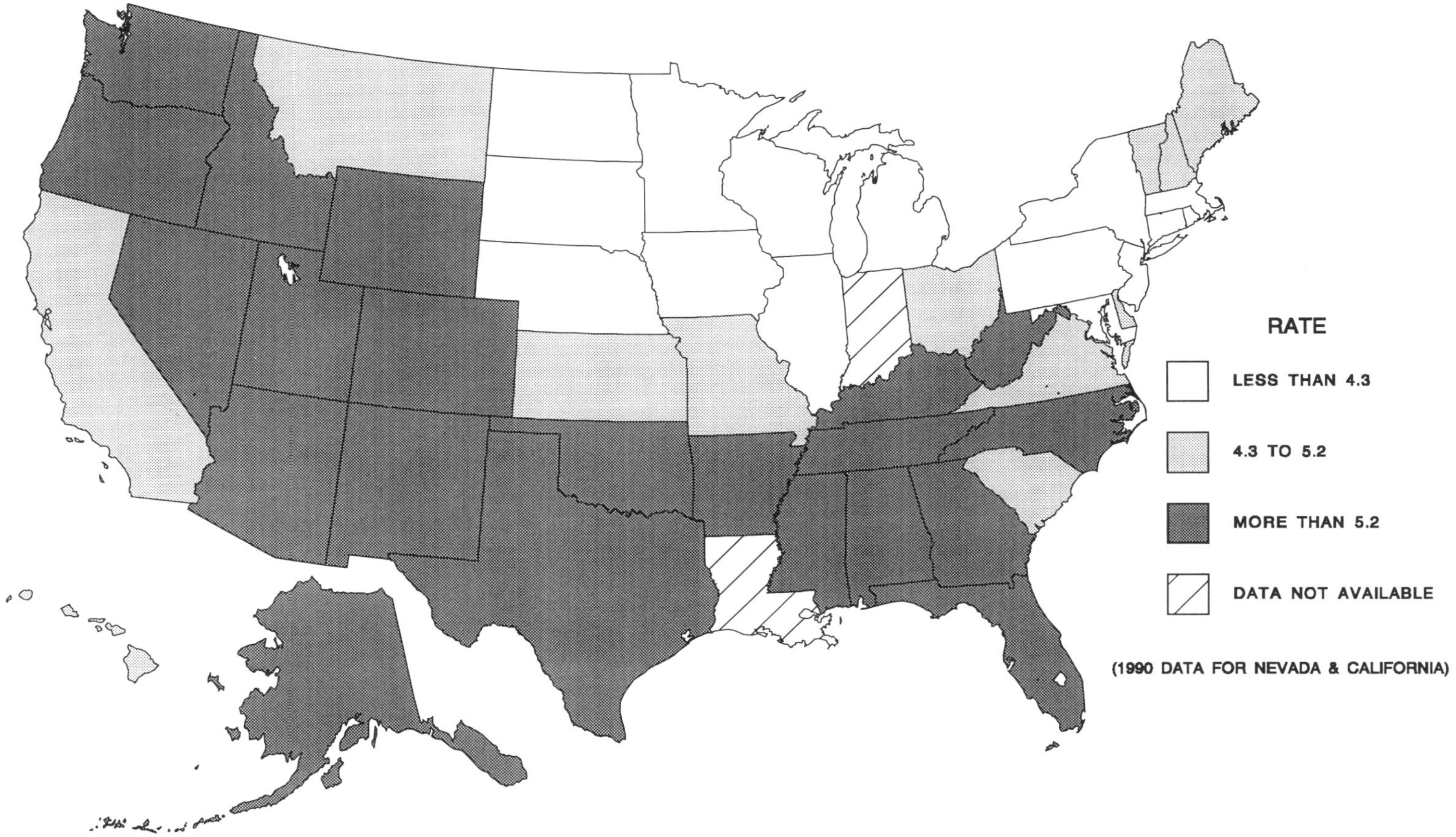

RATE

- [ ] LESS THAN 4.3
- [ ] 4.3 TO 5.2
- [ ] MORE THAN 5.2
- [ ] DATA NOT AVAILABLE

(1990 DATA FOR NEVADA & CALIFORNIA)

Source: National Center for Health Statistics

31

2.6   SEX RATIO

This is one of the more dramatic maps in the demographic series, showing a strictly east-west division of the country in terms of the sex ratio, with higher sex ratios in the West. The sex ratio is demographically defined as the number of males per 100 females. A sex ratio of 100 indicates equal numbers of males and females, while ratios above 100 indicate an excess of males and below 100 an excess of females. Developed countries and most developing countries today have sex ratios below 100, reflecting the fact that life expectancy is higher for females. Higher sex ratios are found in frontier-like situations, where large numbers of males have migrated. Inequalities in the number of males and females are influenced by several factors. More boys are born than girls, but death rates are sex-selective and usually higher for males. Migration is also sex-selective; for example, traditionally it has been males who moved first into newly opened frontiers. Women, on the other hand, have often dominated in the migration streams moving to large cities, because their opportunities were more limited in the countryside. The stereotype of "government girls" moving to Washington, or of farm girls going to New York to find employment, is commonplace in recent American folklore. All three of the demographic dynamics that cause populations to grow and decline—birth, death, and migration—also influence the sex ratio.

A look at historical maps of the sex ratio reveal that some version of the east-west divide has existed since the very beginning of the country. Data from the first census in 1790 have been used to calculate sex ratios for the states in their present borders. At that time only the states in New England had sex ratios of less than 100, indicating a preponderance of females; they were the least frontier-like and the most developed. The ratio for the new country as a whole was about 105, in keeping with the times and with its frontier character. Since that time, the pattern of the sex ratio has shifted westward with the frontier. Continued immigration into the area, both from Mexico and into California from Asia as well, undoubtedly plays a role in maintaining this characteristic.

The table below shows how the sex ratio has changed over the past several decades, projects it into the near future, and shows how it varies by age group.

SEX RATIO BY SELECTED AGE GROUPS
1950–91, WITH PROJECTIONS FOR 2000 AND 2025

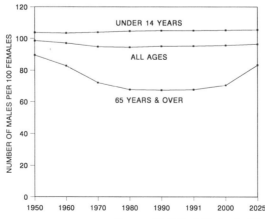

Source: *Statistical Abstract of the United States: 1993*, Table 15

32

2.6 SEX RATIO
MALES PER 100 FEMALES, 1992

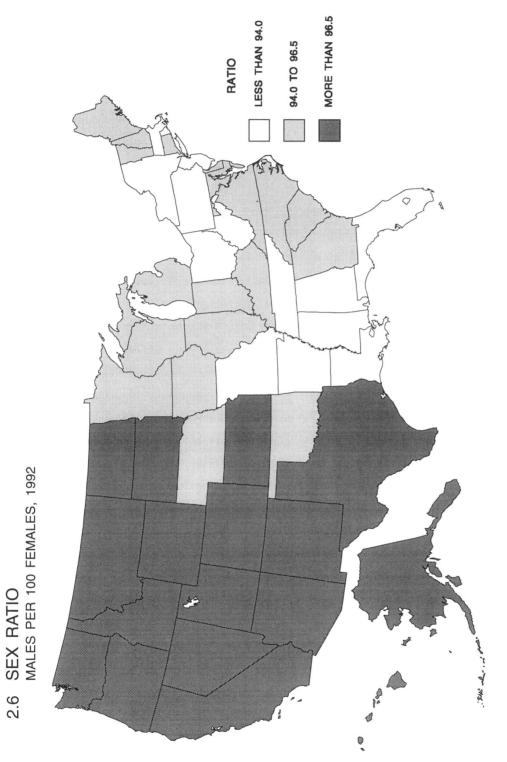

RATIO

LESS THAN 94.0

94.0 TO 96.5

MORE THAN 96.5

Source: U.S. Bureau of the Census

33

3

Migration, Mobility and Population Change

3.1   POPULATION CHANGE

From 1980 to 1993, America's population grew by 31,362,000, or 13.8 percent. These figures take into account natural increase (births minus deaths) and immigration. Population change is not at all evenly distributed among the states or regions. California had the greatest absolute gain, more than 7,500,000 people, followed by Florida with 4,000,000 and Texas with 3,800,000. Meanwhile West Virginia had an absolute loss of 135,000 people and Iowa lost 100,000. The highest rate of growth was in Nevada where a gain of 589,000 people translated into a population growth rate of 76 percent; Alaska (49%) and Arizona (45%) were similarly high. Florida stands out as an exceptional state in having both a very high rate of growth (40%) and a large absolute increase. West Virginia's population loss was significant (7%) while losses in Iowa (3.4%) and North Dakota (2.8%) were not as severe.

Population change varies greatly by region. The West and Southwest, from Texas to California, and the South Atlantic coast, from Maryland and Delaware to Florida, are the two areas that experienced greatest population growth. Alaska, Hawaii and New Hampshire are the only other states that gained more than 15 percent in population from 1980 to 1993. Low-growth states (less than 5%) and those with actual population losses are also quite concentrated. One bloc of slow growth is in the Northeast from Massachusetts, New York and Pennsylvania extending into all of the eastern Midwest and adjoining Kentucky, West Virginia and Iowa. Another bloc is made up of Louisiana and Mississippi. A third area is made up of Wyoming, the Dakotas and Nebraska. States growing at an intermediate rate (5% to 15%) are quite scattered but with concentrations in New England, New Jersey, the Central Interior and the upper Midwest.

Why this pattern? To some extent the map reflects the Sunbelt versus the Rustbelt. This however is an overly broad generalization as some Sunbelt states, such as those of the lower Mississippi, are slow-growth states, and some Rustbelt states, such as much of New England, Minnesota, and Wisconsin, are experiencing moderate growth. The primary explanation can be seen by comparison of this map with earlier ones. The birth rate is a major factor, and comparison of this map with Map 2.1 shows no surprise in that many of the fastest growing states also have high birth rates. There are exceptions, such as Mississippi, with a high birth rate and yet low population growth due to out-migration, or New Hampshire with a low birth rate yet rapid population growth due to in-migration from Massachusetts. A comparison with the maps of internal migration (Map 3.3, Where Did Former Residents Go, and Map 3.2, Where Were Residents Born) shows many flows that correspond to the population change map. Examples are the huge flows from New York to California and Florida; from Illinois to California, and from Pennsylvania to Florida. Lastly, immigration from abroad is also a factor. Most of the rapidly growing states shown on this map are also ones receiving large numbers of immigrants, as shown in Map 3.5, Foreign-Born Population. California, Florida and Texas are notable ex-amples. There are exceptions, however. New York and Illinois are slow-growth states despite the large number of foreign-born population, indicating that huge numbers of American-born residents must be leaving these states. Some recent research has demonstrated this quite clearly. William Frey, a demographer at the University of Michigan, has shown that large numbers of native-born population, particularly poorer Americans, migrate out of certain states in iden-tifiable paths: New Yorkers to North Carolina, Virginia, Florida and Massachusetts; Illinoisans to Wisconsin; Texans to Colorado, New Mexico and Arizona; and Californians to Washington, Oregon, Nevada and Arizona.

3.1 POPULATION CHANGE
PERCENT CHANGE, 1990–93

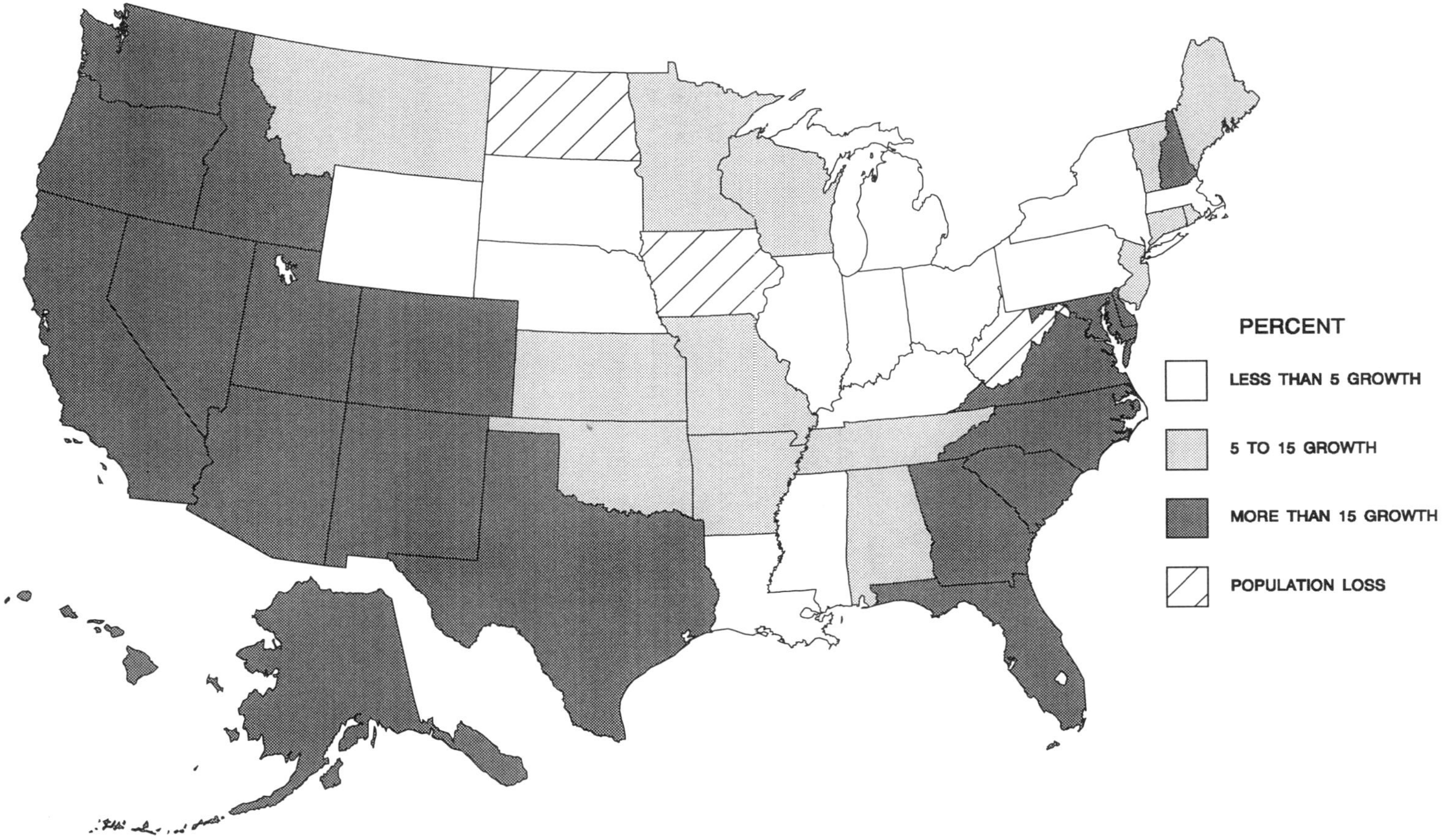

PERCENT

LESS THAN 5 GROWTH

5 TO 15 GROWTH

MORE THAN 15 GROWTH

POPULATION LOSS

Source: U.S. Bureau of the Census

37

3.2   WHERE WERE RESIDENTS BORN?

This is a flow map showing the predominant state of origin of in-migrants into each state. Expressed another way, the arrow that ends in each state originates in the state that in 1990 had contributed the largest number of migrants to that state. For example, the arrow connecting New York to Florida indicates that of all Floridians in 1990 who were born in another state, New York State contributed more people to that flow than any other state. This flow from New York to Florida also happens to be the largest flow shown on the map: 1,270,667 people. As the map shows only the largest flows, it is important to note that the total of many smaller flows may be greater than the single largest flow.

The map illustrates a number of interesting regional patterns. There is a distinct westward flow through most of the center of the nation. Of Montana residents born out-of-state, more were born in North Dakota than any other state; but among migrants to North Dakota, more were born in Minnesota than anywhere else, and among Minnesotan migrants, more were born in Wisconsin. This pattern prevails for states between the Mississippi and the Rockies with the notable exception of Texas.

Texas, like other very populous states including California, New York and Illinois, has a large enough population base to act as the main regional supplier of migrants to neighboring states. Texas is the birthplace of more born-out-of-state residents of New Mexico, Oklahoma, Arkansas and Louisiana than any other state. California is the main supplier of immigrants to all states west of the Rockies (including Alaska and Hawaii). Similarly, New York has supplied migrants to all its immediate neighbors as well as to Florida and California; Illinois has sent large flows to Wisconsin, Iowa and Missouri. There are other smaller regional centers of migrants: Massachusetts supplies Rhode Island, New Hampshire and Maine; Ohio, Maryland and Delaware receive their largest flows from Pennsylvania; Michigan, West Virginia and Kentucky get most of their newcomers from Ohio. The map does not reveal how far migrants are moving between states; sometimes it may just be a short distance. The flow from Massachusetts to New Hampshire is undoubtedly mainly the expansion of exurban Boston suburbanites across the state line; similarly many in the Illinois to Wisconsin flow are staying within metropolitan Chicago. Much of the movement of New Yorkers into Connecticut and New Jersey is migration within the New York metropolitan area.

A third pattern evident is that populous neighbors often exchange migrants; they are, in effect, each other's best customers. Examples abound such as New York and Pennsylvania; Virginia and North Carolina; Georgia and Alabama; Mississippi and Tennessee; Texas and Louisiana.

It is important to view this map as a reflection of long-term patterns. Because the arrows reflect migration for all 1990 residents, including elderly residents, the map is a long-term summary of migration trends. (The next map looks at more recent movements.) As a long-range perspective, the map reflects many important migrations of the twentieth century, some of which began even earlier: Kentucky Appalachian people north to Indiana; African Americans north from Mississippi to Illinois (primarily to Chicago); New Yorkers to south Florida; and those following the great American propensity to "go west."

3.2 WHERE ARE RESIDENTS BORN?
ARROW ORIGINATES IN STATE THAT HAS CONTRIBUTED THE LARGEST
NUMBER OF RESIDENTS AS OF 1990

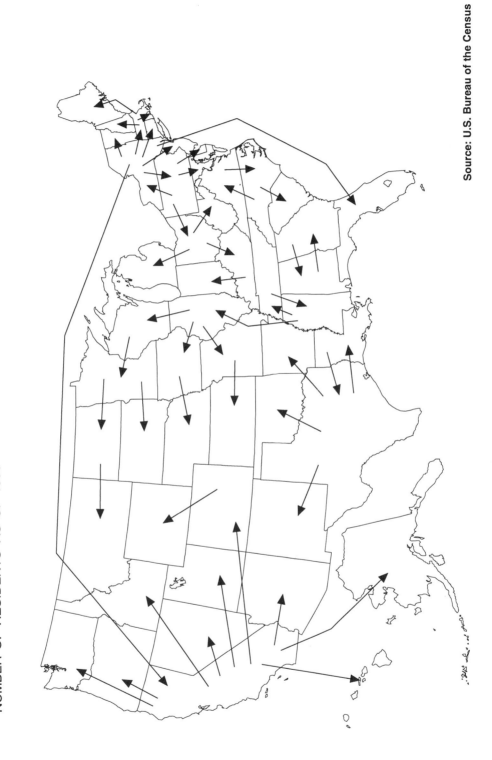

39

3.3 WHERE DID FORMER RESIDENTS GO?

On this map, each arrow indicates the most popular destination of migrants who left each state between 1985 and 1990. It differs from the previous map in two ways; first, the focus is on out-migrants rather than in-migrants, and second, it illustrates more recent patterns of movement, unlike Map 3.2, which gave a longer-term historical perspective.

Flows to three states, California, Florida and Washington, dominate the map. California is the most popular destination for residents of almost all states west of the Mississippi, with a few exceptions. Those exceptions are Oklahoma and Louisiana, whose residents move primarily to Texas, and North Dakota, where out-migrants mostly go to Minnesota. In addition, California is also the most popular destination of three states east of the Mississippi, all in the Midwest: Illinois, Wisconsin and Michigan. Perhaps the most surprising pattern revealed by the map is the popularity of Washington state as a destination. Residents of five states are more attracted to Washington than anywhere else. These five are California, Alaska, Oregon, Montana and Idaho.

Florida is the third state that dominates the national map. Florida is the most popular destination for three clusters of states: its immediate neighbors, Georgia and Alabama; two midwestern states, Indiana and Ohio; and four northeastern states, New York, New Jersey, Connecticut and Massachusetts. At one time, Florida's immigrants were retirees, but now there is a more general migration trend of all age groups into the state.

With the exception of the clear pattern of migration to Florida, the out-migration flows in the East are much more complex than those in the West because several states act as magnets for regional clusters of states, although they do not affect as large an area as do California, Florida or Washington. Massachusetts acts as a regional magnet for residents of Maine, New Hampshire and Rhode Island. Ohio attracts migrants from Kentucky and West Virginia. Georgia attracts residents from Florida and Tennessee; Virginia from North Carolina and Maryland, and North Carolina from Virginia and South Carolina. There are also a few local flows: Vermont to New York, New York to New Jersey, and Delaware to Maryland. One longer-distance flow is that of Mississippi migrants to Chicago, Illinois, partly a continuation of the historic migration of African Americans from south to north. As on Map 3.3, not all the flows between states are long-distance. Much of the flow from Pennsylvania to New Jersey, for example, takes place within metropolitan Philadelphia; many migrants from Maryland to Virginia are moving within metropolitan Washington; many of those moving from Kentucky to Ohio stay within greater Cincinnati.

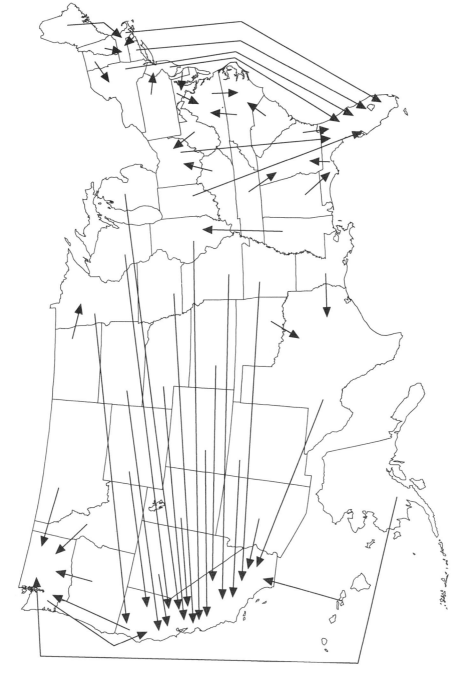

3.3 WHERE DID FORMER RESIDENTS GO?
ARROW INDICATES THE MOST POPULAR DESTINATION
OF OUT-MIGRANTS BETWEEN 1985 AND 1990

Source: U.S. Bureau of the Census

41

3.4   RESIDENTIAL STABILITY

Traditional measures of population growth and in-migration, while reflecting well on the economic health of a state, have a human cost in terms of family disruption. Changing one's neighborhood, city or state often entails a new school, a new job and other adjustments in addition to a new home. Census statistics identify the proportion of the population aged five and over who lived in the same house in 1990 as they did in 1985. (The age five restriction is necessary because the question has no meaning for a three-year-old in 1990 who didn't "live" anywhere in 1985. Also, a person who moved across the street or from city to suburb in the same area is counted the same as someone who moved across the country; that is, neither person is still in the same house.)

The area of the country with the greatest residential stability is primarily the Rustbelt: the older industrial and heavily urbanized states of the Northeast and the Midwest. In these states, more than 55.5 percent of the population resided in the same house in 1990 as in 1985. North Dakota, Nebraska and four southern states (South Carolina, Mississippi, Louisiana and Alabama) are also in this group, reflecting rural residential stability rather than urban residential stability. West Virginia had the highest percentage (64.2%), followed by Pennsylvania (63.4%).

As one would expect, the lowest percentages are in states that experienced tremendous population growth between 1985 and 1990 with waves of new arrivals moving into new homes. These states with lower residential stability are mainly western and Sunbelt states. In Nevada, only 34.7 percent of its 1990 population lived in the same house as in 1985; Alaska was next lowest at 40.6 percent. In addition to the Sunbelt and Pacific states, Virginia, Colorado and Wyoming also had less than 50 percent residential stability. States in the intermediate category (50% to 55.5%) were mainly west of the Mississippi River, but not in the Sunbelt or on the Pacific Coast. In addition, Hawaii, two New England states and four southern states east of the Mississippi were among this group.

This map is closely related to Map 3.1, Population Change, and to the two maps showing internal migration (Maps 3.2 and 3.3).

ANNUAL MOBILITY RATES IN SELECTED METROPOLITAN AREAS
1990 AND 1991

	PERCENTAGE OF HOUSEHOLD HEADS WHO MOVED IN LAST YEAR	
METROPOLITAN AREA	ALL MOVES	MOVES WITHIN METRO AREA
Atlanta, GA (1991)	22.5	14.0
Baltimore, MD (1991)	14.7	9.9
Chicago, IL (1991)	16.3	10.5
Denver, CO (1990)	24.3	20.3
Houston, TX (1991)	22.9	16.6
New York-Nassau-Suffolk (1991)	12.3	6.8
Pittsburgh, PA (1990)	12.5	9.9
Portland, OR-WA (1990)	22.6	17.4
San Diego, CA (1991)	25.2	16.9

Source: Gober, *Population Bulletin*, November 1993

3.4 RESIDENTIAL STABILITY, 1985–90
PERCENT OF POPULATION AGE FIVE AND OLDER
WHO LIVE IN THE SAME HOUSE IN 1990 AS IN 1985

PERCENT

LESS THAN 50.0

50.0 TO 55.5

MORE THAN 55.5

43

3.5   FOREIGN-BORN

Almost 20 million American residents (19,767,316 in 1990) were born outside the United States. They make up about 8 percent of America's population. This is the largest number of foreign-born residents ever living in the United States and a sharp increase from 14 million in 1980. As a proportion of America's population, however, the foreign-born residents have made up a relatively larger share many times in the past and as recently as 1950. In 1910, 13.6 million American residents had been born outside its boundaries, representing 14.8 percent of total population. Census statistics show that in addition to language differences (80% of newcomers speak a language other than English at home), the foreign-born tend to be older than the native population; they are less likely to have graduated from high school and more likely to live below the poverty line. Occupation and median family income vary greatly by country of origin. For example, 40 percent of American residents born in the United Kingdom are classified as managerial workers and only 6 percent as laborers; for Italy, the split is about even, at 20 percent in each category, but less than 6 percent of those born in Mexico are employed in managerial positions and almost one-third are classified as laborers.

States with a large proportion of foreign-born (more than 9%) are clustered around the periphery of the nation. Five states stand out in the Northeast—New York, New Jersey, Massachusetts, Connecticut and Rhode Island. This area of large urban centers, especially New York, Philadelphia and Boston, has welcomed immigrants for more than 350 years, particularly from Europe, although more recent immigrants arrive at this region from all over the world. Illinois, with its Great Lakes entry port of Chicago, is similar in this respect. Florida has a large proportion of foreign-born, especially from Cuba and more recently Haiti. Most of the foreign-born population in Texas is from Mexico. California and Nevada, also in the highest category, receive large numbers of Hispanic immigrants. California is an entrepot, like New York, welcoming immigrants for more than a century from Southeast and South Asia, Central and South America, the Middle East and Europe. Hawaii's foreign-born population came mostly from Asia, especially Japan, the Philippines, and Vietnam.

States with an intermediate proportion of foreign-born, 2 percent to 9 percent, are located generally in areas adjacent to those states in the highest category. In this category are the remaining states of the Northeast and Virginia; most of the midwestern states; the Pacific Northwest and Alaska, and southwestern and southern Great Plains states experiencing continuing migration from Mexico. Georgia and Louisiana are also in the intermediate category. States with the smallest percent of foreign-born population, less than 2 percent, are in the interior of the nation, away from the coastal ports, especially in the northern Great Plains and Rocky Mountain states and in the South. The two Carolinas are the only Atlantic or Pacific Coast states in the lowest category.

The difference in percentage of foreign-born population between the highest and lowest ranked states is remarkable—less than 1 percent in Mississippi, but almost 22 percent in California. Consider California's percentage (and also that of New York, almost 16%). Of California's almost 29,760,000 people, 21.7 percent, or 6,460,000, are foreign-born, surely reflecting one of the greatest mass migrations in human history. The largest number of foreign-born are from Mexico, almost 4,300,000 people; another 900,000 are from the Philippines, the second largest group. More than a half-million American residents have also arrived from Canada, Cuba, Germany, the United Kingdom, Italy, Korea, Vietnam and the People's Republic of China.

3.5 FOREIGN-BORN
PERCENT OF TOTAL POPULATION, 1990

PERCENT

LESS THAN 2

2 TO 9

MORE THAN 9

Source: U.S. Bureau of the Census

45

3.6 NATURALIZED CITIZENS

On this proportional circle map, the size of the circle reflects the number of immigrants who became American citizens in 1992. An immigrant who has resided in the United States for at least five years, who is conversant in English and who has a general knowledge of principles of American government may apply for citizenship. Spouses of U.S. citizens need only wait three years. More than 240,000 resident foreigners became citizens in 1992, a figure that has been fairly constant since 1985 (except for 1990–1991 when about 300,000 were naturalized due to a special amnesty). In 1992, numbers by state ranged from highs of 52,400 in California and 43,400 in New York, to less than 100 new citizens each in South Dakota and Wyoming. Other states with large totals were Florida (21,100), Texas (17,600), New Jersey (16,600) and Illinois (10,900).

The map shows two huge concentrations of naturalized citizens in 1992—California and the Northeast. Combined, New York, New Jersey and the three states of southern New England added more than 75,000 citizens to the U.S. population in 1992. (Note that for clarity, the proportional circle for Massachusetts includes figures for Rhode Island.) There is a close correlation between this map and the previous map showing percent foreign-born (Map 3.5) as all the states with the largest numbers of naturalized citizens are also states with more than 9 percent foreign-born population. With the exception of Illinois and its interior port city of Chicago, all the large concentrations of naturalized citizens, like the foreign-born population, are concentrated along the perimeter of the nation where immigrants enter.

The chart below shows the ten countries that produced the largest number of naturalized citizens in 1992. Six of the top ten nations and four of the top five are Asian countries. A comparison of the numbers of foreign-born and naturalized citizens shows that those who become American citizens are disproportionately from Asia. Asians make up 27 percent of American foreign-born; 37 percent of immigrants between 1980 and 1990, and almost 47 percent of naturalized citizens. Immigrants from certain countries are more disposed to become American citizens sooner than immigrants from other countries. For example, Filipinos become American citizens at about ten times the rate in proportion to numbers as do Mexicans, even though about equal proportions of both groups have been in the United States for the same length of time.

ORIGINS OF NATURALIZED CITIZENS, 1992
TEN LARGEST NATIONS

Philippines	28,579
Vietnam	18,357
China (People's Republic)	13,488
India	13,413
Mexico	12,880
Dominican Republic	8,464
Korea	8,297
United Kingdom	7,800
Cuba	7,763
Iran	6,778

Source: U.S. Immigration and Naturalization Service

3.6 NATURALIZED CITIZENS
NUMBER OF PERSONS NATURALIZED, 1992

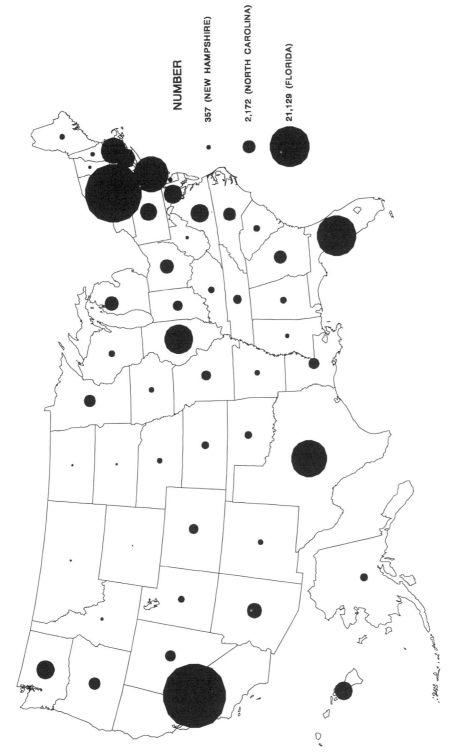

NUMBER

357 (NEW HAMPSHIRE)

2,172 (NORTH CAROLINA)

21,129 (FLORIDA)

Source: Immigration and Naturalization Service

47

4

Affluence versus Poverty

4.1   HOUSEHOLD INCOME

The discussion of poverty versus affluence among the states of the United States logically begins with the geographical distribution of income. Median household income is shown as a three-year average from 1990 to 1992. Because of the economic recession, household income declined during these years. Census Bureau statisticians analyzed household incomes by comparing a two-year average from 1990–1991 with a two-year average for 1991–1992 (adjusted for inflation as shown by the Consumer Price Index, or CPI). The analysis showed that no state had an increase in income; 38 states and the District of Columbia showed no significant change, and 12 states showed a significant decline in household income: Florida, Illinois, Kentucky, Maryland, Massachusetts, New Hampshire, New Jersey, New York, Rhode Island, South Carolina, Texas and West Virginia.

The regional aspects of the distribution of income are striking. Two distinct areas had the highest average income (more than $34,000 on average, between 1990 and 1992): many of the Megalopolis strip of states from New Hampshire to Virginia, and the Pacific states of California, Washington, Alaska and Hawaii. Connecticut was highest at $42,069 followed by Alaska, Hawaii and New Jersey. Lowest average incomes over the three-year period (less than $29,000) were in the South, overlapping into Missouri, Indiana and New Mexico. A second bloc of low-income states was located in the northern Great Plains and northern Rocky Mountain region including both Dakotas, Montana and Idaho. The lowest income state was Mississippi with $20,769, less than half the income of Connecticut. Next lowest (in order of increasing incomes) were West Virginia, Arkansas and Tennessee.

This map partly reflects the distribution of high-income, white-collar, professional and technical jobs that are particularly concentrated in large metropolitan areas, so there is some correspondence with Maps 1.3, Metropolitan Population, and 10.4, College Graduates, especially along both the East and West Coasts. These same states and metropolitan areas are also more likely to offer employment opportunities for two-income families, boosting household income. There is an inverse correspondence with the map of Rural Population (1.4) in that many of the more rural southern and western states are in the lowest income category. Also related are the maps in Section 5 on Ethnic and Cultural Diversity because of the lower incomes of many minority groups. Every state has unique factors too numerous to detail, such as the inflated incomes due to the high cost of living in Alaska and Hawaii and the lower income in Florida, due to retirees and recent waves of low-income immigrants.

Early data for 1993 showed that the declining trend in household income was continuing, down to $31,241 in 1993 from $33,585 in pre-recession 1989. Another continuing trend was concentration of income away from the "have-nots" and toward the "haves." Between 1968 and 1993, the proportion of income earned by the wealthiest 20 percent of the population grew from 42.8 percent to 48.2 percent, while the share of the poorest 20 percent of the population declined from 4.2 percent to 3.6 percent. Secretary of Labor Robert Reich called this distribution the most unequal of any industrial nation in the world. Regionally, it is interesting to note that six of the twelve states mentioned above that had significant declines in household income were among the 11 states in the high-income category. Three of the states, however, were in the low-income category: Florida, Kentucky and West Virginia.

50

4.1 HOUSEHOLD INCOME
THREE-YEAR AVERAGE OF MEDIAN INCOME, 1990–92

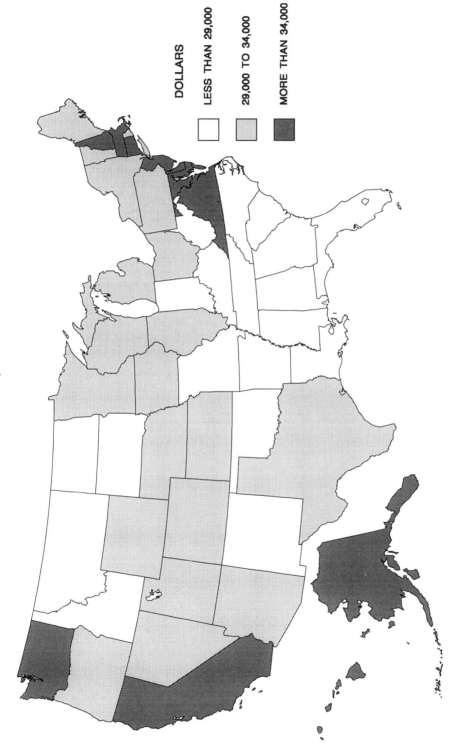

DOLLARS

LESS THAN 29,000

29,000 TO 34,000

MORE THAN 34,000

Source: U.S. Bureau of the Census

51

4.2   UNEMPLOYMENT

Unemployment in the United States in 1993 averaged 6.8 percent, down from 7.3 percent in 1992, but still slightly higher than the rate of 6.7 percent in 1991. The graph below shows the fluctuation in the numbers of unemployed and the unemployment rate since 1980. The most striking regional characteristic of the distribution of unemployment is the large bloc of states in the western interior of the country with relatively low unemployment, less than 6.1 percent. This bloc of states with low unemployment rates stretches from Wisconsin west to Montana and south along the Great Plains and Rocky Mountains to Utah in the west and Oklahoma in the east. Many of these states are the less urbanized states of the nation as shown on Map 1.4, Rural Population. In contrast, most of the more urbanized, more industrial states have the highest unemployment rates (more than 6.9%). The list of high-unemployment states reads like a roll-call of the most important states in the electoral college: California, Texas, New York, Florida, Illinois, Michigan, Pennsylvania, New Jersey.

West Virginia had the highest unemployment rate in 1993, 10.8 percent, and was the only state over 10 percent. California was second highest with 9.2 percent, followed by Maine, 7.9 percent, and New York and Rhode Island, both at 7.7 percent. Undoubtedly, defense downsizing plays a role in California's economic troubles. Some analysts have remarked how striking it is to see California with higher unemployment than Michigan (Michigan almost fell into the medium unemployment category—only 0.1 percent kept it in the high category). The lowest unemployment rates were in Nebraska (2.6%), South Dakota (3.5%), Utah (3.9%) and Iowa (4.0%). Low unemployment rates in many rural states are partly a function of fewer two-income families in the labor force. In non-rural states such as Virginia and Georgia, the economy is fueled by high-tech employment growth and the expansion of urban centers such as metropolitan Washington and Atlanta.

NUMBERS UNEMPLOYED AND UNEMPLOYMENT RATE, 1980–93

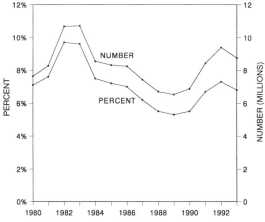

Source: Bureau of Labor Statistics, U.S. Department of Labor

4.2 UNEMPLOYMENT
AVERAGE ANNUAL UNEMPLOYMENT RATE, 1993

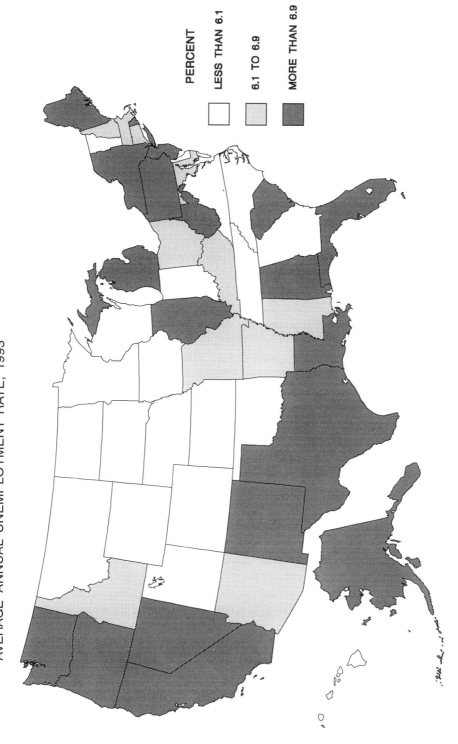

PERCENT

LESS THAN 6.1

6.1 TO 6.9

MORE THAN 6.9

Source: Bureau of Labor Statistics

53

4.3 FEDERAL FUNDS PER CAPITA

Any analysis of poverty and affluence in the United States must take into account the importance of federal taxes, federal government spending and federal assistance programs in the economy of the states. The Advisory Commission on Intergovernmental Relations calculated this federal impact in terms of the net flow of federal funds per capita over a three-year period, 1989–1991. This measure takes into account all forms of payments by residents of each state for income taxes, Social Security taxes, excise taxes, and other fees ranging from passport fees to National Park fees. From these federal receipts by state were subtracted all forms of federal funds dispersed to states or the individuals within each state. These payments are amazingly diverse and include direct assistance to individuals such as Social Security payments, Medicare, Medicaid and AFDC payments; agricultural subsidies; direct federal employment; federal contracts (whether for services or tangible items such as naval vessels); defense spending, including military bases, and federal cost-sharing with states and localities (such as for school and highway construction programs).

From these measures of federal income and expenditure (inflow and outflow of federal funds by state) a net flow of federal funds per capita has been mapped. The range of net flow of federal funds per capita is quite wide, from a net gain of $2,942 per capita in New Mexico (reflecting the numerous military installations and federal research laboratories in the state) to a new loss of $2,107 in New Jersey. Generally, the older urban, industrial states of the North, California and adjoining Oregon and Nevada have net losses. Texas, North Carolina and Georgia are also in the net loss column. For the most part, these states are those with higher income, as can be seen by comparison with Map 4.1, Household Income. This reflects the relatively progressive aspect of the U.S. income tax. There are exceptions to this generalization, however, as seen in North Carolina and Indiana, both states low on the income map and yet also experiencing net losses in the flow of federal funds per capita.

The redistributive aspect of federal spending can be seen in many of the states with substantial net gains per capita in federal funds. Many of these states are more rural and many are in the West or South. The typical state in this category is one with small population where federal civilian or military installations or agencies are major employers and have a big impact on the state's economy. The numerous military bases and federal research laboratories in New Mexico are examples of such employers, as are the numerous military bases in South Carolina or the community of relatively well-paid federal scientists in Huntsville, Alabama. Maryland and Virginia benefit much more directly from direct federal paychecks and payments to local contractors due to their proximity to the federal capital. In Virginia's case, there is an additional benefit from numerous military bases and naval vessel construction in the Hampton Roads area. Other than Alaska and Hawaii, where income figures are somewhat distorted by the high cost of living, Maryland and Virginia are the only other states that are in both the high-income category and the highest category of gains in flow of federal funds. (Data are not available for the District of Columbia itself as this study was restricted to impacts on states.)

4.3 FEDERAL FUNDS PER CAPITA
NET FLOW OF FEDERAL FUNDS, 1989–91

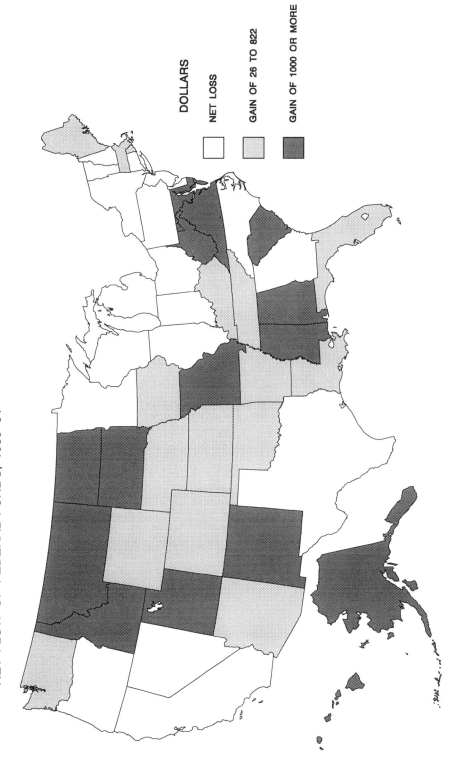

DOLLARS

☐ NET LOSS

☐ GAIN OF 26 TO 822

■ GAIN OF 1000 OR MORE

Source: Advisory Commission on Intergovernmental Relations, p.12

4.4   POVERTY

In 1992, 14.5 percent of the population, or 36,900,000 people, fell below the poverty line. The poverty line varies by size of family; in 1992 it was $7,143 for a single person and $14,335 for a family of four. The poverty estimates are based solely on money income before taxes and do not include the value of noncash benefits such as food stamps, Medicare, Medicaid, public housing, and employer-provided fringe benefits. The accompanying map shows a three-year average of the proportion of the population under the poverty line for 1990, 1991 and 1992. The percentage of people living in poverty varies by state by a magnitude of more than 3:1. Delaware has the smallest percentage of poor persons: 7.3 percent, followed by New Hampshire (7.4%) and Connecticut (8.0%). The largest percentages were in Mississippi (24.6%, three times the percentage of Delaware); Louisiana (22.3%); and New Mexico (21.4%).

The maps of Poverty and Household Income (4.1) are similar but not identical. The strip of Megalopolis states stands out again in having the smallest proportion of poor people, less than 11.4 percent. New York is an exception in that it has a larger proportion of poor people than its northeastern neighbors. The Pacific Coast has a relatively small proportion of persons below the poverty line. Like New York, California differs from its neighbors in falling into the medium class (11.4% to 16.4%) of percent of persons in poverty. Only 13 states have a larger proportion of poor persons than California; yet on the income map, California ranks ninth and falls in the highest income category, indicating an income distribution issue probably related to California's Hispanic and immigrant population. There is a large bloc of states with a relatively small proportion of poor people in the western interior of the country from Wisconsin through Iowa, Kansas, Nebraska, Wyoming and Utah. There is surprisingly little relationship between the map of Poverty and Map 4.2, Unemployment.

Once again, the South has the lowest rank on this index. All the southern states have more than 16.4 percent of their populations below the poverty line, with the exception of Virginia and Maryland (in the low-poverty Megalopolis strip), North Carolina and Florida, which fall in the medium category. The distinct appearance of the South on the map is related to the distribution of minority population. As shown by the graph below, minorities (except Asians and Pacific Islanders) are more likely to be poor than the population at large; thus the map closely resembles Maps 5.1, Ethnic-Racial Diversity, and Map 5.2, African American Population. Children are especially affected by poverty; 21.9 percent of children (14,600,000 children) lived in poverty households in 1992 and there is an obvious overlap with Map 13.3, Hungry Children.

ETHNIC DIVERSITY AND POVERTY
PERCENT OF PERSONS LIVING IN POVERTY, 1992

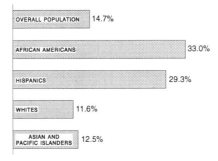

Source: U.S Bureau of the Census

4.4 POVERTY
THREE-YEAR AVERAGE PERCENTAGE OF PERSONS BELOW THE POVERTY LINE, 1990–92

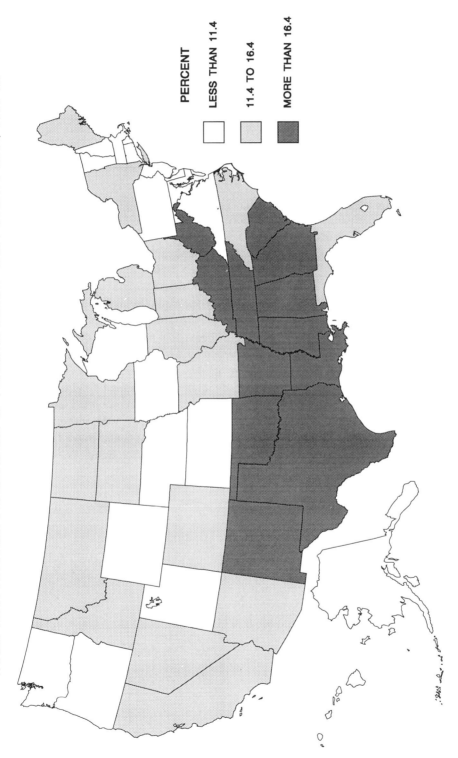

PERCENT

LESS THAN 11.4

11.4 TO 16.4

MORE THAN 16.4

Source: U.S. Bureau of the Census

4.5   CHANGE IN POVERTY RATE

How has the poverty rate changed among the states over time? The map on the facing page tries to answer this question by showing the ten-year change in the poverty rate from 1982 to 1992. The graph below shows how the overall poverty rate has changed over time. Thirty-five states experienced a decrease in the poverty rate; fifteen states experienced an increase. As the national rate was similar in 1982 and 1992 (15.0% and 14.5%, respectively), this implies that poverty became more concentrated in those states that experienced an increased rate. The magnitude of change among states was considerable; from increases in Nevada (6.6%), Kentucky (3.5%) and Oklahoma (3.0%), to decreases in Tennessee (6.6%), Arkansas (6.4%) and Utah (5.2%).

The distribution of rates on the map shows little pattern by large regions. Some of the sharpest increases in poverty and some of the sharpest decreases occurred in adjacent states (Nevada and Utah; Kentucky and Tennessee, for example) indicating that state-by-state change dominated rather than broad regional trends. One aspect in explaining the map is immigration (compare Map 3.5, Foreign-Born). This reflects, in part, the arrival of many low-income new-comers in states such as California, Texas, Florida, New York and Illinois. The increase in poverty in Nevada and Arizona probably reflects the phenomenon noted by demographer William Frey, that California is exporting large numbers of poor persons to neighboring states. Hardest hit are those southern states that are already in the lowest income category on Map 4.1 and have fallen even further behind. These states are Oklahoma, Louisiana and Mississippi, already among the bottom ten states in household income. Two neighboring states of the South, Missouri and Kentucky, are also in the low-income and increasing percentage of poverty categories.

On the positive side, nineteen states experienced a decrease of 2.0 percent or more in persons in poverty. Some of these states were in the northeast corridor, including Vermont, New Jersey and Delaware. Another bloc was made up of Virginia, West Virginia, North Carolina and South Carolina. Other states in this category varied by region and type of economy, ranging from Michigan and Montana to Arkansas and Hawaii. Three states with substantially declining poverty rates were already high-income states (New Jersey, Virginia and Hawaii). More common were low-income states where poverty declined, particularly in the South: West Virginia, both Carolinas, Tennessee, Arkansas and Alabama. Two western states, Montana and South Dakota, also fell in this group.

POVERTY 1959–92
NUMBER AND PERCENT OF POOR PERSONS

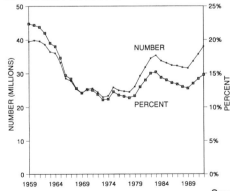

Source: U.S. Bureau of the Census

4.5 CHANGE IN POVERTY RATE, 1982–92

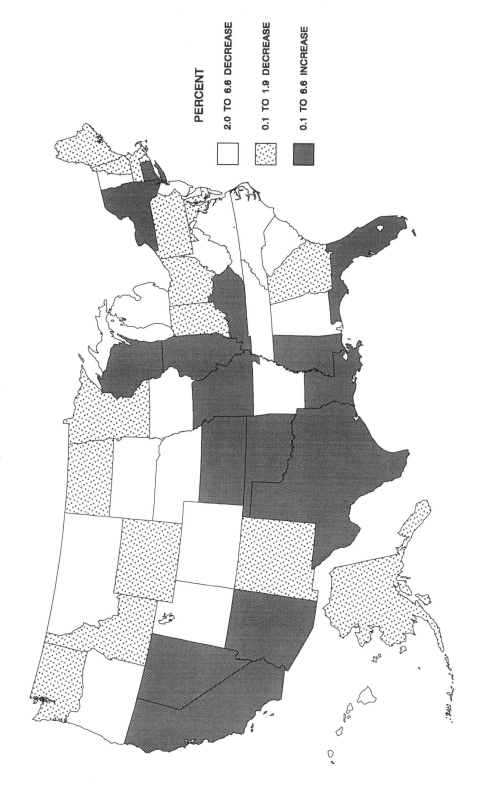

PERCENT

2.0 TO 6.6 DECREASE

0.1 TO 1.9 DECREASE

0.1 TO 6.6 INCREASE

Source: U.S. Bureau of the Census

4.6 WELFARE BENEFITS

Two of the most important programs in fighting poverty are the Food Stamp Program and Aid to Families with Dependent Children (AFDC). About 11,000,000 households and 27,000,000 individuals benefitted from the Food Stamp Program in 1993. About 14,000,000 people benefitted from AFDC in 1993, with substantial overlap between the two programs. The Food Stamp program, initiated in 1977, is administered by the U.S. Department of Agriculture. The purpose of the program is to enable low-income households to obtain a more nutritious diet. The USDA issues food purchase coupons through state and local welfare offices to low-income households. The AFDC Program is a provision of the Social Security Act. It provides cash assistance to needy children who lack financial support from one parent. The costs are shared by federal and state governments and some states require local governments to share the state costs.

As children are the primary beneficiaries of these programs, the Annie E. Casey Foundation has analyzed these data by combining the two major forms of assistance received by families and expressing that amount as a percentage of the poverty line for each state. The amount varies greatly by region because supplementary payments made by states vary based on generosity and differential costs of living. There is no state in which benefits from these two programs bring recipients above the poverty line. In Hawaii and Alaska, which both have high costs of living due to distance from the contiguous 48 states and due to restricted amount of land for agriculture, benefits come close to the poverty line, 98.1 percent and 92.7 percent, respectively. On the other hand, Mississippi, the state with the lowest average household income ($20,769) and the largest proportion of persons living below the poverty line (24.6%), has the lowest benefits from these two programs, benefits that bring recipients only to 43 percent of the poverty line. Alabama, Texas and Tennessee are the other states that fall below 50 percent.

The regional pattern shown on the map is familiar. It bears a close resemblance to Household Income (Map 4.1) and Poverty (Map 4.4) as well as the series of maps illustrating the distribution of minority population. States in which benefits bring income up to at least 68 percent of the poverty line are concentrated in the high-income states of the Northeast, all the Pacific states, and the northern Midwest (Michigan, Wisconsin, Minnesota and adjoining Iowa and North Dakota). Kansas is the only state in this category outside these three clusters. Almost all southern states are in the lowest category (less than 61%). Exceptions are Virginia, Maryland, Delaware and Oklahoma, which fall in the intermediate class. A number of neighboring states expand the southern bloc toward the interior: Kentucky, West Virginia, Indiana and Missouri. One other regional bloc is distinct on the map: a huge area in the intermediate category (61% to 68%) made up of almost all the western states from the Great Plains to the Pacific Coast states.

Many factors help explain this pattern. The states with higher income and higher cost of living have both the means to pay higher benefits and the necessity to do so to compensate somewhat for higher prices for food, clothing, housing and utilities. The southern half of the nation is faced with lower incomes and a more conservative philosophy relating to public assistance. In addition, in many of the more rural areas of the southern states, costs of living are substantially lower than in urban areas in the South or elsewhere.

4.6 WELFARE BENEFITS
AFDC AND FOOD STAMP BENEFITS AS PERCENT OF POVERTY LINE, 1993

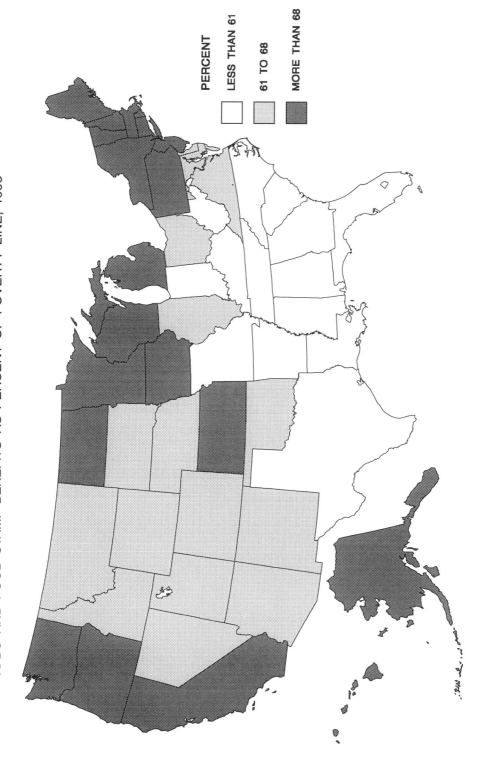

PERCENT

LESS THAN 61

61 TO 68

MORE THAN 68

Source: Annie E. Casey Foundation

61

4.7 LIFE INSURANCE

Life insurance is a measure of future financial security for the beneficiaries of the insurance, usually spouses and children of the insured. This map of life insurance in force per capita in 1991 is based on figures compiled by the American Council of Life Insurance. The total of life insurance in force by state, including individual and group policies, was divided by the population of each state to obtain this measure. Life insurance in force varies by more than a 2:1 ratio, from almost $63,000 in Connecticut to less than $28,000 in West Virginia.

An east-west division is evident on the map. Most of the states with the largest amounts of life insurance in force per capita, more than $41,000, are concentrated in the East, especially in the high-income states of the Megalopolis corridor from Massachusetts to Virginia. Georgia, Illinois, Hawaii and a bloc of three states made up of Colorado, Nebraska and Kansas, are also in the highest category. The largest bloc of states with smaller amounts per capita, less than $36,500, are in the Rocky Mountain region and West. A number of southern states fall in the lowest category also, including Florida, Oklahoma, the three states of the lower Mississippi, and West Virginia and Kentucky. Only two eastern states outside the South and adjoining states are in the lowest category—Maine and Wisconsin.

Clearly income is the most important variable explaining this pattern. Connecticut, the state with the highest household income, is also the state with the most heavily insured population. Connecticut, particularly Hartford, is also recognized as a concentration of some of the nation's largest insurance companies and employment in the insurance industry. Four of the bottom five states on the insurance map, West Virginia, Arkansas, Kentucky and Mississippi, are also among the bottom five states in household income. A second factor is evident in the east-west pattern. The West has a relatively younger population and a higher percentage of children, meaning younger families who cannot yet afford large sums for life insurance and more persons to divide insurance among when the per capita index is calculated. The eastern half of the nation is also home to more of the larger, established firms that are more likely to offer group insurance policies to employees. Many rural states are also in the low category, whether northeastern (like Maine), southern, or western. This may simply be another reflection of the income factor at work, but it may also represent many farmers not covered by group policies through corporations, as would be the case in more metropolitan states.

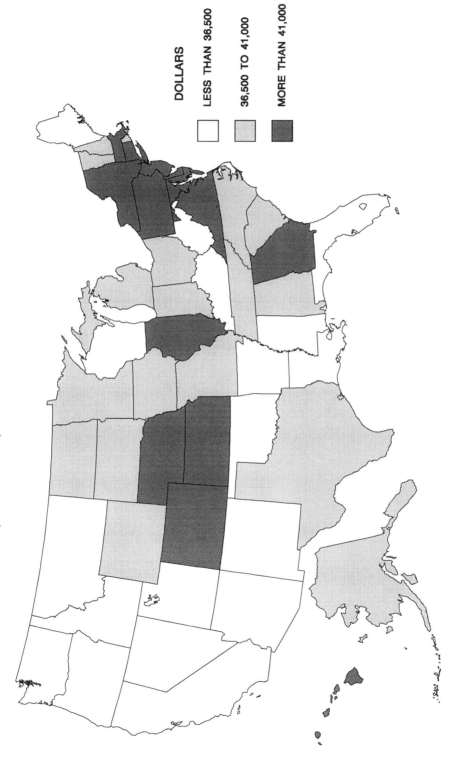

4.7 LIFE INSURANCE
INSURANCE IN FORCE, PER CAPITA, 1991

DOLLARS

LESS THAN 36,500

36,500 TO 41,000

MORE THAN 41,000

Source: American Council of Life Insurance

5

Ethnic and Cultural Diversity

5.1   RACIAL-ETHNIC DIVERSITY

This map uses data from a *USA TODAY* article and map that appeared in April 1991. The newspaper's researchers ranked states in terms of their racial and ethnic diversity by devising a statistical index "based on the chance that two randomly selected people in a particular area are different from each other racially or ethnically." The index used the Census Bureau categorization of the population by race and Hispanic origin. The four racial groups are white, black, Native American (American Indian, Eskimo, or Aleut), and Asian and Pacific Islander. (The census also uses the category "other races," not included in the diversity index.) The Hispanic group is linguistically defined and may include persons of any race. The diversity index calculated for the United States has a value of 40, meaning that there is a 40 percent chance that any two Americans picked at random are ethnically or racially different. The state with the highest diversity index is New Mexico, at 60; California ranks second with 59. At the other end of the scale are the diversity index values of New Hampshire (5), Vermont (4), and Maine (4). Iowa and West Virginia also have low diversity index figures. All five of these states with diversity figures of less than 10 are more than 95 percent white.

The map shows a pattern in which a southern rim of states from California all the way to Virginia and Maryland are in the high category, with index figures of more than 38. This region, commonly called the Sunbelt, includes many states with large African American and/ or Hispanic populations. Outside this southern rim, only New York, New Jersey, and Illinois are in the high diversity category, all with huge metropolitan areas that have attracted ethnically diverse migrants. Hawaii, with its majority Asian population, and Alaska, with a significant Native American population, are also in the high category. States in the middle category, with diversity index figures of 19 to 38, are mostly adjacent to the states with higher figures. They include the rest of the Northeast, several border states, and the state of Washington, which has attracted small percentages of all minorities. The least diverse states are in the northern half of the country, particularly in northern New England and in a band stretching from Wisconsin west to Oregon. West Virginia and Kentucky also are in this category. They have offered relatively few opportunities to migrants, have smaller proportions of minority groups, and their populations are over 90 percent white.

The map mirrors the prominence of minorities, almost exactly matching Map 10.3, which shows the percentage of minority enrollment in higher education. Two issues with the diversity index should be clarified. First, a state might have a high index value simply by having a very large percentage of a single minority group, rather than being truly diverse. For example, Mississippi ranks seventh on the list with a high diversity index of 48, solely on the basis of its large African American population (about 36%, three times the national figure). It has less than one percent each of the other three minority groups. Second, the diversity index does not take account of ethnic groups of European ancestry (except as they may fall into the Hispanic group). Thus northern New England is at the very bottom of the diversity index rankings, although its considerable population of French Canadians affords it a very real ethnic diversity.

USA TODAY also listed the 25 metropolitan areas with the highest values on the index. At the top of the list was Los Angeles-Long Beach (71), followed by Miami-Hialeah, New York, and Jersey City (all 66 or more). Of the remaining 21 MSAs on the list (all 53 or higher), 11 were in California, and many were in the Southwest. Honolulu and Chicago were also in the top 25.

5.1 RACIAL-ETHNIC DIVERSITY
USA TODAY DIVERSITY INDEX, 1990

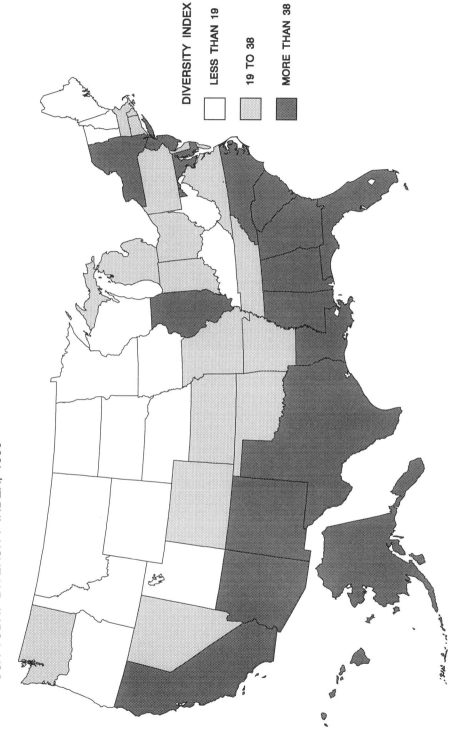

DIVERSITY INDEX

LESS THAN 19

19 TO 38

MORE THAN 38

Source: Data Copyright 1991, *USA TODAY*. Reprinted with permission

5.2   AFRICAN AMERICAN POPULATION

In l990, there were 30 million African Americans, making up about 12 percent of the total U.S. population.   At the time of the first census in 1790, blacks had numbered about three-quarters of a million, a number that grew to 4.4 million at the start of the Civil War.   The population doubled by l900, reaching 8.8 million people, who made up about 12 percent of the population. That proportion declined to 9.7 percent by l930, due to the floods of European immigrants in the early twentieth century, and then gradually increased again to the present percentage, almost exactly what it was in l900.

Within the United States, the distribution of this population has gradually changed over time. The map, which uses both choropleth and proportional circle techniques to show both percentages and actual numbers, helps in understanding how that pattern has evolved. The largest bloc of states with an African American population of over 12 percent (higher than the national proportion) are in the South, a region where the large African American population is a legacy of the era of slavery and plantations. Mississippi has the largest percentage (nearly 36%), followed by Louisiana and South Carolina (each around 30%). Percentages fall to about 16 on the fringes, in Arkansas, Tennessee, and Delaware. Then there are the big industrial states of the Northeast, which began to attract black migrants early in this century. As late as 1910, 90 percent of African Americans were still in the South, but then the Great Migration, in which thousands of blacks moved north seeking better jobs and living conditions, began to change the pattern. Today, New York State has the largest actual numbers of African Americans (2,859,000), who make up about 16 percent of the population. Illinois, Michigan, and New Jersey are all between 13 and 15 percent. Finally, another generalization that can be related to the map is that African Americans, like the rest of the population, have tended to be pulled westward in recent decades, so that now California has over 2.2 million. States with large numbers of African Americans are readily seen on the map by means of the proportional circles. African Americans are now primarily an urban population; 84 percent lived in metropolitan areas in 1990, 57 percent in central cities and 27 percent in suburban areas. In 1990, about 40 percent of the black population lived in 10 metropolitan areas. They were, in order: New York, Chicago, Philadelphia, Washington, Detroit, Atlanta, Houston, Baltimore, and Miami. In the Washington area, blacks made up 27 percent of the population of the metropolitan area; in the District of Columbia itself, they made up nearly 66 percent.

Some demographic characteristics of African Americans as a group may help to explain certain patterns in other maps. For instance, the age composition of a population is a prime explanatory variable. The African American population is a young one, with 33 percent of the population under 18 (compared to 13 percent for whites). In 1990, black median family income was still only 58 percent of white median family income, despite increases in the last two decades. The poverty percentage for black families was still 29 percent in 1990, down from 34 percent in 1967. A very high percentage (48%) of black woman-headed families were poor in 1990. Very striking is the change in the composition of black families over the last four decades. In 1950, 78 percent of black families were classified as married-couple families, while 18 percent were female-headed households with no husband present. By 1991, married-couple families made up only 48 percent, while the female householder proportion had risen dramatically to 46 percent. These changes help to explain why blacks are disproportionately represented in such maps as income, poverty, and non-marital teen births.

5.2 AFRICAN AMERICAN POPULATION
PERCENT AND NUMBER, 1990

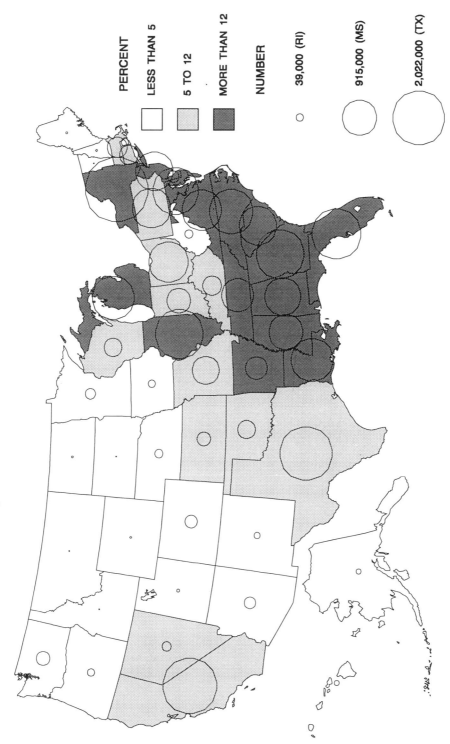

PERCENT

LESS THAN 5

5 TO 12

MORE THAN 12

NUMBER

39,000 (RI)

915,000 (MS)

2,022,000 (TX)

Source: U.S. Bureau of the Census

69

5.3   HISPANIC POPULATION

Between 1980 and 1990, the Hispanic population grew by 53 percent, a rate more than seven times that of the country as a whole. The Hispanic population grew most rapidly in the Northeast, South Atlantic, and Pacific regions. Fueled by immigration and by relatively high birth rates, it will continue to grow. In 1990 the total Hispanic population was 22.4 million; at present growth rates, the projected figure for the year 2050 is 80.7 million. Thus in 2050 Hispanics would make up 22.5 percent of the population, compared to 9 percent in 1990.

The pattern of distribution of the Hispanic population of the United States is one of concentration in the states bordering Mexico from California to Texas, in Florida, and in the large urban areas of the North, especially in the New York-New Jersey and Chicago areas. Expansion from the border states has placed both Nevada and Colorado into the high category. In the 1990 census, two states, California (with over 7.6 million Hispanics) and Texas (with over 4.3 million), together accounted for over half the total number of Hispanics. Both have large populations; in each, Hispanics accounted for close to 26 percent of the population. Both numbers and percentages help to tell the whole story. New Mexico, a relatively sparsely populated desert state, had about 579,000 Hispanics, but they made up over 38 percent of the total population, the largest proportion of any state. In contrast, Hispanics accounted for less than 2 percent of the population in the 21 states making up the lowest category on the map.

Hispanic is a linguistic term, not a racial or national one, and the origins of the U.S. Hispanic population are varied, as shown below. Some of the Hispanic population of the Southwest is of old origin, dating back to the days of Spanish settlement, though the largest numbers come from recent immigration from Mexico. Florida has many Cubans and some Central Americans, and the Hispanic population of New York City is distinguished by a large proportion of Puerto Ricans. Different Hispanic groups have different demographic characteristics, particularly in terms of education and income, but also in terms of fertility.

HISPANIC POPULATION BY ORIGIN, 1990

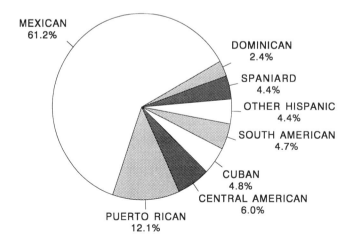

Source: *We the American...Hispanics*, November 1993, Fig.5

5.3 HISPANIC POPULATION
PERCENT AND NUMBER, 1990

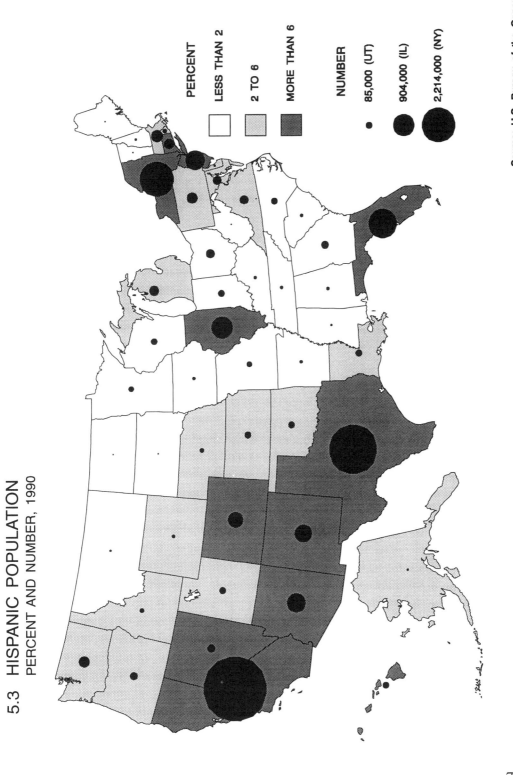

PERCENT

LESS THAN 2

2 TO 6

MORE THAN 6

NUMBER

85,000 (UT)

904,000 (IL)

2,214,000 (NY)

Source: U.S. Bureau of the Census

71

5.4   ASIAN AND PACIFIC ISLANDER POPULATION

In 1990, the census counted about 7.3 million in this racial/ethnic category, of which Asians made up the huge majority (6.9 million) and Pacific Islanders made up only about 365,000. This was a 99 percent increase of Asians and a 41 percent increase of Pacific Islanders over the 1980 population. For the decade of the 1980s was one in which the immigration of people in this category soared. Their proportion grew by 40 percent or more except in Hawaii, where they already formed the majority and grew by only 17 percent. In 1990, 54 percent of the Asian population lived in the West, which had only 21 percent of the total population.

The largest numbers of API population (Census shorthand for this long name) are found in California and New York, as is only to be expected. Percentages are high also, 9.6 in California and 3.9 in New York. Hawaii is in a class by itself, where the API population made up nearly 62 percent in 1990. The overall map pattern shows that Asians form a significant minority (in this case the high category is over 2% of the total population) only in Alaska, all West Coast States and Nevada, a belt of states in the Megalopolis area of the East Coast, and in Illinois. In other words, Asians have settled in the American states that are part of the Pacific Rim, in the big urban areas of the East, and in the Chicago metropolitan area. Some states in the Megalopolitan region (Connecticut, Rhode Island, Pennsylvania, and Delaware) do not rise to the two percent figure, but fall into the middle category of one to two percent. Also in this middle category are Georgia and Florida in the South; Michigan, Wisconsin, and Minnesota in the Midwest, and all of the Southwestern states except New Mexico. Louisiana, which has attracted many Indo-Chinese, is also in this category. Remaining are 22 states where the API population falls below one percent, mostly in the North and interior.

Outstanding characteristics of the API population are its great ethnic diversity, the relative youth of the population (median age of 30 years), the high proportion of foreign-born due to recent immigration, larger family size than the average American family, high educational attainment (though this varies by nationality group), high level of labor force participation, and the fact that nearly two-thirds still speak an Asian language at home. The population as a whole has poverty rates slightly higher than the national average, an apparent contradiction to the high educational levels, and a tendency toward higher-paying occupations. This is explained by the foremost characteristic of this broad group: diversity. The high poverty rate group includes the Hmong (64%), Cambodians (43%), Laotians (35%), and Vietnamese (26%), all recent arrivals, many of whom came as refugees from agrarian countries. Filipinos and Japanese had very low poverty rates.

POPULATION COMPOSITION
1992 AND 2050 PROJECTION

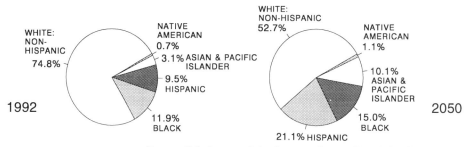

Source: U.S. Bureau of the Census, *Current Population Reports*, P25-1092

5.4 ASIAN AND PACIFIC ISLANDER POPULATION
PERCENT AND NUMBER, 1990

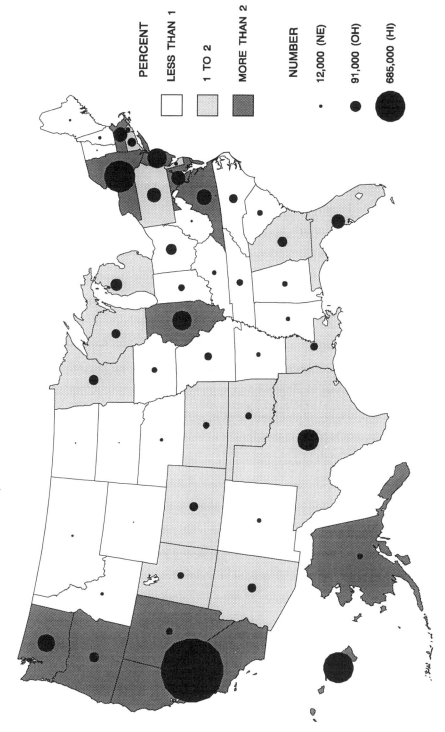

PERCENT

LESS THAN 1

1 TO 2

MORE THAN 2

NUMBER

12,000 (NE)

91,000 (OH)

685,000 (HI)

Source: U.S. Bureau of the Census

73

5.5   NATIVE AMERICAN POPULATION

It is ironic that by far the smallest of the racial groups recognized by the census is that which includes the indigenous population of our country—American Indians, Eskimos, and Aleuts, who are collectively referred to as Native Americans. In 1990, they numbered slightly less than two million people, or less than one percent of the total population. The Native American population was essentially stable from 1890 to 1920, then grew at a slightly higher rate from 1930 to 1950. In the last four decades the Native American population has grown rapidly, and is projected to reach 4.6 million by 2050.

As the map shows, every state has at least a few Native Americans, although only in some states of the West do they reach two percent or more of the population. More than half the total live in just in six states: Oklahoma, California, Arizona, New Mexico, Alaska, and Washington. Oklahoma has about a quarter of a million; this population dates from the 1840s, when the Cherokee and other eastern tribes were forcibly removed from their eastern homelands and relocated in Oklahoma. California is not far behind in total numbers.

Total numbers shown on the map show a remarkable degree of concentration for this population, but the percentages shown on the map are also useful. Alaska is highest in the top percentage category; nearly 16 percent of its small population is composed of Eskimos, Aleuts, and American Indians. New Mexico (9%) and Oklahoma (8%) are next. These states, together with Arizona, form a southern belt of high percentages, while the Dakotas, Montana, and Wyoming form a northern bloc. In the middle category (0.5% to 2%) the states are mostly west of the Mississippi, but include Wisconsin and Michigan, a continuation of the northern belt. On the East Coast, only Maine and North Carolina, both with small reservations, fall in this category. Over half the states are in the low category, with less than 0.5 percent Native American population.

A sizeable percentage of Native Americans (about 38%) lives on reservations or in specially designated tribal statistical areas (prominent in Oklahoma). The largest reservation population (143,000) is found on the Navajo Reservation covering parts of Arizona, New Mexico, and Utah. Other large reservations are located in South Dakota, Arizona, and Montana. The remaining 62 percent live distributed throughout the United States, mostly in cities, and roughly in proportion to the size of the population.

TEN RESERVATIONS WITH THE LARGEST NUMBER OF NATIVE AMERICANS, 1990

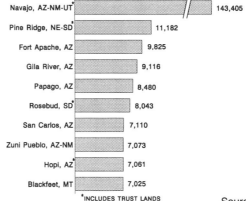

Navajo, AZ-NM-UT*	143,405
Pine Ridge, NE-SD*	11,182
Fort Apache, AZ	9,825
Gila River, AZ	9,116
Papago, AZ	8,480
Rosebud, SD*	8,043
San Carlos, AZ	7,110
Zuni Pueblo, AZ-NM	7,073
Hopi, AZ*	7,061
Blackfeet, MT	7,025

*INCLUDES TRUST LANDS

Source: U.S. Bureau of the Census

74

5.5 NATIVE AMERICAN POPULATION
PERCENT AND NUMBER, 1990

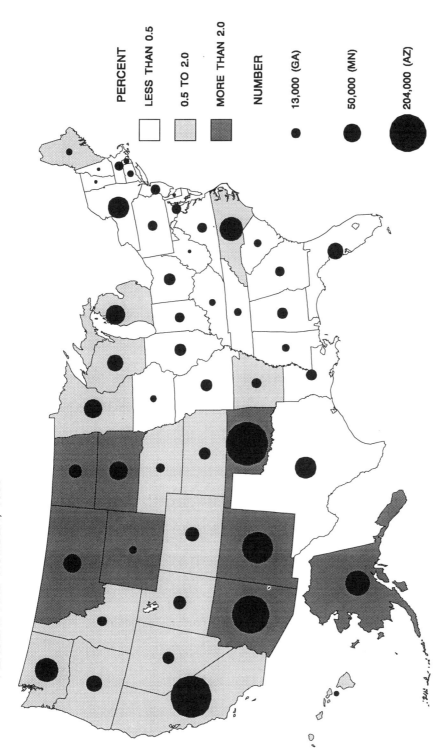

PERCENT

LESS THAN 0.5

0.5 TO 2.0

MORE THAN 2.0

NUMBER

13,000 (GA)

50,000 (MN)

204,000 (AZ)

Source: U.S. Bureau of the Census

6

Health and Disease

6.1   OVERALL HEALTH

The Northwestern National Life Insurance Company has developed a comprehensive ranking of the relative healthfulness of the 50 states based on 17 components that measure disease, lifestyle, access to health care, occupational safety and disability, and mortality. The 17 components include: prevalence of smoking; motor vehicle deaths; violent crime; risk for heart disease; high school graduation; unemployment; adequacy of prenatal care; lack of access to primary medical care; support for public health care; occupational fatalities; work disability status; heart disease; cancer cases; infectious disease; total mortality; infant mortality; and premature death. Many of these variables are mapped in this atlas. The overall pattern of social and bodily health serves as an excellent introduction to this section on Health and Disease.

The states are divided into categories of average, above average and below average health based on Northwestern National Life's scores for 1993. Two regions stand out as areas of above-average health: New England (except Rhode Island), and a band of western and interior states from Utah to Wisconsin. Virginia and Hawaii are the only two states with above-average scores that lie outside these two regions. States scoring below average are even more distinctly clustered. They form one large bloc throughout the South east of Texas and Oklahoma, and extend north into Kentucky and West Virginia. Alaska, New Mexico and Nevada are outliers in the below-average category. In this ranking system, Michigan has the most average or typical pattern of overall health. The highest ranked state, Minnesota (with a score of +22), lies at the opposite end of a north-south axis from the lowest-ranked state, Mississippi (with a score of minus 19).

Many of the indicators of health selected by Northwestern measure diseases that will be shown on the maps in this section. As an introduction to these maps, the chart below shows the leading causes of death in the United States. Heart disease alone kills one-third of Americans; cancer accounts for another 24 percent. After these two leading causes of death, only stroke (6.6%) is responsible for a significant portion of American deaths. The chart also shows several causes of death not related to disease: accidents (4% of deaths); suicide (1.4%); and homicide (1.2%).

LEADING CAUSES OF DEATH, 1992

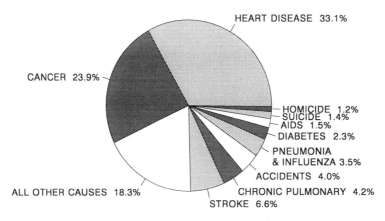

Source: National Center for Health Statistics

78

6.1 OVERALL HEALTH
NORTHWESTERN NATIONAL LIFE RANKINGS, 1993

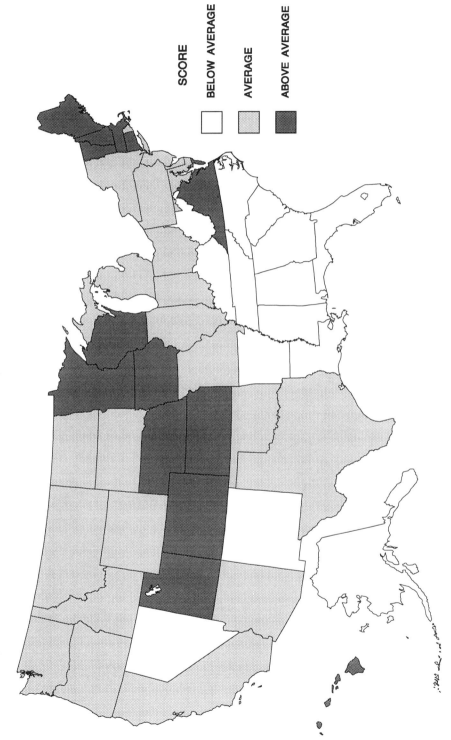

SCORE

☐ BELOW AVERAGE

▨ AVERAGE

■ ABOVE AVERAGE

Source: Northwestern National Life Insurance Company, used by permission

6.2　HEART DISEASE

Heart disease is the leading cause of death in the United States. It accounts for one-third of deaths, more than cancer, which accounts for about 24 percent. Coronary disease killed almost half a million Americans in 1990, about 300,000 of whom died before reaching a hospital. The most obvious form of heart disease is heart attack. Other important forms of heart disease include rheumatic heart disease, congenital heart defects and congestive heart failure.

The death rate from heart disease is highest for white males (148 deaths per 100,000 population) but slightly lower (143) for black males. While women had significantly lower rates than men, the rate was higher for black women (91) than for white women (71). Women, however, are more likely to have a second heart attack within four years after the first than men; they are more likely to die within a year from the attack than are men (39% to 31%), and at older ages, women are twice as likely as men to die from their heart attack within a few weeks. Older people, of course, are more likely to suffer heart attacks than younger ones, but 45 percent of heart attacks occur in those under 65; 5 percent to those under 40. Less educated people are more likely to die from heart attacks. Cigarette smoking, high cholesterol levels and high blood pressure are all associated with predisposition to heart attack, and combinations of any two or three of these risk factors produce even higher risk. Fortunately, the death rate from heart attack has declined by half since 1950; in 1950 the death rate was 226 per 100,000; in 1990 it was 114.5.

There is a distinct pattern to the distribution of death rates from heart attack. All the states with high death rates are concentrated on the Great Plains and eastward. States on the periphery of this region have intermediate rates as in New England (except Maine and Rhode Island); the Atlantic Coast from Delaware to Georgia, Louisiana, and the northern Midwest. Not a single state in the lowest rate category lies east of the Mississippi. Differences from highest to lowest states are striking: West Virginia's rate of 393 per 100,000 is almost five times that of Alaska's rate. There is an obvious correlation with age as shown by a comparison of this map with Map 14.1, Senior Citizens, particularly in the east-west component, as the western half of the nation has relatively younger population than the eastern half. The reader is also invited to compare this map with maps showing some of the risk variables associated with heart attacks: the overweight population (Map 8.3); physical activity (Map 8.1); education (Maps 9.4 and 10.4), and smoking (Map 8.2). While there are no simple explanations of this pattern, it is clear that there are states, such as Alaska, that rank "healthy" on maps of all these variables, and other states, such as West Virginia, that rank high in heart attacks and also rank poorly on all or most of the maps measuring lifestyle risks.

6.2 HEART DISEASE
DEATH RATE PER 100,000 POPULATION, 1991

RATE

LESS THAN 241

241 TO 299

MORE THAN 299

Source: National Center for Health Statistics

6.3 STROKE

Cerebrovascular disease, commonly called stroke, is the leading cause of death after heart disease and cancer. Stroke refers to a variety of conditions involving blood vessels in the brain; most common are the blockage of the flow of blood to a portion of the brain due to thickening of the walls of the arteries (cerebral thrombosis, related to arteriosclerosis); rupture of blood vessels in the brain (cerebral hemorrhage, often associated with high blood pressure); a blood clot formed elsewhere in the body but lodging in the brain (cerebral embolism); and a sac-like dilation of a blood vessels which then bursts (aneurysm). Perhaps half of strokes are related to blockage of the carotid arteries, the two main arteries in the neck supplying blood to the brain. The carotid arteries can become blocked with plaque, an accumulation of calcium and fatty tissue, reducing the flow of blood to the brain, or a portion of the plaque can break off resulting in an embolism. In 1994 the National Institutes of Health praised studies that endorsed carotid endarterectomy, a procedure that strips accumulated plaque from the carotid arteries and significantly reduces the chance of stroke for men (but not women). The result of a cerebrovascular accident, if not death, may often be brain damage. This leads to diminished speech ability, and diminished use of limbs usually on the opposite side of the body from the portion of the brain where the damage occurred.

About 500,000 people suffer a new or recurrent stroke each year. Stroke is also the leading cause of serious disability in the United States. Incidents are concentrated among older Americans (about 19% higher incidence for men than for women) but 28 percent of people who suffer stroke in a given year are under age 65. The incidence of stroke has declined about one-third just since 1980.

Stroke affects African Americans almost twice as frequently as whites. The age-adjusted death rate from stroke per 100,000 population was 54 for black men compared to 28 for white men; 45 for black women compared to 24 for white women. These differences by race and sex are in part related to differences in occurrence of high blood pressure (hypertension) between blacks and whites. While a third of white men have high blood pressure, 38 percent of black men have it. Among women, the difference is more pronounced—25 percent of white women; 39 percent of black women. Men have a greater risk of high blood pressure than women until about age 55; after age 65, the disease is more common among women.

The distribution of deaths from stroke shows a striking pattern. The east-west differential due to older average age in the eastern half of the country is evident again as it was on the map of heart disease. The highest death rates from stroke are in the South, in the western and upper Midwest, and in the northern Great Plains states. Most of the states of the Megalopolis corridor and those in the West and Southwest are in the lowest category. The classification of most southern states in the highest category is partly explained by the African American population with its higher incidence of stroke. The inclusion of many states of the northern interior of the United States in the same class is most likely a function of higher percentages of senior citizens in these states. The variation among states is substantial; Arkansas is highest, at almost 90 deaths from stroke per 100,000 population; Alaska is lowest with a rate of 15.4, one-sixth that of Arkansas. As with the map of cardiovascular disease, many of the states with low rates of death from stroke stand out as having healthy characteristics on lifestyle risk maps, such as those showing exercise, smoking, and overweight population.

6.3 STROKE
DEATH RATE FROM CEREBROVASCULAR DISEASE PER 100,000 POPULATION, 1991

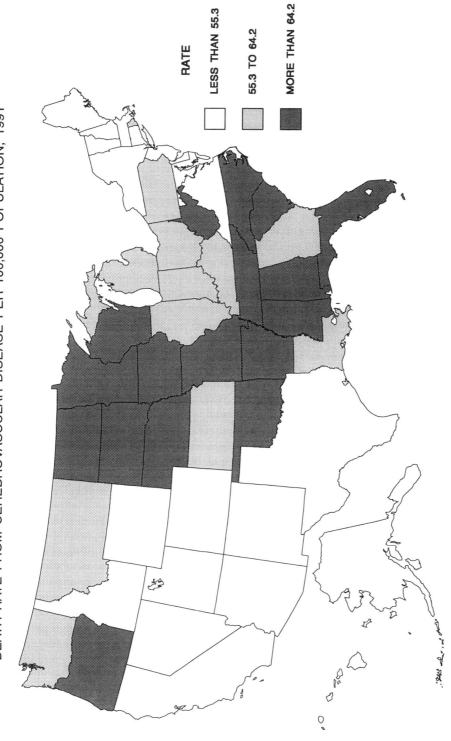

RATE

LESS THAN 55.3

55.3 TO 64.2

MORE THAN 64.2

Source: National Center for Health Statistics

6.4   CANCER

Cancer is the second leading cause of death for Americans. Cancer is responsible for 24 percent of deaths, second only to heart disease. Cancer (malignant neoplasms) is a group of diseases characterized by the uncontrolled growth and spread of abnormal cells. One in three Americans now living will eventually have cancer, but not all will die from the disease. While older Americans are more susceptible to cancer, it can strike at any age. Cancer causes more deaths among children ages 1–14 than any other disease. Cancer is caused both by factors external to the body such as chemicals, radiation and viruses, as well as internal conditions including inherited mutations, hormones and immune conditions. In 1993, about 1,170,000 new cancer cases were diagnosed as well as an additional 700,000 cases of the less severe form of the disease classified as skin cancer. Over 8,000,000 Americans alive today have a history of cancer, of whom 5,000,000 were diagnosed as having the disease more than five years ago, and are generally considered cured. About 526,000 people die of cancer each year (about 1,400 people a day).

The death rate from cancer was 143 per 100,000 population in 1930 and has increased to 171 per 100,000 in 1989, mostly due to lung cancer. Lung cancer caused fewer than ten deaths per 100,000 males in 1930 and now causes more than 70; lung cancer deaths for women have grown from less than 5 per 100,000 women in 1930 to more than 30. Comparison of this map with the map of smokers (8.2) shows a good deal of correspondence. The death rate from almost all other forms of cancer in men and women has declined or stabilized. Two dramatic examples are stomach cancer in men and cancer of the uterus in women. Stomach cancer was the leading cause of cancer deaths for males in 1930 (almost 40 deaths per 100,000 males) and has declined to less than 10 deaths per 100,000. Uterine cancer among women has seen a similar decline from slightly more than 30 deaths per 100,000 women in 1930 to about 7 deaths per 100,000 women.

Death rates from type of cancer vary significantly by sex, although lung cancer from smoking is the most serious killer for both sexes. For women, the major kinds of cancer by site are lung (responsible for 21% of female cancer deaths); breast (19%); colon (11%); pancreas (5%); and ovaries (5%). These five kinds of cancer are responsible for 61 percent of cancer deaths among women. For men, the leading killers are lung cancer (34%); prostate (12%); colon (9%); pancreas (5%); and leukemia (4%). The five types combined cause 63 percent of male cancer deaths.

Deaths from cancer vary significantly by state. Florida has the highest death rate (260 cancer deaths per 100,000 population) related to its having the highest percentage of senior citizens. West Virginia has the second highest rate (257). Alaska has the lowest rate (88), followed by Utah (112). As is true on many maps relating to disease and health, the West stands out as having lower rates of deaths from cancer while states east of the Great Plains have higher rates. Three New England states, Florida, and a cluster of states in the interior, eastern Midwest and Middle Atlantic are the states with high rates. Many (but not all) of these states have concentrations of the nation's heavy industry such as steel-making and petrochemicals, which contribute to the environmental causes of cancer. Most states ranked in the intermediate category are located in the eastern half of the nation. The South Atlantic states from Maryland to Georgia stand out with many western states as having lower death rates from cancer. Vermont, Minnesota, Alaska and Hawaii also have low rates of cancer deaths. The following two maps deal with the distribution of sex-specific forms of cancer: breast cancer in women and prostate cancer in men.

84

6.4 CANCER
DEATH RATE FROM MALIGNANT NEOPLASMS PER 100,000 POPULATION, 1991

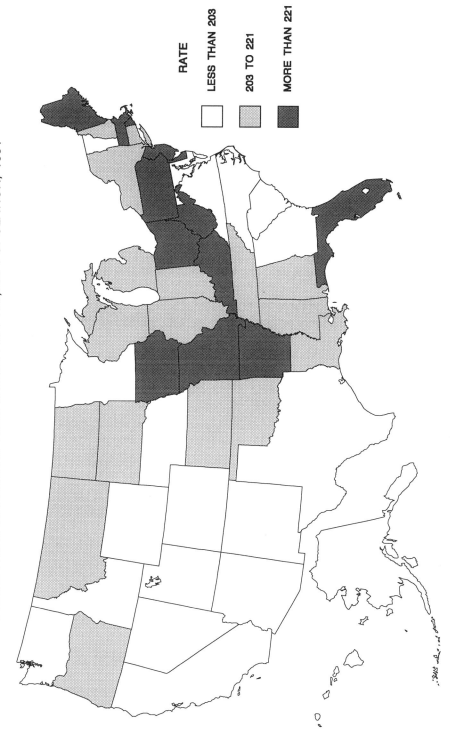

RATE

LESS THAN 203

203 TO 221

MORE THAN 221

Source: National Center for Health Statistics

85

6.5   BREAST CANCER

Breast cancer is a disease that arouses fear in American women, fear of the disease itself and fear of the disfigurement that surgical treatment may bring. In a 1994 report on breast cancer, the Centers for Disease Control stated that the disease is the most frequently diagnosed cancer among women and ranks as the second leading cause of cancer death among women. The CDC states that a health objective for the year 2000 is to bring the national death rate from breast cancer down to no more than 25.2 per 100,000 women. The main weapon against death from this disease is early screening, both mammograms and clinical examinations, in order to detect the disease in its early stages, when it is more treatable. Many of the established risk factors for breast cancer are things that cannot be changed, such as a family history of the disease, early age at menarche, and late age at menopause, so the strategy has to be geared toward early detection.

The two major factors that underlie the pattern that appears on the map are age and race. Women over 50 have a death rate from breast cancer that is over 15 times as great as that of women under 50. Black women have a higher incidence than white women, and both have higher death rates than women of "other races," which numerically means mainly Asians and Pacific Islanders. This is demonstrated in the very high death rates for the District of Columbia, with its heavily black population, and in the low death rates for Hawaii, with its majority Asian and Pacific Islander population. The table below shows deaths from breast cancer by age and race.

The map shows the age-adjusted average death rate for breast cancer for the three years from 1988 to 1990. The regional pattern is striking, with the higher death rates concentrated in the states of the Northeast and Louisiana. Such a pattern is suggestive of some kind of link with urban conditions and with pollution, though such links have not been proven. It can also be tied to the urban poor, who are often disproportionately black. The fact that West Virginia stands out with a low rate, a state which is not affluent, but is mostly white, is suggestive. Yet, states of the Deep South with large proportions of African American population are in the middle category, as are the remaining New England states and the states of the northern Midwest and Great Plains. In fact, Mississippi and Arkansas fall into the low category, in striking contrast to neighboring Louisiana. The other states in the low category are in the West, as is true on many other maps of disease.

DEATHS FROM BREAST CANCER
AGE-ADJUSTED RATES PER 100,000 WOMEN, 1991

RACE	NUMBER OF TOTAL DEATHS	RATES		
		ALL WOMEN	WOMEN UNDER 50	WOMEN 50 AND OVER
White	38,250	26.8	5.7	92.0
Black	4,809	31.9	9.1	102.1
Other	519	12.4	3.7	39.0
Total	43,583	27.0	6.0	91.8

Source: *MMWR*, Vol. 43, No. 15, 1994

6.5 BREAST CANCER
AGE-ADJUSTED DEATH RATE PER 100,000 FEMALES, 1988–90

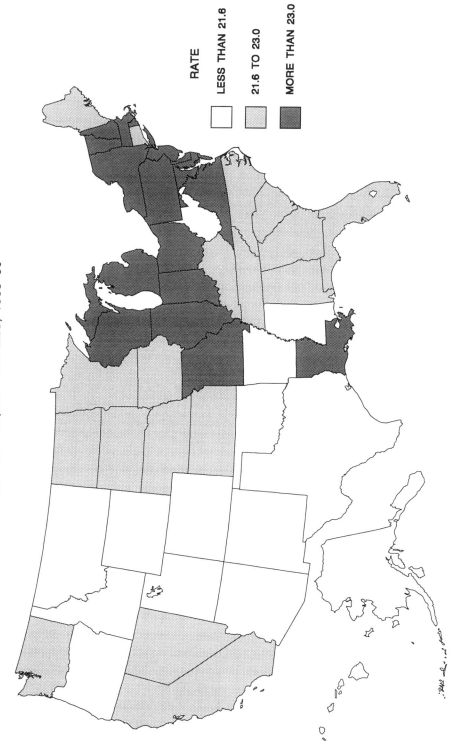

RATE

LESS THAN 21.6

21.6 TO 23.0

MORE THAN 23.0

Source: National Center for Health Statistics

6.6   PROSTATE CANCER

Like breast cancer for women, prostate cancer for men is the leading cause of death from cancer after lung cancer. Prostate cancer accounts for almost 12 percent of male cancer deaths (lung cancer accounts for 34%). Cancer of the prostate gland is by far the primary cause of these cancers, although the map also includes data for cancers for other sites in the male genital organs. The prostate gland is located near the outlet for the urinary bladder. Almost all men experience a slow enlargement of the gland in middle age, a condition called benign hypertrophy. Between 10 and 20 percent of men past age 50 will develop cancer of the prostate. The disease becomes increasingly more common with age, so that among men who live to be 90 almost all will have some prostate tissue that can be termed malignant. In most men, the cancer activity is slow and most will succumb to other diseases. The disease produces few, if any, symptoms in its early stages and thus annual examination by a doctor is recommended for men over 50. A prostate-specific antigen (PSA) screening test is available. The decision to treat or not treat prostate cancer with radiation, chemotherapy or surgery is tricky because the cancer can lie dormant indefinitely in some men, yet advance quickly in others. Since treatment can result in serious side effects such as incontinence and impotence, the decision to treat or not to treat the disease presents doctor and patient with a dilemma.

The death rate from prostate cancer in African American males is about twice that of white males. The death rate is increasing slightly for both groups, perhaps reflecting a stable occurrence of the cancer that kills more men as the average male life span lengthens; that is, as men live longer, prostate cancer, which was dormant or growing very slowly in many men who died of other causes, now becomes the cause of death. Age-adjusted death rates from prostate cancer range from a high of 21 per 100,000 males in South Carolina to a low of about 10 in Hawaii. The regional concentration of prostate cancer in the Southeast from Louisiana to Maryland is largely explained by the larger proportion of African American population in these states. This is borne out by statistics for the District of Columbia, which has a higher proportion of African Americans than any of the states and higher death rates from prostate cancer (29.5). This fact does not help explain high rates in states such as New Jersey and a group of northern states from northern New England to Montana and south along the Rockies to Utah. Note that Hawaii with its large population of Asian and Pacific Islanders has the lowest rate of prostate cancer deaths (as was true for breast cancer). States with either low death rates or intermediate rates are scattered throughout the nation without much pattern, except for a distinct concentration of states with low rates in California and Nevada and along the southwestern rim of the country.

6.6 PROSTATE CANCER
AGE-ADJUSTED DEATH RATE PER 100,000 MALES, 1988–90

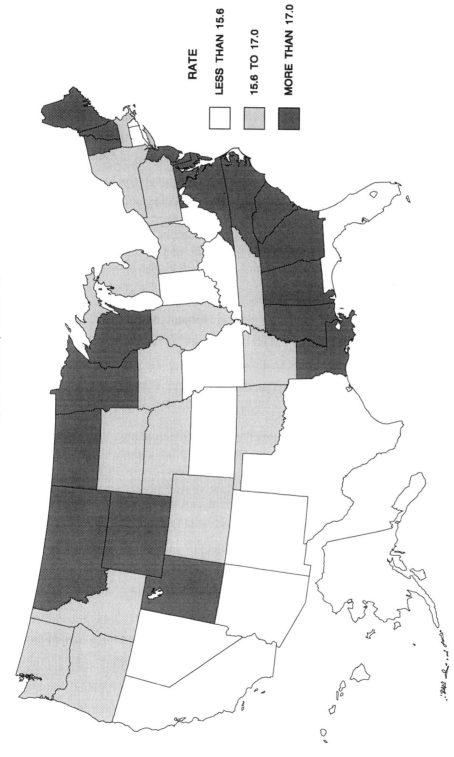

RATE

LESS THAN 15.6

15.6 TO 17.0

MORE THAN 17.0

Source: National Center for Health Statistics

6.7   AIDS CASES

Acquired Immune Deficiency Syndrome (AIDS) is a generally fatal viral disease that attacks the body's immune system. AIDS is the disease that results from exposure to the human immunodeficiency virus (HIV). There may be a long time between exposure to HIV and the development of AIDS symptoms. HIV may be acquired by several means but by far the most common cause of contagion is male homosexual contact, which is responsible for 53 percent of AIDS cases. Contamination by sharing needles among intravenous drug users is the second major cause, responsible for 20 percent of cases. In an additional 6 percent of cases, victims reported both homosexual contact and shared needle use, so these two methods of acquiring the virus combined account for 79 percent of AIDS cases. An additional 7 percent of cases resulted from heterosexual contact and 2 percent from infection during blood transfusions.

AIDS was first detected as a disease in 1981. By 1991 it had grown to be the ninth leading cause of death in the United States when it claimed almost 30,000 lives. Because males more commonly acquire the disease, it is the eighth leading killer among males (but is not among the top ten causes of death among women). Because the disease disproportionately affects African Americans, it is the sixth leading cause of death among that group. AIDS is very age-specific; 69 percent of deaths are among 30- to 50-year-olds, and another 18 percent fall in the 13- to 29-year-old group. Unlike many other diseases, AIDS strikes in the prime of life. AIDS is the leading killer of black males between the ages of 25 and 44. (The second leading killer of black males in the 25–44 age group is homicide, which AIDS replaced as the leading killer in 1991.) AIDS is the second leading killer of Hispanic males aged 25–44.

The map shows the distribution of AIDS cases reported (not death rates) in 1992–93. The states with a high incidence of AIDS cases (more than 32 per 100,000 population) reflect a combination of the factors discussed above. Because of the preponderance of the disease among African Americans, comparison of this map with Map 5.2 showing the distribution of African Americans is helpful in explaining the map, but that is only partially accurate. Generally, the concentration of African American males with AIDS is not coincident with the African American population as a whole, but with the urban African American population. Thus, not all southern states are in the high category, only those with major metropolitan areas such as Florida, Georgia and Texas. The Megalopolis corridor states from Massachusetts to Maryland also stand out (as well as the District of Columbia with a rate of 184 per 100,000, almost triple the rate of any individual state). Concentrations of homosexual males, as in San Francisco (which has the highest AIDS infection rate of all large metro areas, 235 per 100,000), and New York (138, second highest among metro areas), help explain why California and New York State are included in the highest category. New York State has the highest rate of cases per 100,000 population (77.8), followed by Florida (64.4) and California (49.7). In addition to the high rate of AIDS infection among the Hispanic population, other ethnic groups such as Haitians have high rates of infection. This phenomenon contributes to the high rates in Texas, California, New York and Florida (Miami has the third highest metro AIDS rate). Generally, states with low rates of reported AIDS cases lack substantial presence of the groups most affected by AIDS, as in a large area including the northern Midwest, northern Great Plains and northern Rocky Mountains. For the same reason, northern New England, West Virginia and Kentucky are in the lowest category. North Dakota has the lowest rate (less than 1 case per 100,000 population).

90

6.7 AIDS CASES
RATE PER 100,000 POPULATION, 1992–93

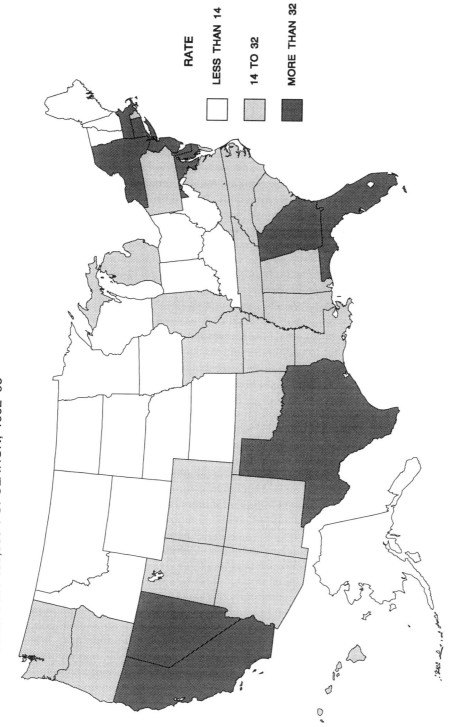

RATE

LESS THAN 14

14 TO 32

MORE THAN 32

Source: National Center for Infectious Diseases

6.8   TUBERCULOSIS

Tuberculosis is a disease that many had assumed to be almost eliminated in the United States. It had been in steady decline from the turn of the century until 1988. Then cases began increasing again to more than 26,000 cases in 1991 and a rate of 10.4 per 100,000 population (both figures about 10% higher than in 1988). Although this recent increase is serious, cases are substantially lower than in 1953, for example, when there were more than 84,000 cases of tuberculosis in the United States, a rate of 53 per 100,000 population. Fortunately, the death rate from the disease has stabilized despite the increasing incidence of infection. About 6 percent of infected individuals now die compared to almost 23 percent in 1953.

Tuberculosis is an infectious disease caused by the tubercle bacillus. The primary locus of infection (about 80% of cases) is the lung, but the disease can also lodge in other tissues such as the intestines, bladder, kidney and even the brain. The disease is spread by infected persons through coughing, sneezing, spitting and kissing. The bacterium can be transferred from one person to another by food and from animals to humans through untreated cow's milk.

Because the presence of the disease is partly related to sanitation and living conditions, particularly overcrowding, minority groups are more often affected. This is especially true for recent immigrants from countries where the disease is more common than in the United States. Mexico, El Salvador, Vietnam, Philippines, Haiti and Ethiopia are examples. Whites make up about half of the cases of tuberculosis; African Americans for about 37 percent of cases; Asians or Pacific Islanders for 13 percent; and Hispanics for 20 percent. (The figures add to more than 100% because Hispanics may also be counted in totals for the other groups.)

Tuberculosis is primarily found in urban areas where new immigrants concentrate and where minority populations of all types often live in overcrowded conditions. The graph below shows a clear correlation of the disease with size of area. States with high incidence of the disease are states that have a large proportion of minority population (compare this map with Map 5.1, Ethnic-Racial Diversity) and/or large urban centers receiving numerous immigrants (compare Map 3.5, Foreign-Born). States having all these characteristics have the highest rates of tuberculosis: New York (24.5 per 100,000 population); Hawaii (17.7); and California (17.4). Less urbanized states without much ethnic diversity and with few new immigrants have very low rates of incidence. Examples are New Hampshire (1.0) and Wyoming (1.3). Kentucky's high rate is an anomaly that may be explained by the fact that the bacillus can spread on dust particles in close quarters, such as in coal mines.

TUBERCULOSIS CASES BY POPULATION SIZE OF AREA
RATE PER 100,000 POPULATION, 1991

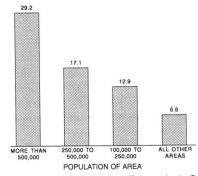

Source: *Tuberculosis Statistics in the U.S.*, CDC, 1991, p. 83

6.8 TUBERCULOSIS
CASES OF TUBERCULOSIS PER 100,000 POPULATION, 1991

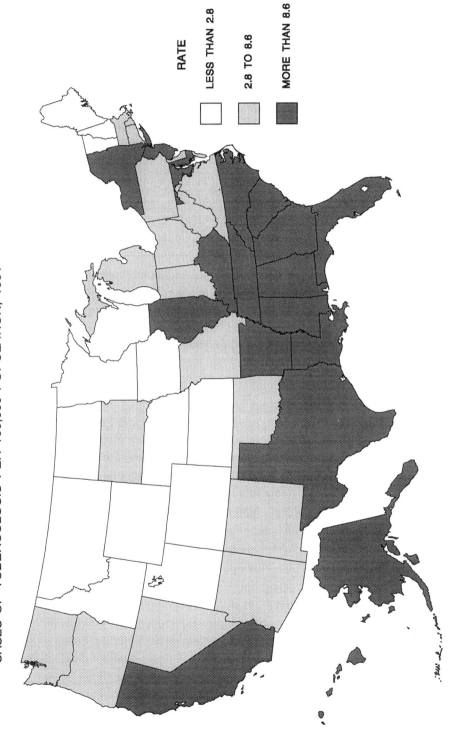

RATE

LESS THAN 2.8

2.8 TO 8.6

MORE THAN 8.6

Source: CDC, National Center for Prevention Services

6.9   SUICIDE

As noted on the chart of causes of death accompanying Map 6.1, suicide accounts for 1.4 percent of U.S. deaths, a proportion about equal to deaths by AIDS and to deaths by homicide. Who decides to take his or her own life? The occurrence of suicide varies greatly by age, by sex and by race. White men, by far, are the most likely to commit suicide. The rate increases by age from 37 occurrences per 100,000 white men aged 64 to 74 to more than 72 suicides per 100,000 white men over age 85. Obviously the increasing infirmities of old age, and in many cases, the presence of an incurable disease are factors in the decision to take one's own life. The suicide rate among black men is considerably less and does not show the same increased rate with age as for white men. While white women are more likely to kill themselves than black women, for both groups the rate is substantially less than for men. Among those over age 85, for example, the white male suicide rate is 14 times that of white women.

The map shows a distinct pattern of higher rates of suicide (more than 13.5 per 100,000 population) in the western half of the nation. Every state from the Rocky Mountains to the Pacific is in the highest category except California. Oklahoma, Missouri, Florida, Vermont and Maine also have high suicide rates. States in the lowest category (less than 11.8 suicides per 100,000 population) are concentrated in the North, particularly in many states of the Midwest, the Middle Atlantic and southern New England. States in the intermediate category are scattered, but most of the southern states (except Florida and Oklahoma) are included in this group.

What factors help explain this map? The rates are not age-adjusted, so one factor is surely the age of the population. Comparison of this map with Map 14.1, Senior Citizens, shows that the high suicide rate of some states such as Florida and South Dakota is very likely related to the large proportion of older persons in those states. Second, states with higher ratios of males to total population will have more suicides (see Map 2.6, Sex Ratio). This factor helps explain why the West stands out so prominently on the suicide map. In addition, the mythic tradition of the "Wild West"—the gun-toting, physically active, free male spirit—could also be a factor as many male suicides occur by gunshot, especially older males in their declining years. In any case, the seven states with the very highest rates are all western states. Nevada is highest at almost 25 suicides per 100,000 population. Nevada is followed by Montana (19.9), Wyoming (18.9) and New Mexico (18.3). This outdoor tradition may also be a factor in the high suicide rate in the Northeast's two most rural states, Maine and Vermont. In addition, religion undoubtedly plays a role, particularly among Catholics who regard suicide as mortal sin. Comparing the map of suicide with Map 15.3, Leading Religious Denominations, shows that many of the most Catholic states have the lowest suicide rates. New Jersey is lowest at 6.6 per 100,000 population, followed by Rhode Island (8.2); Massachusetts (also 8.2); Maryland and New York (both 8.8). The ethnic factor can also be seen by the suicide rate in the District of Columbia, which has a larger proportion of African Americans than any state and a suicide rate of 5.7, lower than any of the fifty states.

6.9 SUICIDE
DEATHS BY SUICIDE PER 100,000 POPULATION, 1991

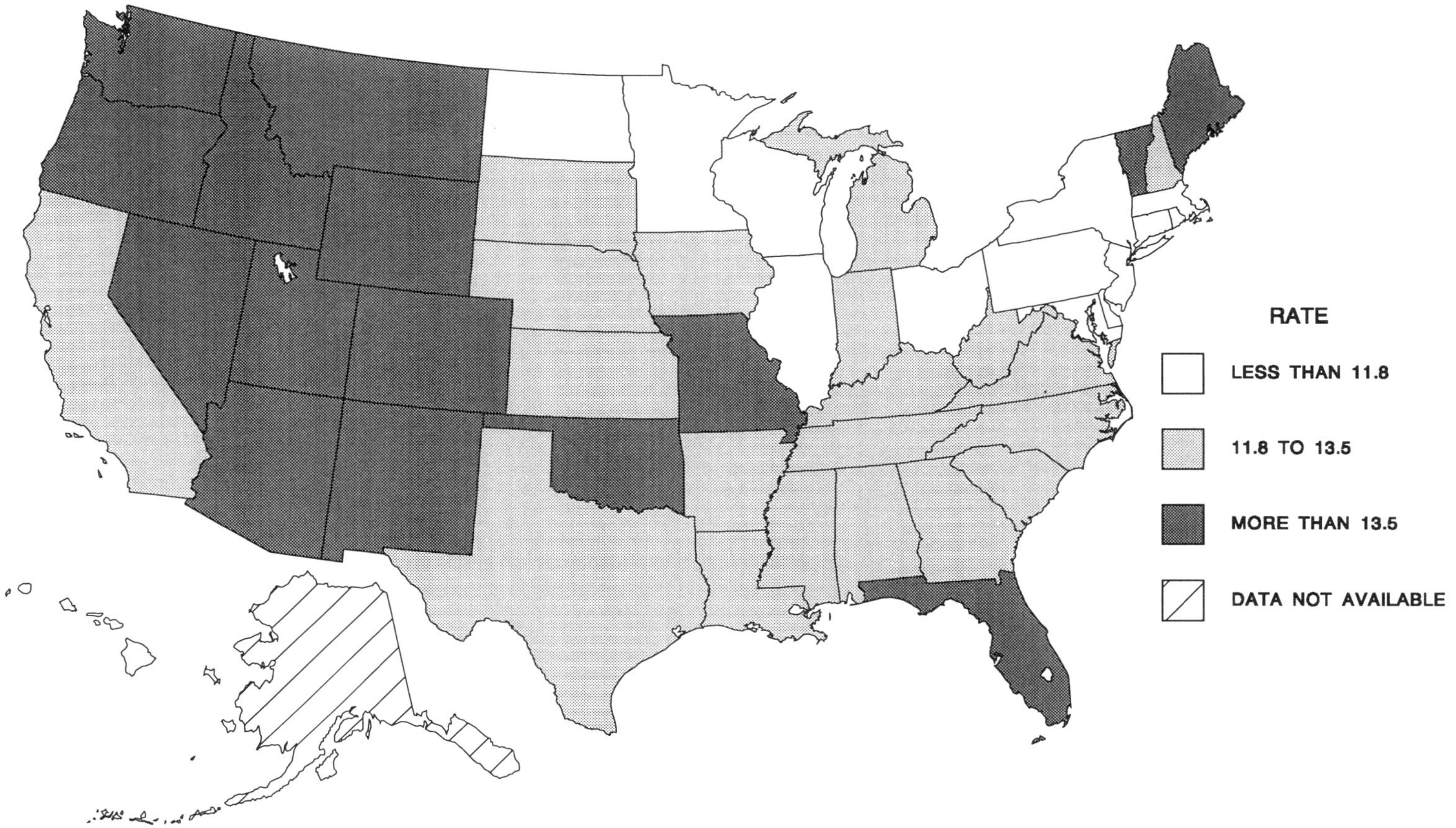

RATE

LESS THAN 11.8

11.8 TO 13.5

MORE THAN 13.5

DATA NOT AVAILABLE

Source: National Center for Health Statistics

7

Medical Care and Costs

7.1 PHYSICIANS

Physician supply is not the sole criterion for judging the adequacy of health care; there are other demographic and socioeconomic variables that affect both availability and quality. The ratio of physicians to population, however, is certainly one of the most commonly used indicators and it is an important one. The value for the United States as a whole (about 260 physicians per 100,000 people), falls within the range of the top third of states on this map. This is because large numbers of doctors are concentrated in certain medical meccas, most of them in metropolitan areas, while many remote rural areas remain underserved.

The lowest ratios of physicians per 100,000 population are found in some large, sparsely populated states of the West (Idaho, Alaska, Wyoming, and Nevada) and in Mississippi, which has a large population of rural African Americans with low incomes. Regionally, the low category includes a number of southern states (South Carolina to Texas, excepting Louisiana). Similarly low ratios are found in West Virginia, Kentucky, and Indiana. Also included are a bloc of sparsely populated states in the Rockies; this group extends eastward to include South Dakota and Iowa.

The high value of nearly 400 is reached in Maryland (totally urban DC, with a ratio of 765, is an anomaly). Maryland has major medical centers in both Baltimore and in the suburbs of Washington, where many federal physicians are occupied at the National Institutes of Health and in military medical centers. The high category (top third of states) has an interesting regional distribution. It includes two groups of states: the three Pacific Coast states and Hawaii, and the urban northeastern bloc from Massachusetts to Maryland (which is joined, surprisingly, by rural Vermont). Other states in the top category are scattered; they include Illinois and Minnesota in the Midwest, Florida (with an affluent population of retirees needing medical facilities) and Colorado (where Denver is a major medical center for a very large area including neighboring states). States in the middle group are quite scattered.

Physician services are a major component in the costs of American health care. The graph below shows that of the $666 billion spent on health care in 1990, 19 percent was spent for physician services. Hospital care accounted for twice that amount, 38 percent. Drugs and medical supplies (8%) and nursing home care (also 8%) were other major categories of expenses.

WHERE DO HEALTH CARE DOLLARS GO?
NATIONAL HEALTH EXPENDITURES: $666.2 BILLION IN 1990

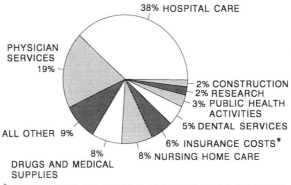

Source: American Medical Association, "Factors Contributing to the Health Care Cost Problem," March 1993

7.1 PHYSICIANS
PHYSICIANS PER 100,000 POPULATION, 1992

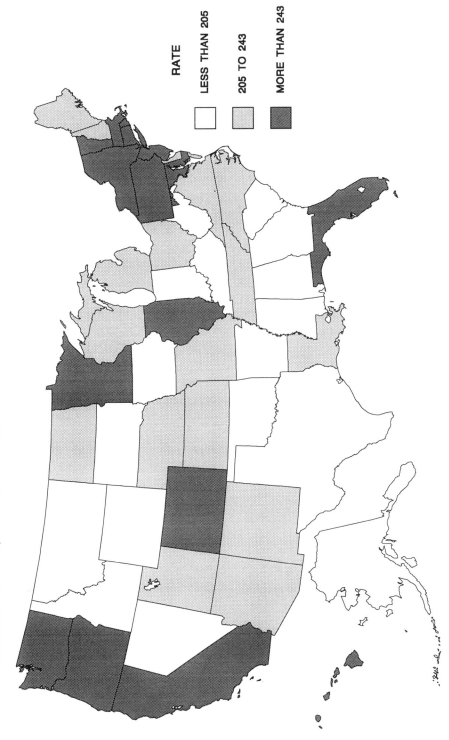

RATE

LESS THAN 205

205 TO 243

MORE THAN 243

Source: *Physician Characteristics and Distribution in the U.S.*, 1993 Edition, American Medical Association. Used by permission

7.2   HEALTH MAINTENANCE ORGANIZATIONS (HMOs)

By 1994, the year of the great health care debate, the acronym HMO (Health Maintenance Organization) had become a household word in America. HMOs are prepaid health care systems, either nonprofit or for profit. The Group Health Association of America, the national group representing HMOs, annually publishes information on the industry; this summary is drawn from its publications. HMOs vary greatly within the industry, from staff plans employing salaried physicians to contract arrangements with one or more independent group practices, or directly with independent physicians. They also vary greatly in size, with the ten largest HMOs together accounting for 44 percent of all enrollees in 1992. The giant of the industry is Kaiser Foundation Health Plans, which enrolled 6.6 million in 1992. The HMO industry is of recent vintage. As the graph below shows, HMO enrollment grew slowly but generally steadily from 6 million enrollees (who were in 175 HMOs) in 1976 to 45 million in 1993 (in 545 HMOs). The actual number of HMOs peaked in 1987, then gradually declined in a period of consolidation when larger and more successful organizations absorbed smaller ones.

The proportion enrolled in HMOs varies greatly from state to state, from 35 percent in California to zero in Alaska, Wyoming, and West Virginia. The major factor underlying this map is that HMOs thrive in metropolitan areas, where high population densities give the critical mass of members needed for convenient delivery of medical services. States that are more rural and/or small in population do not have high proportions of HMO enrollment. In the top category are California, Oregon, Arizona, Utah, and Colorado in the West. On the East Coast, this category includes a metropolitan bloc of states extending from Massachusetts to Maryland (except New Jersey) and also Florida. In Florida the enrollment in HMOs has recently increased, in keeping with its rapid urbanization and with the in-migration of people from northern states. In the northern Midwest, three states are in the high category: Minnesota, Wisconsin, and Michigan. In the low category are most southern states except Virginia and Georgia (both with large metropolitan areas), Iowa, and a group of states in the northern Great Plains and Rockies.

HMO characteristics vary by region. In the Pacific states, the large number of enrollees are generally in very large HMOs. The South Central and South Atlantic regions are most likely to have for-profit plans. New England plans are least likely to be for-profit but most likely to be qualified to participate in federal programs. The Middle Atlantic region, due to its location, is most likely to have HMOs that participate in the Federal Employee Health Benefit program.

HMO ENROLLMENT, 1980–93

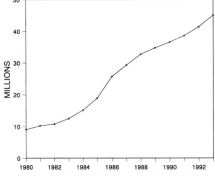

Source: Group Health Association of America, *Patterns in HMO Enrollment, 1993*

7.2 HEALTH MAINTENANCE ORGANIZATIONS (HMOs)
PERCENT OF POPULATION ENROLLED, 1993

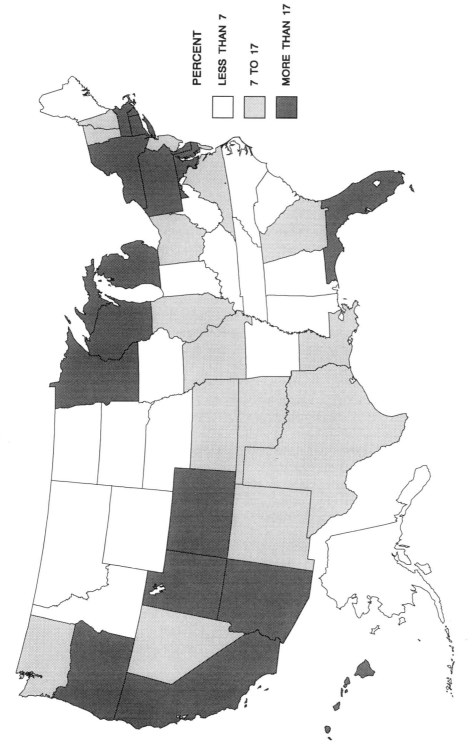

PERCENT

LESS THAN 7

7 TO 17

MORE THAN 17

Source: GHAA, *Patterns in HMO Enrollment, 1994*

101

7.3 PERSONS NOT COVERED BY HEALTH INSURANCE

One of the major issues in the health care debate has been the gap in health insurance coverage. As health care costs have increased, as shown in the graph below, the number of people without health insurance has risen. Despite the controversy over health care, there seems to be general agreement among government and private sources on several key points: that the number of Americans without private or public health insurance climbed above 38 million in 1992, that the percentage of the population that is uninsured is somewhere between 14 and 17 percent, that this percentage has risen considerably since 1980 (when it was 12 percent), and that as many as two million people lost employment-based health insurance between 1991 and 1992. While the number with health insurance has declined, the need for health insurance is increasing in importance as health expenditures rise. The graph below shows this dramatic increase in health care expenditures from $74 billion and 7.4 percent of the nation's Gross Domestic Product in 1970 to $752 billion (13.2% of GDP) in 1991.

The percentage of people who are not covered by health insurance varies among the states, for there are really 50 different health care systems in operation. It also varies according to certain demographic and socioeconomic characteristics. The map shows a three-year average percentage of persons who were without health insurance in the period 1990 to 1992. There is a wide range, from only 6.8 percent without health insurance in Hawaii, a state that has led in health care reform and has offered comprehensive coverage since 1974, to 22 percent in Texas (and also in the District of Columbia). The map displays a strong regional pattern. It is chiefly the Sunbelt states that have high percentages without insurance, although Virginia and Idaho are also in this group. In general, low coverage is associated with low income, with workers in small firms, part-time workers, and with the age of the population. The over 65 population is well covered; 96 percent are covered by Medicare and many also by supplementary private insurance. The age group with the highest percentage of people not covered by health insurance is the group in the 18 to 35 year category.

The states with low percentages (in white on the map) are mostly located in New England and in the northern Midwest and Great Plains. Low percentages without insurance are associated with affluence, with large firms employing many workers, and with higher levels of education. Some states that seem to have these characteristics fall into the middle category because of their large low-income minority populations; such states include New York and Illinois. Many border states and western states are also in the middle category.

NATIONAL HEALTH EXPENDITURES, 1970–91

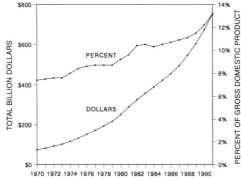

Source: U.S. Health Care Financing Administration, *Health Care Financing Review,* 1992

7.3 PERSONS NOT COVERED BY HEALTH INSURANCE
THREE YEAR AVERAGE PERCENTAGE, 1990–92

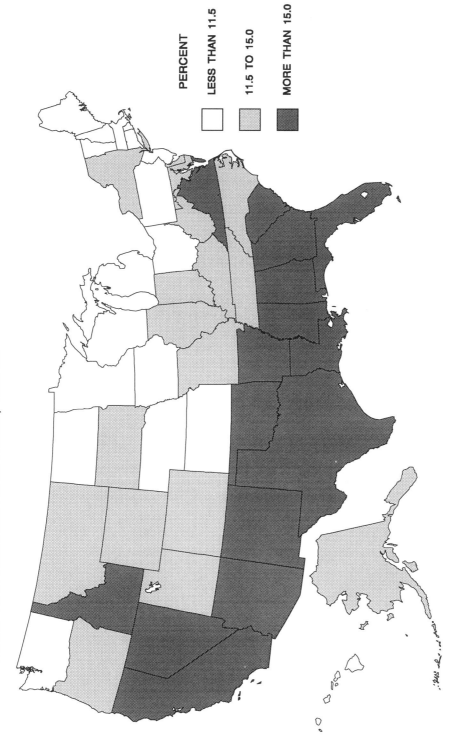

PERCENT

LESS THAN 11.5

11.5 TO 15.0

MORE THAN 15.0

Source: U.S. Bureau of the Census: 1993

103

7.4 ACCESS TO PRIMARY MEDICAL PRACTITIONERS

A problem often cited in the debate over American health care has been the lack of congruence between the supply of medical personnel and the populations who need them. The lack of access may be geographic; there may simply not be enough practitioners to serve a population in a given area, particularly one in which transportation is inadequate. This kind of access problem is usually associated with rural areas. Most physicians are located in urban areas with the technical infrastructure provided by large hospitals, medical schools, laboratories, and research facilities. The lack of access can also be economic; access can be blocked by lack of money and health insurance, problems often associated with poverty. This kind of access problem is often found in inner city populations located within blocks of doctors and hospitals.

In order to alleviate these problems, the Division of Shortage Designation within the Public Health Service is charged with designating geographic areas, population groups, and facilities (federal and state institutions) that have shortages of health professionals. These professionals include those engaged in primary medical care, dental care, and mental health care. Requests are channeled through state health system agencies to have certain geographic areas (often counties) or populations (such as poverty populations, migrant workers, or the homeless) designated as shortage areas or shortage populations. These designated areas or populations are then eligible for various federal benefits and the total percentage of eligibility for each state can be calculated. The map portrays lack of access to primary medical practitioners, the first line of defense in maintaining health. One of the arguments for health care reform has been that the United States has an overabundance of specialists but a shortage of primary medical practitioners.

There is a predictable pattern on the map. There are two regions and three states that are in the high category, where more than 11 percent of the population is underserved by primary medical practitioners. One region is the Deep South, states from South Carolina to Arkansas and Louisiana, an area identified with rural populations, poverty, and a high percentage of minority population. The other region includes states in the northern Plains and Rockies, from the Dakotas to Idaho. Here the greatest problem is a very dispersed rural population, sometimes forced to travel considerable distances for medical care. In some of these states, the presence of a substantial Native American population contributes to the underserved total. Among the single states in the high category is West Virginia, with a substantial rural population and problems of poverty and out-migration; it lacks the minorities often associated with the high percentage of underserved population. New Mexico, on the other hand, has a higher percentage of Hispanic population and also a substantial Native American population. Finally, the medical shortage in Alaska is perhaps easiest to understand—a small, scattered population in a huge, rugged area.

In the low category, with less than 7 percent underserved, are the East Coast states from Maine to Virginia (excepting New York and Rhode Island) and seven other states: Minnesota, Kansas, Colorado, Florida, Arizona, Oregon and Hawaii. These are areas well supplied with physicians and medical facilities especially in metropolitan regions. Most of the country falls into the middle category, with 7 to 11 percent of the population underserved.

7.4 ACCESS TO PRIMARY MEDICAL PRACTITIONERS
PERCENT OF POPULATION UNDERSERVED, 1993

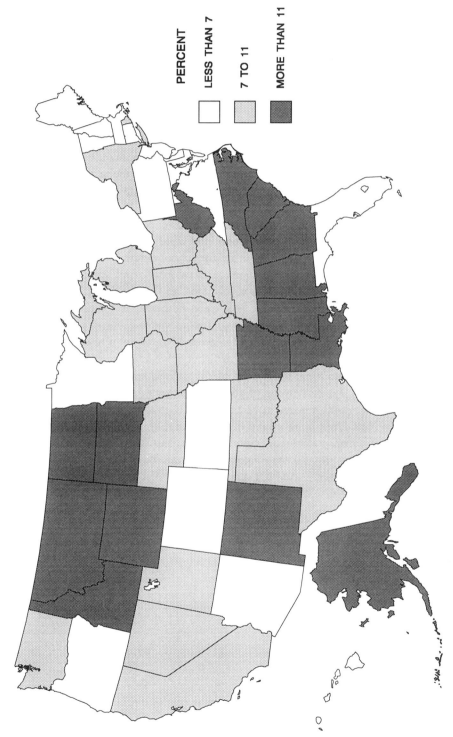

PERCENT

LESS THAN 7

7 TO 11

MORE THAN 11

Source: Department of Health and Human Services

105

7.5 IMMUNIZATION STATUS OF CHILDREN

The immunization of children has been a high priority for public health officials at all levels of government (local, state, and federal). In 1993, the new Democratic administration made a major proposal, that the government would provide enough vaccine to immunize all children in the country without charge, regardless of income. The proposal met with opposition from the pharmaceutical industry and some members of Congress, and eventually a much more modest plan was passed as part of the budget bill. The program approved would provide free vaccine to children on Medicaid, or who were either uninsured or had insurance that did not cover immunization.

The need for closing the gap in immunizations is recognized, but it is difficult to get data for the states or even for the country as a whole. Probably about 55 percent of children were fully immunized as of 1994, but many more are partially immunized. The series of immunizations for children are one dose of MMR (measles-mumps-rubella vaccine), at least three doses each of OPV (oral polio vaccine), and three doses of HIB (Haemophilus influenzae type b, which is a major cause of meningitis). These immunizations should take place by age two.

The Centers for Disease Control and Prevention have been making annual estimates of the level of vaccination coverage of young children since 1991, through a National Health Interview Survey. The most recent data are those for school enterers in 1992–93, children who were two years old in 1989. Data from the survey show that for all states, 90 percent or more of children had been immunized against *some* diseases. In fact, in the state of Tennessee, 100 percent had received some immunizations. But when percentages for the different series are examined, the needs are great. In terms of the oral polio vaccine, for example, the percentage ranged from lows around 60 percent in New Mexico and Michigan to highs of 87 to 88 percent in some New England states (New Hampshire, Rhode Island, and Massachusetts).

We have shown the data by state for the MMR (measles-mumps-rubella) immunization, the one for which the largest percentage of children had been immunized in almost all states. The range was from about 69 percent in Michigan to 91 percent in Vermont. All of the New England states plus New York were in the high category, as were Delaware, Tennessee, and Kentucky. Illinois, Wisconsin, Michigan, South Dakota, and Wyoming were also in the high group. In contrast, the states in the lowest category tended to be in the West and South, although Michigan and New Jersey were also low. Data were not available for six states, so the regional picture is incomplete.

IMMUNIZATION STATUS OF CHILDREN
PERCENT VACCINATED FOR MEASLES, MUMPS, AND RUBELLA, 1992–93

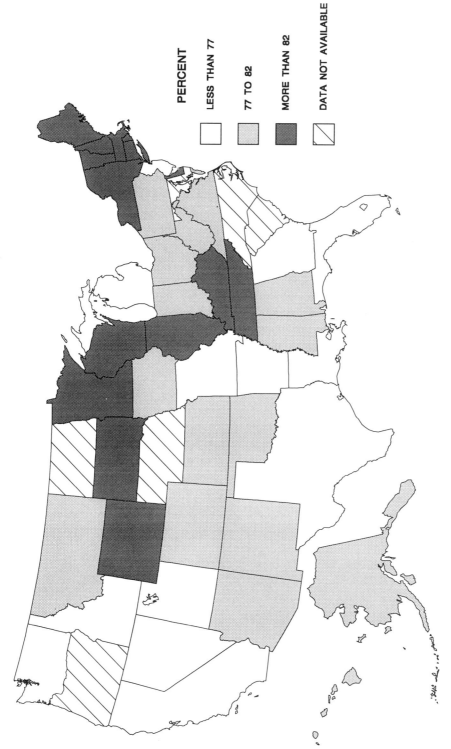

PERCENT

LESS THAN 77

77 TO 82

MORE THAN 82

DATA NOT AVAILABLE

Source: Centers for Disease Control and Prevention

7.6   HOSPITAL EXPENDITURES

Despite the great concern about the health care system and its costs, data about actual cost to patients and how costs vary by state are hard to come by. One source of information is the Statistical Abstract, which reports data from the American Hospital Association's annual survey of hospitals. The data mapped, costs to community hospitals, are not the same as billing charges to patients, but they are useful in giving an overall perspective on the variation of hospital costs among the states. Community hospitals are the (often large) public and private regional and metropolitan hospitals open to the general public; the category excludes military and specialized facility hospitals.

In 1991 costs per patient varied from $1,130 per patient per day in Alaska, with its high cost of living, to $436 in South Dakota. A fairly clear regional pattern is shown on the map. The states with the highest costs to community hospitals, more than $800 per patient per day, form a broad band across the Southwest and West from Texas to Washington and include Alaska. Other than these ten states, only Florida, Delaware, Connecticut and Massachusetts are in the high-cost category. Hospitals with the lowest costs, less than $650 per patient per day, are clustered in the interior of the nation in a large bloc in the northern Rocky Mountain states, northern Great Plains and upper Midwest. Several southern states are in this category, including Arkansas, Mississippi, Alabama, Kentucky and West Virginia. Outside these areas, Vermont and Maine are the only other two low-cost states. The remaining states, those in the $650 to $800 category, are concentrated primarily in the eastern half of the country in the remaining Midwest, most of the Northeast and along the South Atlantic Coast.

The pattern of costs defies easy explanation. Cost of living is undoubtedly a factor as many of the high-cost states have high costs of living, such as Alaska, which was noted as the state with the highest average costs to hospitals; were this the sole factor, many of the states of the Northeast would be ranked in the high category. There is clearly a rural versus urban component to the map. All of the states with large proportions of rural population, regardless of region, ranging from Idaho and the Dakotas in the West to Mississippi in the South and Maine and Vermont in New England, are states with low hospital costs. Partly this urban-rural difference may reflect cost-of-living differences, but it may also reflect less medical attention received by rural residents given the lesser accessibility of rural residents to health care, as was shown on Map 7.4, Access to Primary Medical Practitioners. More metropolitan states also face the costs of subsidizing low-income urban residents utilizing hospital emergency room services for non-emergency health needs. Age may be a factor in some states, such as Florida and Arizona, with large numbers of retirees who make extensive demands on hospital services, but many of the high-cost states are those with relatively youthful populations, particularly in the West.

HOSPITAL EXPENDITURES
AVERAGE DAILY COST TO COMMUNITY HOSPITALS, PER PATIENT, 1991

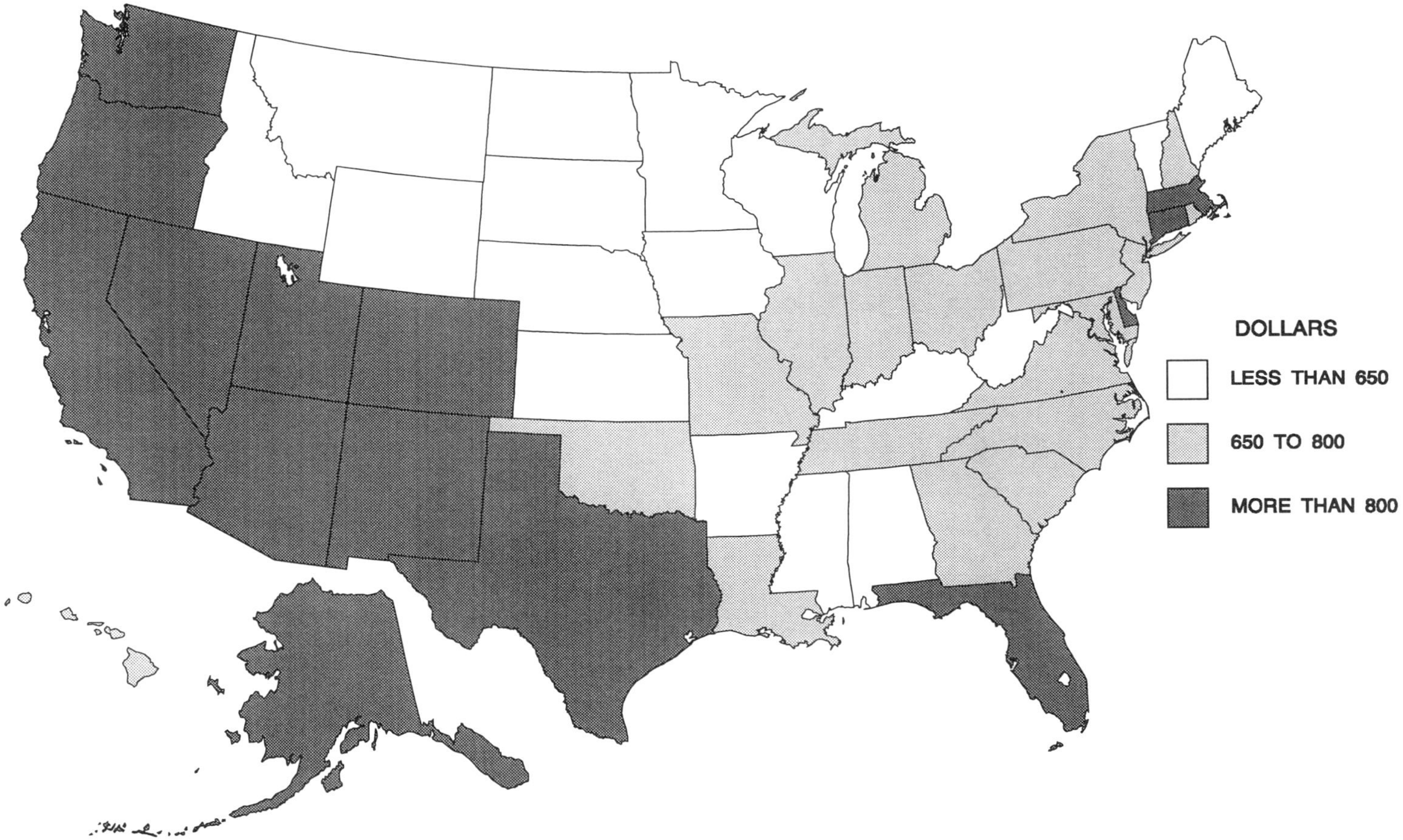

DOLLARS

LESS THAN 650

650 TO 800

MORE THAN 800

Source: Statistical Abstract

109

7.7   MEDICARE PAYMENTS

Medicare is probably the best-known of all the social programs enacted during the period of the Great Society. It dates from 1965 and it has or will affect almost all Americans. Not all are poor, which is the criterion for many social programs, but all will grow old. At age 65, many Americans become eligible for Social Security benefits and also qualify for Medicare, which is essentially health insurance for the elderly. Spouses of persons who are eligible for Social Security are also eligible for Medicare, as are some categories of disabled people and people with kidney diseases. While Medicaid was designed to help the poorer people of our society and is a welfare program, Medicare is supposed to pay part of the cost of medical care for all citizens over 65, regardless of need. Because of it, the elderly are perhaps the best-insured age group in the country. Many of them rely on Medicare as a basic insurance, but also supplement it with private insurance, usually acquired from employers before retirement. For the poor, Medicaid may be used to supplement Medicare, and it provides an important additional benefit: long-term care.

Medicare comes in two parts, Part A and Part B. Part A refers to hospitalization insurance and there is no charge for it; it comes automatically with eligibility for Medicare at age 65. Part B essentially covers physician services, and people pay a monthly premium (relatively low), which for most people is simply deducted from their monthly Social Security benefits. The Medicare administration sets standard amounts for physicians' fees and other medical work (laboratory, x-rays, etc.). If medical providers agree to "accept assignment" of the fees that are set by Medicare, then the senior patient is responsible only for a 20 percent copayment. Medicare comprises a major source of income to doctors and clinics.

Medical fees vary according to standard of living and local norms and the Medicare clientele varies from state to state. Thus the map displays some variation, even though this is a federal program and the many state options that make Medicaid so variable do not enter in. Average benefit payments per Medicare enrollee in fiscal year 1993 varied among the states from a low of $2,400 in Idaho to a high of $4,920 in Massachusetts. The map pattern is not easy to understand or explain. One important explanatory factor is that the benefits were reported according to the state of the medical care provider, rather than the residence of the enrollee. Thus states whose excellent medical facilities attract many out-of-state residents have high values on the map. The map shows that Medicare expenditures are higher in the northeastern Megalopolitan region and in many Sunbelt states.

DOCTORS AND CLINICS: SOURCES OF INCOME
ESTIMATED RECEIPTS FOR TAXABLE FIRMS, 1992

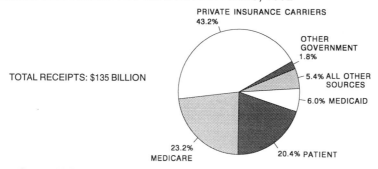

TOTAL RECEIPTS: $135 BILLION

PRIVATE INSURANCE CARRIERS 43.2%
OTHER GOVERNMENT 1.8%
5.4% ALL OTHER SOURCES
6.0% MEDICAID
20.4% PATIENT
23.2% MEDICARE

Source: U.S. Bureau of the Census, *Current Business Reports, BS/92, Service Annual Survey: 1992*, Fig. 7.5

110

7.7 MEDICARE PAYMENTS
BENEFIT PAYMENTS PER MEDICARE ENROLLEE, 1993

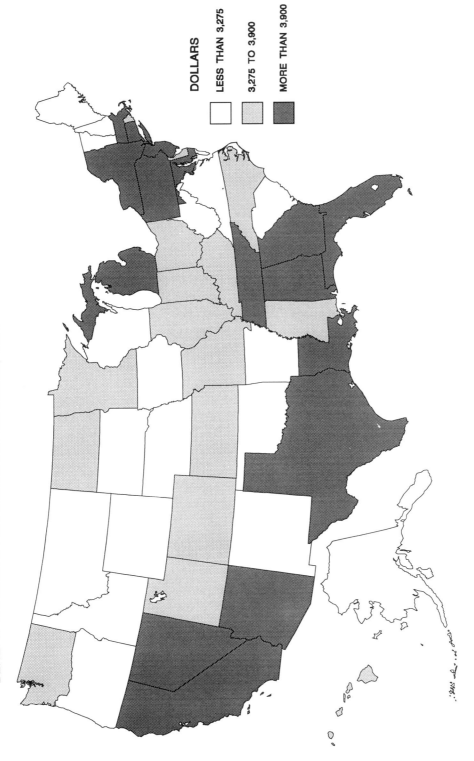

DOLLARS

LESS THAN 3,275

3,275 TO 3,900

MORE THAN 3,900

Source: Health Care Financing Administration

111

7.8   MEDICAID ELIGIBILITY

Medicaid is a government welfare program designed to help pay for health care for people and families with low incomes and limited resources. The program became law in 1965 and is a cooperative federal-state venture, with the federal government providing broad guidelines and the states having considerable powers in determining eligibility, providing a variety of services, and setting the rate of payment for services. This means that the Medicaid program varies from state to state, as this and the next map show.

Some groups are mandated by the federal government as being eligible. Such groups include recipients of Aid to Families with Dependent Children (AFDC), Supplemental Security Income (SSI) recipients, some Medicare beneficiaries, and some others. The emphasis is on pregnant women, infants, children, the blind, persons with disabilities, and the elderly, as shown by the graph below. States have the option to expand the definition to include more people who are not necessarily below the poverty line or receiving other government aid. They can also include "medically needy" persons who may have too much income to qualify under the mandatory rules, but who have unusually heavy and continuing medical expenses.

The map shows the percentage of each state's population that was eligible for Medicaid in 1992. The percentage eligible varies with the percentage in poverty (as determined by the mandatory federal guidelines) and with the liberality of the state programs in adding other groups. More affluent states, or states with a heavy emphasis on human services and welfare, may expand the number of eligibles. Thus the map does not simply mirror the poverty map. There is a considerable range, from only 7.1 percent of the population eligible for Medicaid in New Hampshire to 21.3 percent in West Virginia and in the District of Columbia.

The national average proportion of the population receiving some Medicaid assistance is about 14 percent, and all states in the highest category are above the national average. Perhaps because of the numerous state options, there is no real regional pattern except for the California-Arizona-New Mexico grouping. However, all thirteen of the other states in the high category are located in the eastern half of the country. The high category includes states that range from rural to metropolitan, from northern to southern, with and without large minority groups. The low group, states with less than 11 percent of Medicaid eligibles, presents a somewhat more regionalized picture. It includes a large bloc of states in the Great Plains and Rockies, some East Coast states, Hawaii and Indiana.

MEDICAID RECIPIENTS AND VENDOR PAYMENTS
BY BASIS OF ELIGIBILITY, FISCAL YEAR 1992

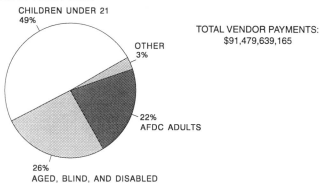

TOTAL VENDOR PAYMENTS:
$91,479,639,165

Source: Health Care Financing Administration, Division of Medicaid Statistics

112

7.8 MEDICAID ELIGIBILITY
PERCENT OF POPULATION ELIGIBLE FOR MEDICAID, 1992

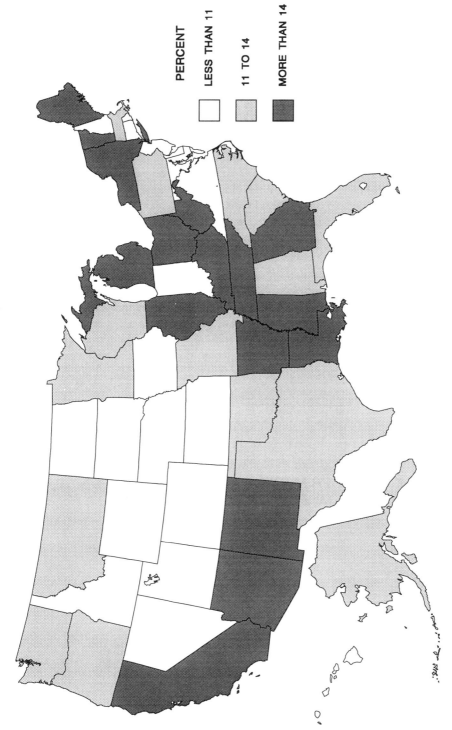

PERCENT

LESS THAN 11

11 TO 14

MORE THAN 14

Source: Health Care Financing Administration

7.9 MEDICAID EXPENDITURES

Medicaid expenditures have risen steadily over the years. Both the number of recipients and the average expenditure per recipient have increased, as shown on the graph below. In 1971, the average payment per recipient was a little over $300; by 1992, that amount had risen to close to $3,000. Medicaid operates as a vendor payment program, paying directly to the health providers. The amount of federal expenditure has no set limit but must at least match what the states provide, and is often more. The federal percentage is determined annually for each state by a formula that compares the average per capita income of the states with the national average, so that the wealthier states pay a larger share. By law, the federal portion cannot be lower than 50 percent nor greater than 83 percent. In 1992, the federal share was 50 percent in 17 states and the District of Columbia, but it ranged up to 80 percent in Mississippi and 78 percent in West Virginia.

All states provide certain basic services mandated by law. They include both in-patient and out-patient hospital services, laboratory and x-ray services, and the services of physicians, as well as some others. Above and beyond these basic services, however, states provide a large range of optional benefits, ranging from the services of podiatrists, optometrists, and psychologists to occupational therapy and Christian Science Sanitoriums.

The map focuses on the average payment to health care vendors (physicians, hospitals, and all other services provided) per Medicaid recipient in 1992; the national average was $2,936. Two regions stand out in which expenditures per recipient were quite high, over $3,600. They are the East Coast region from Maine to Maryland, the region including Megalopolis, where living costs are high, and a region that stretches along the Canadian border from Wisconsin to Montana. What do these regions have in common? One is highly metropolitan, while the other is more rural and oriented to agricultural industries. It may be that in the one case the higher Medicaid payments arise from necessity—the cost of medical care—and in the other case from conviction, in a region noted for emphasis on meeting human needs. Indiana and Nevada are also in the high category. States with the lowest medicaid expenditures, less than $2,700 per recipient, are located primarily in the Sunbelt states and along the West Coast.

AVERAGE PAYMENT PER MEDICAID RECIPIENT AND PERCENTAGE CHANGE, 1971–92

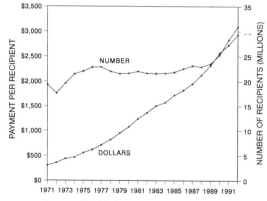

Source: Health Care Financing Administration, Division of Medicaid Statistics

114

7.9 MEDICAID EXPENDITURES
AVERAGE COST PER RECIPIENT, 1992

DOLLARS

LESS THAN 2,700

2,700 TO 3,600

MORE THAN 3,600

Source: Health Care Financing Administration

115

8

Lifestyle Risks

8.1   LEISURE-TIME PHYSICAL ACTIVITY

An examination of health care and disease would not be complete without reference to American lifestyle characteristics that affect health. Americans make choices in the lifestyle and use of leisure time that impact their personal health and in turn, the overall societal costs of health care. The Centers for Disease Control and Prevention, which compiled most of the data in this section, titled their 1991 study "Behavioral Risk Factor Surveillance." Data are from a sample of thousands of adults across the United States (the number of those surveyed ranged from 1100 to 3400 by state).

One lifestyle risk examined by the CDC is leisure-time physical activity. Map 8.1 shows the distribution of the adult population who reported no exercise, recreation or physical activity (other than regular job duties) during the previous month. There is a distinct regional bias to the data. Westerners tend to engage in more leisure physical activities than easterners and southerners. All the states west of the Great Plains for which data were available, including Alaska and Hawaii, fell in the lowest category with less than one-quarter of the population not engaging in some kind of activity the previous month. Westerners appear to take their outdoors seriously. A few East Coast states, mainly in New England—New Hampshire, Connecticut, Massachusetts and Virginia—fell in the low category as well. Are these the metropolitan residents who jog at lunch hour and fill the aerobic clubs at night and the suburban hillsides on weekends? Minnesota and Wisconsin also are in the lowest category.

The South and Midwest have the largest proportion of population not engaging in physical activity, more than 30 percent. The broad band from Oklahoma to North Carolina and from Ohio and Illinois to the Gulf Coast is distinct on the map. A few northeastern states, notably New York and New Jersey, also have large percentages of inhabitants not engaging in regular physical activity. New Mexico is the only state west of the Great Plains with more than 30 percent of its population not reporting regular physical activity. States in the intermediate category, 20 percent to 26 percent, are scattered but include some of the most populous states in the nation: Texas, Florida, Pennsylvania and Michigan.

Part of the explanation for this pattern may lie in the nature of the question asked, which targets physical activity outside of work. Many states of the South and Midwest have larger proportions of their population engaged in farm work and heavy manufacturing work than the rest of the nation. A farmer or factory worker may not be as inclined as a white collar worker to work out in the gym after a day on the job. The CDC's survey found that age and income are also factors. While the median percentage not engaging in physical activity was 28 percent, for people 65 and over, it was 42 percent. Lower income families (those with incomes less than $20,000) also had high percentages not engaged in regular physical activity (37%). Many of the states in the highest category include some of the lowest income states and the highest average age states as well. Differences among states are substantial. In Montana, Oregon and California, less than 20 percent of the population reports no regular physical activity; but in Kentucky, West Virginia and Mississippi, more than 40 percent do not engage in regular physical activity. Comparison with Map 6.1, Overall Health, shows a close correspondence between states with low percentages of physical activity and low scores of overall health.

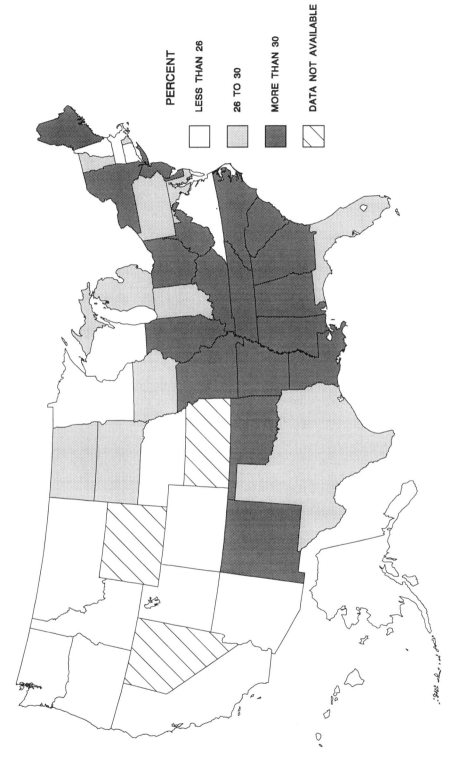

8.1 LEISURE-TIME PHYSICAL ACTIVITY
PERCENT OF POPULATION AGE 18 AND OLDER
REPORTING NO REGULAR EXERCISE OR PHYSICAL ACTIVITY, 1991

PERCENT

LESS THAN 26

26 TO 30

MORE THAN 30

DATA NOT AVAILABLE

Source: *MMWR*, Vol. 42, no. SS-4, 1993

8.2 SMOKERS

The Centers for Disease Control and Prevention reports that 20 percent of all deaths were related to smoking. The American Heart Association states that in 1988 about 430,000 adults aged 35 and over died of voluntary cigarette smoking. Smoking is a clearly identified risk. Despite that fact and the required warning labels on tobacco products, in 1991 23 percent of the American population reported that they smoked regularly, that is, they have smoked at least 100 cigarettes and report that they currently smoke regularly. While the states with the largest percentage of smokers, more than 23.8 percent, are scattered on the map, they are clearly clustered in the eastern half of the country. Of the eighteen states in the highest category, only two, Alaska and Oklahoma, are in the Great Plains or West. The eastern half of the country also contains most of the states in the middle category (22.4% to 23.8%). Of these thirteen states, only South Dakota, Colorado, Arizona and Washington are in the West. This doesn't mean that there aren't any states in the eastern half with fewer smokers (less than 22.4%), but such states are few. The two states with the highest percentage of smokers (Kentucky, 30.2% and Tennessee 28.1%—interestingly, both are among the top three tobacco producing states) are in the eastern half of the country. Undoubtedly, the religious prohibition on smoking is a key factor in the very low rate in predominantly Mormon Utah (14.3%).

Many factors underlie the distribution of smokers. Education is important because those with only high school or less smoke more (28% compared to 23%). The graph below shows this relationship in more detail. A comparison of this map with Map 10.4, College Graduates, shows that many states with the lowest proportion of college graduates also have the highest percentage of smokers. The sex ratio is a factor, too. Although the rate of women smokers has moved closer to men, among the older population more males have smoked for longer periods of time and the CDC reports that twice as many male deaths are due to smoking. Recent improvements in the death rate from smoking have come not primarily from a decrease in smoking but rather from improvements in medical care. The good news? More than 55 percent of smokers succeeded in quitting for at least one day during 1991.

CIGARETTE SMOKING
ADULTS AGE 25 AND OLDER, BY EDUCATION, 1974–90

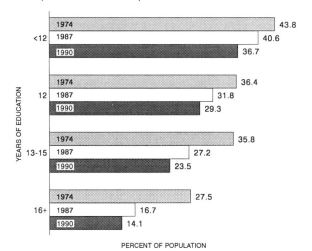

Source: CDC, National Center for Health Statistics, Health Interview Data

120

8.2 SMOKERS
PERCENT OF POPULATION 18 YEARS AND OLDER WHO SMOKE REGULARLY, 1991

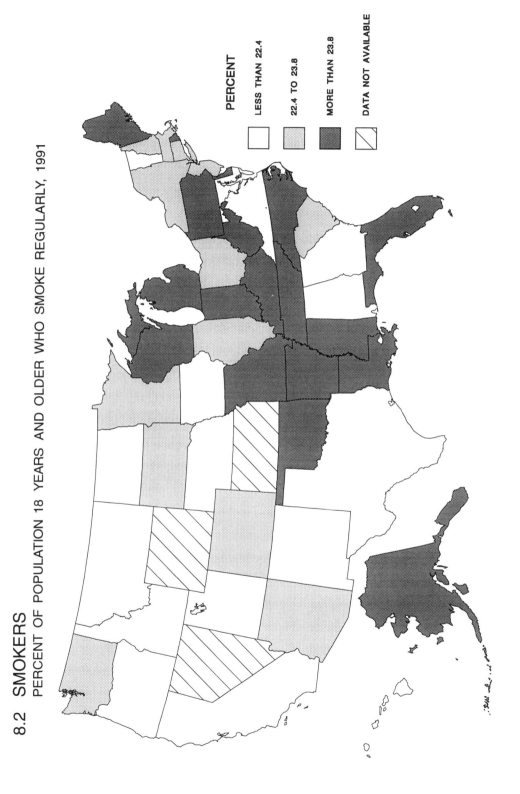

PERCENT

LESS THAN 22.4

22.4 TO 23.8

MORE THAN 23.8

DATA NOT AVAILABLE

Source: *MMWR*, Vol. 42, no. SS-4, 1993

8.3 OVERWEIGHT POPULATION

About 23 percent of the American population is overweight, a lifestyle risk that has well-known implications for health; one example: the Centers for Disease Control and Prevention notes that 40.5 percent of women and 42.5 percent of men who report high blood pressure were overweight. The CDC uses a very specific definition of overweight people: it is a measure called the Body Mass Index (BMI) that is based on weight in comparison to height. Someone is "overweight" if their BMI exceeds the 85th percentile average weight of 20- to 29-year-olds of their sex.

Like states with a high proportion of smokers, those with larger proportions of overweight people tend to be located in the eastern half of the country. With the exception of Texas, all thirteen states in the highest category (more than 25%) are east of the Great Plains, and these states tend to be more in the interior, including many states of the Midwest and Deep South. Michigan (28.7%), West Virginia (28%) and Mississippi (27.8%) have the highest proportions of overweight adults. States in the lowest category, less than 23 percent overweight population, are primarily located west of the Great Plains (all western states except Alaska are in this group) or they are along the Atlantic Coast, including most of the states of Megalopolis as well as Georgia and Florida. Colorado (17.8%), Virginia and New Mexico (both 18.9%) had the "slimmest" populations. States in the intermediate category, 23 percent to 25 percent, are somewhat scattered, but most lie in the middle of the nation, between east and west in the upper Great Plains and Minnesota, and in a band from Illinois to Oklahoma.

Many factors affect the proportion of overweight population, including education and income, which impact nutritional concern, and physical activity. It is not surprising to see a number of states with a large proportion of overweight population also in the lowest categories on Map 4.1, Household Income; Map 6.1, Overall Health; Map 8.1, Leisure-Time Physical Activity, and Map 10.4, College Graduates. In fact, six states with the largest proportion of overweight population are in the lowest category on all four other maps: Kentucky, West Virginia, South Carolina, Mississippi, Louisiana and Alabama. Income and education are two of the important variables because of the high-calorie, low nutritional diets often consumed by persons of low income; 30.3 percent of people from families with incomes below $10,000 were overweight, about 7 percent higher than the overall median figure.

PERCENT

LESS THAN 23

23 TO 25

MORE THAN 25

DATA NOT AVAILABLE

Source: *MMWR*, Vol. 42, no. SS-4, 1993

8.4   MOTOR VEHICLE TRAFFIC DEATHS

More than 40,000 people died in motor vehicle accidents in 1992, a figure representing 15.8 deaths per 100,000 population. This is a substantial decrease in death rate since 1982 and a drop in actual number of deaths despite a large increase in population: more than 45,000 died in 1982 and more than 56,000 in 1972. The decrease is due to a number of factors, including increased auto safety standards, highway design and safety improvements, seat belts, air bags and tougher drunk driving laws. The National Safety Council estimates that the 3,000,000th American motor vehicle death will occur sometime in mid-1994. As one might expect, the largest proportion of deaths occur from collision with other motor vehicles (43%), but substantial proportions involve collision with fixed objects (27%) and pedestrian deaths (16%).

The distribution of motor vehicle traffic deaths by state shows distinct regional patterns. Generally, most states of the Northeast and two West Coast states, California and Washington, have low rates, less than 13.2 deaths per 100,000 population. There are three main clusters of states with high rates, more than 19.5. One extends through the Deep South and into the Appalachian southern states of Tennessee, West Virginia and Kentucky. A second cluster of high rates is in the northern Rocky Mountain states of Montana, Idaho and Wyoming and adjacent South Dakota. Arizona and New Mexico make up a third cluster. Most of the remaining states west of the Mississippi fall in the intermediate category, 13.2 to 19.5. A few eastern states are in this intermediate category as well, such as Maine, Florida and three of the Middle Atlantic states.

Motor vehicle death rates vary widely among states. The death rate of 29.2 per 100,000 people in New Mexico is more than three times the death rates of the lowest states in southern New England: Rhode Island, 7.9, Massachusetts, 8.1, and Connecticut, 9.0. There is a relation between extent of urbanization and motor vehicle death rates, as can be seen by comparison of this map with Maps 1.3 and 1.4. Apparently, high speed, long-distance travel on poorer quality (and sometimes mountainous) rural roads is more risky than urban travel even if the latter involves more congestion. Other factors come into play in western states. For example, New Mexico has roadside drive-through liquor stores that persist despite repeated attempts to outlaw them. Liquor is involved in an estimated 40 percent of serious auto accidents. Other factors influence death rates, such as average age of a state's population. Of the driving-age population, the 45–64 age group has the lowest rate, 13.2; the 15–24 and over-75 age group have much higher rates, 28.5 and 26.0, respectively. Rates for selected cities (urban jurisdictions, not metropolitan areas) are listed in the table below.

MOTOR VEHICLE DEATHS IN SELECTED CITIES, 1992

CITY	AUTO FATALITIES	DEATHS PER 100,000 POPULATION
Atlanta	72	18.3
Boston	27	4.7
Chicago	239	8.6
Dallas	158	15.7
El Paso	90	17.5
Los Angeles	323	9.3
Miami	49	13.7
Minneapolis	19	5.2
New York	566	7.7
Seattle	40	7.7

Source: *Accident Facts, 1993*, National Safety Council

8.4 MOTOR VEHICLE TRAFFIC DEATHS
RATE PER 100,000 POPULATION, 1992

RATE

LESS THAN 13.2

13.2 TO 19.5

MORE THAN 19.5

Source: National Safety Council

125

8.5   SEAT BELT USE

This map shows the percentage of persons who report always using a seat belt. Nationally, 58.2 percent of the population uses a seat belt, but the figure varies greatly by state from a remarkable high of 87.8 percent in Hawaii to an equally remarkable low of 22.8 percent in South Dakota. Nationally, seat belt use shows an interesting pattern of coastal states (which tend to be the more urban states) with high usage versus interior (more rural) states with lower usage rates. All the Pacific states (including Alaska and Hawaii) and a band of southwestern and southern states from Arizona to Louisiana are in the highest category, more than 58.5 percent. Also in the highest category is a band of states along the Atlantic from Florida to Connecticut, except Delaware. Only three states in the highest category, Michigan, Iowa and Colorado, are not located along the periphery. States with the lowest rates of seat belt usage, less than 49 percent, are clustered in a few areas: most of New England, Kentucky and West Virginia, Mississippi, and the northern Great Plains-Rocky Mountain area. States in the middle category, 49.0 percent to 58.5 percent, are concentrated in the Midwest, but include a few southern states such as Arkansas, Tennessee and Alabama, and also Vermont.

The obvious question to ask is how does this map correlate with the previous one, Map 8.4, showing auto vehicle deaths? There is some correspondence: of the thirteen states with the lowest rates of seat belt use, only three states (all in New England) have low vehicle death rates. Conversely, of the fifteen states with highest seat belt usage, only three (New Mexico, Arizona and South Carolina) are high death rate states. Clearly there is not a one-to-one correspondence, however. Perhaps one can argue that driving is so urbanized and relatively safe in some states (such as southern New England) that motorists are lulled into not paying much attention to seat belts; on the other hand, maybe driving is so inherently dangerous in some wide-open western states (Arizona, New Mexico) that even high seat belt usage does not prevent a high death rate from motor vehicles. This map is discussed again in reference to Map 11.5, Firearm and Motor Vehicle Deaths.

8.5 SEAT BELT USE
PERCENT OF POPULATION AGE 18 AND OLDER REPORTING REGULAR SEAT BELT USE, 1991

PERCENT

LESS THAN 49.0

49.0 TO 58.5

MORE THAN 58.5

DATA NOT AVAILABLE

Source: *MMWR*, Vol. 42, no. SS–4, 1993

127

8.6   DRUG USE: MARIJUANA AND COCAINE

Of all the choices available in the American lifestyle, the choice to use drugs is one of the riskiest. Yet almost one-third of Americans over age 12 have used marijuana and 11 percent have tried cocaine, according to a sample survey by the U.S. Public Health Service. Note that cocaine usage includes use of its highly concentrated derivative, "crack." In the West, more than 41 percent have used marijuana at least once and more than 17 percent have tried cocaine at least once. The Northeast has the second highest usage, about 33 percent and 12 percent, respectively. Rates of usage are almost identical for the Midwest and the South; about 30 percent have used marijuana and about 8.5 percent have tried or use cocaine.

In addition to marijuana and cocaine, illicit drug use for which some data are available include hallucinogens (including LSD and PCP), heroin, inhalants, and nonmedical use of psychotherapeutics such as sedatives, tranquilizers, stimulants and analgesics. Taken together with marijuana and cocaine, all kinds of illegal drug use have touched more than 36 percent of the population. Usage varies by sex, as 41 percent of males have used illegal drugs compared to 32 percent of females. Usage also varies by age: about 17 percent of 12–17-year-olds have used illegal drugs, but that figure skyrockets to 52 percent of the 18–25 age group and 61 percent of the 26–34 age group before dropping to 28 percent of those over 35. As the graph below shows, recent drug use (within the past year) is more dramatically biased toward youth.

Drug use also varies by ethnic group: about 34 percent of whites report using marijuana compared to 26 percent of African Americans and 31 percent of Hispanics. The figures for the three groups for cocaine are 12 percent, 9 percent and 10 percent respectively. More than twice as many African Americans have used crack cocaine than have whites, although the total percentage is small in both cases (2.5% and 1.2%); but whites are much more likely to have tried hallucinogens (9.3% to 5.1%).

Alcohol is a popular drug, although not an illegal one. Of the population over 12 years of age, 83 percent have used alcohol (87.3% of men; 79% of women). Alcohol usage is not mapped simply because there is little geographic variation in its usage by region, ranging only from a high of 85.5 percent in the Northeast to a low of 79.5 percent in the South.

ILLICIT DRUG USE WITHIN THE PAST MONTH, 1992

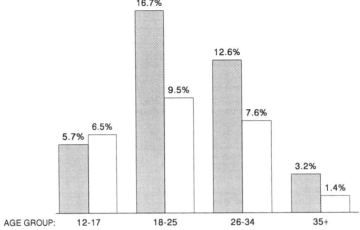

AGE GROUP: 12-17   18-25   26-34   35+

Source: *National Household Survey on Drug Abuse: 1992*, Substance Abuse and Mental Health Service Administration, U.S.H.H.S. 1993

8.6 DRUG USE: MARIJUANA AND COCAINE
PERCENT OF POPULATION AGE 12 AND OLDER
WHO HAVE EVER USED MARIJUANA OR COCAINE, 1992

NATIONAL
USAGE

32.8%-MARIJUANA
11.0%-COCAINE

32.7%
11.8%

29.4%
8.6%

30.0%
8.4%

41.6%
17.2%

Source: *National Household Survey on Drug Abuse: 1992, U.S.H.H.S., 1993*

129

8.7   HOMELESS PEOPLE

What is homelessness, and how can the homeless population be counted or even estimated? The federal government has defined homelessness to include individuals who do not have a regular and adequate nighttime residence, or are accommodated in a public or private temporary sleeping place. A federal plan to break the cycle of homelessness was inaugurated in May 1993. This plan acknowledges that about 7 million Americans were homeless at some point during the late 1980s (not, however, all of them at any one time). An early (1987) count of homeless reported that as many as 600,000 people were homeless during a single week. More recent studies have suggested that the number experiencing a time of homelessness during a period of one or more years may be ten times the number generated by a single count.

Who are the homeless? Probably about three-fourths of them conform to the stereotype of single, unattached adults, with about five times as many men as women. But the other fifth is made up of families with children, and four out of five of these families are headed by a single mother. Most of the homeless are adults in their thirties. Minorities, especially African Americans, are disproportionately represented among the homeless, especially homeless families. Many of the homeless, particularly men, have histories of institutionalization, drug or alcohol abuse, HIV/AIDS, or other diseases, notably tuberculosis. Some 30 to 45 percent of the male homeless are veterans, and a disproportionate number of both men and women were in foster care while growing up.

Governments at all levels, as well as many volunteer agencies, have tried to estimate the number of homeless. Our map presents one such count, that made by the U.S. Bureau of the Census on the night of the "homeless census" that was taken on the evening of March 20 and early morning hours of March 21, 1990. Census enumerators counted persons in established homeless shelters including shelters for runaway, neglected and homeless youths, and shelters for abused women, as well as those entering and leaving places, including abandoned buildings, that had been identified as gathering places of homeless people. The Census Bureau found 240,140 people in such sites. Another 219,075 persons were living in homes for unwed mothers, group homes for drug and alcohol abusers, agricultural workers living in dormitories, and group homes for the mentally ill. The Census Bureau cautions that these figures are not intended to be an accurate count of the homeless, that the count underestimates the rural homeless population, and that it is not accurate to extrapolate from this one night to a year-round count. Nevertheless, the count gives a rough estimate of the relative numbers of homeless living in shelters and visible in street locations.

With these factors in mind, the map, though based on a fragmentary data set, begins to be more understandable. The homeless in shelters and street locations are most numerous as a proportion of population (more than 66 per 100,000 people) in the Pacific Coast states, in the Megalopolis states of the Northeast and in Florida, Illinois, Colorado and Oklahoma. Urbanization is a factor, so that states with large cities stand out on the map: New York, Boston, Philadelphia, Miami and Chicago in the East, and San Francisco, San Diego, Los Angeles, Portland, Seattle, and Honolulu in the West. States with the fewest homeless, less than 42 per 100,000, are located in much of the Midwest and in many of the more rural states.

130

8.7 HOMELESS PEOPLE
HOMELESS COUNT AT SELECTED SHELTER AND STREET LOCATIONS PER 100,000 POPULATION, 1990

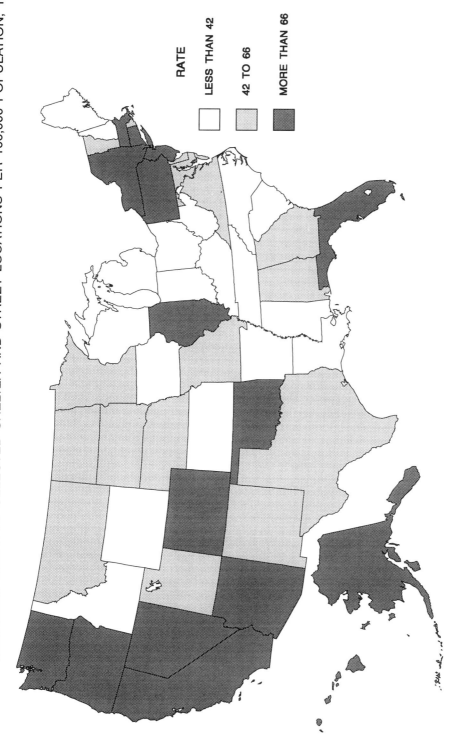

RATE

LESS THAN 42

42 TO 66

MORE THAN 66

Source: U.S. Bureau of the Census

131

9

Education K–12

9.1   HEAD START ENROLLMENT

The Head Start Program was part of the War on Poverty of the mid-1960s and is generally acknowledged to be the most successful and popular of a variety of programs that were authorized by the Economic Opportunity Act of 1964. Other programs for low-income persons included, among others, the Job Corps, College Work Study, and VISTA (Volunteers in Service to America), a domestic analogue to the Peace Corps. Head Start grew out of the realization that nearly half of the country's poverty population were children, and most of them were under the age of 12. The program was popular because it was aimed at children; the country believed that education was the major weapon in the war on poverty. The goal of Head Start was to improve the intellectual capacity and school performance of poor children by helping them prepare for first grade. The aims were soon broadened to include nutrition programs and medical and dental screening, which were recognized as essential adjuncts to preschool education. Immunizations and home visits were also added.

The Head Start program was operated by the Department of Health and Human Services by 1992, and about two billion dollars were allocated to it. Allocations averaged over $3,000 per child, and varied only slightly among the states. Grants were made to both public and private nonprofit agencies; most of these Head Start centers offered half-day preschool programs, though some offered full-day. As shown below, the largest proportion of preschool children served were four-year-olds.

The map shows the percentage of preschool children enrolled in Head Start by state. Percentages ranged from a high of 27 percent in Mississippi to a low of around 7 percent in Nevada and Arizona. It is a relatively small program in some states; 11 states enrolled less than 2,000 children. Enrollment varies according to state and local interest and initiative as well as by demographic factors such as poverty percentage and population composition. In general, western states enroll significantly lower percentages of their preschool population in Head Start programs. Of 25 states west of the Mississippi, only Hawaii, Wyoming, and Arkansas have percentages over 12.

DISTRIBUTION OF HEAD START ENROLLMENT
BY AGE AND RACE/ ETHNICITY, 1992

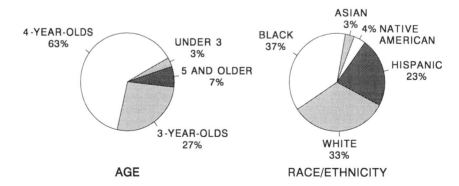

Source: National Center for Education Statistics, *Digest of Education Statistics 1993*, Table 361

134

9.1 HEAD START ENROLLMENT
PERCENT OF PRESCHOOL CHILDREN ENROLLED, 1992

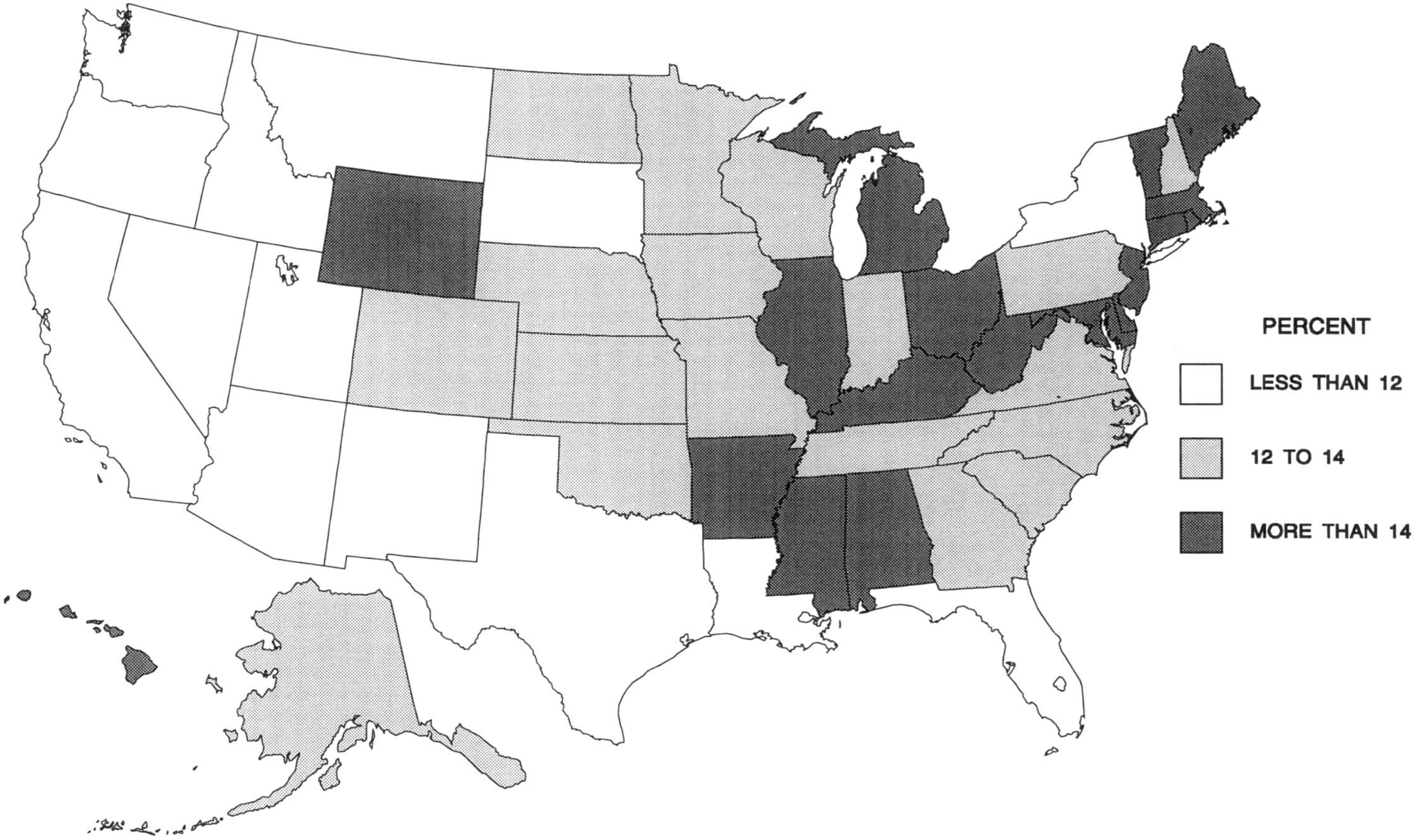

PERCENT

LESS THAN 12

12 TO 14

MORE THAN 14

Source: CQ State Fact Finder

135

9.2   FOURTH GRADE MATH AND READING PROFICIENCY

The National Assessment of Educational Progress (NAEP) is an ongoing project of the National Center for Education Statistics. The NAEP is the only nationally representative, continuing assessment of what the country's students know and can do in various subject areas. It is given regularly to students in grades four, eight, and twelve, at a carefully selected sample of both public and private schools. The process of devising questions, drawing samples, administering tests, and analyzing data is carried out by the Educational Testing Service at Princeton, New Jersey. For the map, we have chosen the regional results of the 1992 NAEP in mathematics and reading at the fourth grade level as a good way of comparing regional accomplishment in two basic areas of schooling.

In 1992, forty-one states and the District of Columbia participated in the math and reading tests. Because of the missing nine states, regional averages are presented on the map. The four regions used for grouping the NAEP data are not identical to the four census regions of the United States that have been used in some other maps. The differences are that here Texas and Oklahoma are included in the West, rather than in the South, and Maryland and Delaware in the Northeast, rather than the South.

In reading, the Northeast came first with 29 percent of participating students testing at or above proficient level, followed by the Central Region (25%), the West (22%) and the South (19%). The same rank order held true for mathematics, with the Northeast first (23%), followed by Central (20%), West (17%), and South (11%). It should be noted that "proficient" is a higher level of achievement than "average." It means that the students have a good grasp of the subject, not just a basic knowledge. Some small-population states in the West had relatively high scores, but the influence of the large California and Texas populations and the absence of four states from the testing resulted in a low overall score for the region.

In terms of actual scores, the overall average proficiency score for the nation in reading was 216 and in math was 217. The table below shows how these scores varied by gender and by race/ethnicity. The influence of minority populations is apparent in the overall results, whether it is Hispanics in the Southwest, non-English-speaking Asians in Hawaii, or low-income African Americans in the South.

AVERAGE MATH AND READING PROFICIENCY, GRADE 4
BY GENDER AND RACE/ ETHNICITY, 1992

		GENDER		RACE/ ETHNICITY		
		MALE	FEMALE	WHITE	BLACK	HISPANIC
MATH	**Nation**	**218**	**216**	**226**	**191**	**199**
	Northeast	225	220	232	194	200
	Southeast	209	209	219	190	198
	Central	224	220	228	192	198
	West	217	217	225	188	200
READING	**Nation**	**212**	**220**	**224**	**192**	**200**
	Northeast	218	224	230	198	201
	Southeast	205	217	221	195	195
	Central	217	221	225	187	210
	West	208	218	222	185	197

Source: National Center for Education Statistics, NAEP 1992

136

FOURTH GRADE MATH AND READING PROFICIENCY
PERCENT OF STUDENTS PROFICIENT AT MATH AND READING, 1992

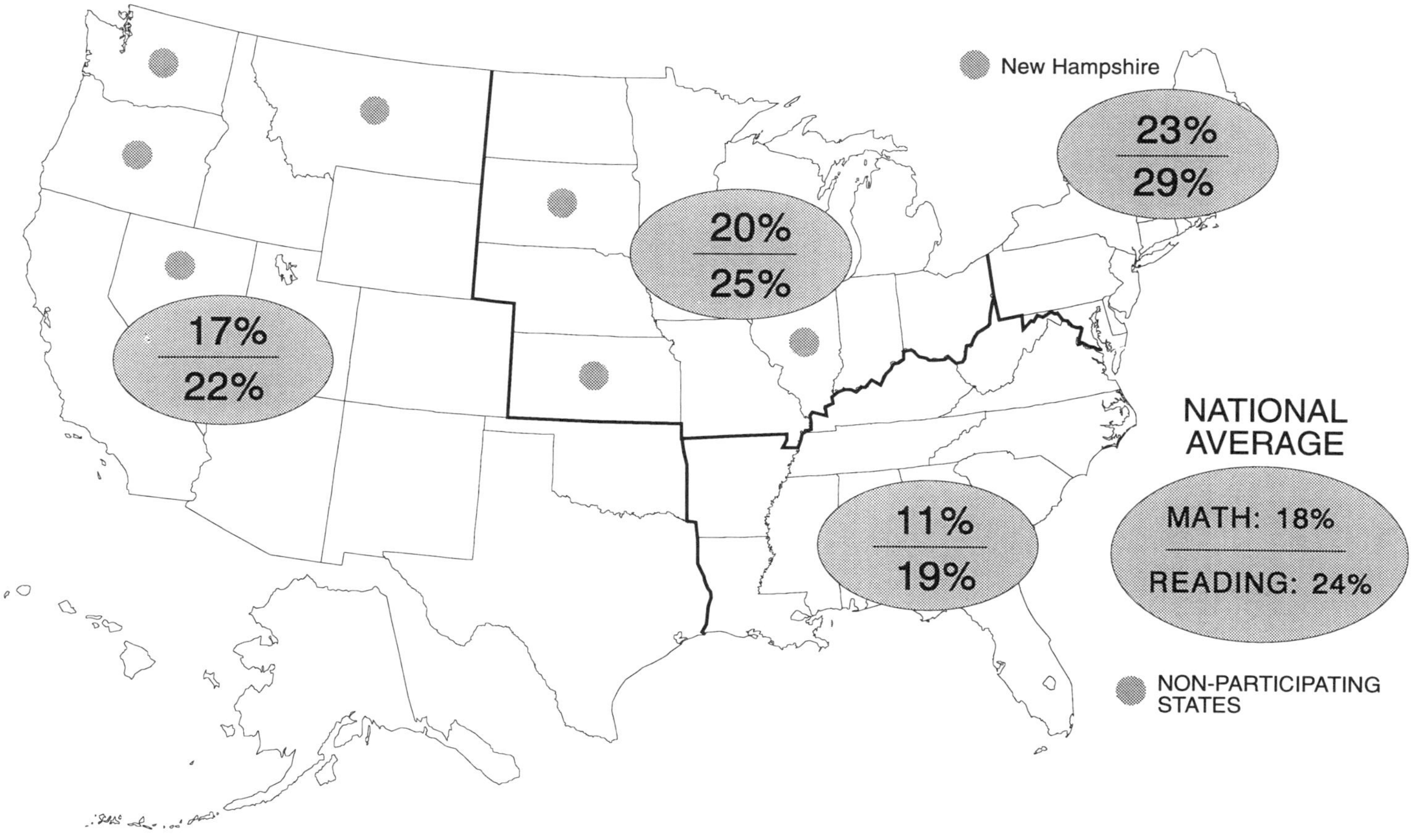

New Hampshire

23%
29%

20%
25%

11%
19%

17%
22%

NATIONAL
AVERAGE

MATH: 18%
READING: 24%

NON-PARTICIPATING
STATES

Source: National Center for Education Statistics

137

9.3   HIGH SCHOOL DROPOUTS

High school dropouts are defined as persons in the high school age group who are not in school and have neither graduated from high school nor received GED credentials. Dropping out of school without acquiring minimum educational competencies constitutes a major problem for young people in finding employment; they find themselves relegated to jobs with lower status and lower pay. Lowering the dropout rate has long been a priority of schools and of society in general, and it has, in fact fallen considerably over the last two decades. The dropout rate has not fallen equally for all groups, as shown by the graph below. The decline has been most impressive for blacks, but their dropout rate was still almost twice that of whites. The dropout rate for Hispanics remains a major problem and was almost four times that of non-Hispanic whites in 1992, a situation that is largely attributable to the language problem.

The dropout rate shown on the map is the percentage of young persons age 16 to 19 who were not in school in 1990. This is another map in which the regional aspects are striking. The Sunbelt is the dropout belt. The whole southern rim of the country from North Carolina across the South to California, Nevada, and Oregon had the highest proportion of dropouts in 1990 (over 11.4%). The highest rate was in Nevada (15.2%), closely followed by Arizona, Florida, and California. All of these are states with significant Hispanic populations. Interestingly, New Mexico, with the highest proportion of Hispanic population of any state, was in the high category, but ranked fifteenth. In the Southeast, there are high percentages of low-income black population, which undoubtedly affect these percentages. All in all, the presence of minority populations is the strongest influence on the map pattern.

In contrast to the southern rim, the western interior again shows up as a distinct bloc of states with relatively low dropout rates (less than 8.8%) from Wisconsin to Montana and south to Utah and Kansas. Only four states with low rates lie outside this bloc; three are in New England—Maine, Massachusetts, and Vermont. The other is Hawaii, an interesting case where "minority" populations are in the majority. These, however, are long-established Asian populations, and the language problem is not acute. States with the very lowest dropout rates are North Dakota (in a class by itself with only 4.6% not in school), Minnesota (6.4%), Iowa (6.6%), and Wyoming (6.9%).

PERCENT OF HIGH SCHOOL DROPOUTS AMONG 16- TO 24-YEAR-OLDS
BY RACE/ ETHNICITY, 1972–92

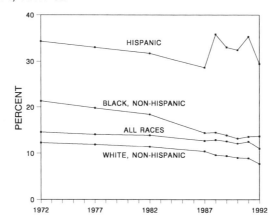

Source: National Center for Education Statistics, *Mini-Digest of Education Statistics 1993*, Table 16

138

9.3 HIGH SCHOOL DROPOUTS
PERCENT OF ALL TEENS (AGES 16–19 NOT IN SCHOOL, 1990

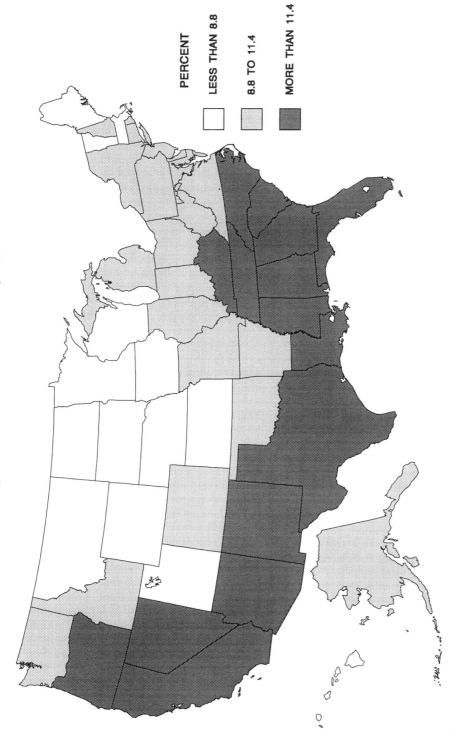

PERCENT

LESS THAN 8.8

8.8 TO 11.4

MORE THAN 11.4

Source: Center for the Study of Social Policy

9.4   HIGH SCHOOL GRADUATES

In contrast to the preceding map, which focused on the problem of dropouts (non-completion of high school), this map focuses on achievement. It shows the percentage of persons 25 years and older who have completed high school. It is not an exact opposite of Map 9.3. The dropout map gives a portrait of a certain age group for a particular year. This map is a cumulative map, for it presents information on the educational achievement of a more inclusive age group. Persons in this group might have completed high school seven years ago, or fifty or more years ago. They might have been earlier dropouts who later completed a high school education. They might have attained their high school education in a different state and then migrated. This map reflects a longer history of American schooling and achievement. The graph below reminds us of some recent parts of that history by depicting the change, over the period 1960 to 1991, in percent of persons 25 and over who have completed various levels of schooling.

The range on this map is from a low of 67 percent in Kentucky to a high of over 88 percent in both Utah and Washington. There are three regions of high achievement. One is in the Northeast, which in this case is a rather restricted area that includes only New England and New Jersey. It does not include New York, New Jersey, Pennsylvania, Maryland, Delaware, or Virginia as many maps have done. A second, very large region extends from Minnesota and Iowa to the West Coast in Washington and Oregon, and south to the tier of states from Kansas to Nevada. Exceptions to this pattern include Idaho and the Dakotas, which fall into the middle category. Third, the non-contiguous states of Hawaii and Alaska are also in the high category. At the other extreme, a contiguous bloc of states in the southeastern quadrant of the country, continuing west to include Texas and with a northern extension in Indiana, comprises a single large region in which less than 77 percent of the adult population has completed high school. Florida is a notable exception to this bloc, falling into the middle category with almost 80 percent high school graduates. This percentage has undoubtedly been affected by the in-migration from the Northeast.

PERCENT OF PERSONS 25 YEARS AND OLDER WHO COMPLETED VARIOUS YEARS OF SCHOOL: 1960–91

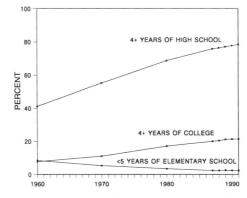

Source: National Center for Education Statistics, *Mini-Digest of Education Statistics 1993*, Table 17

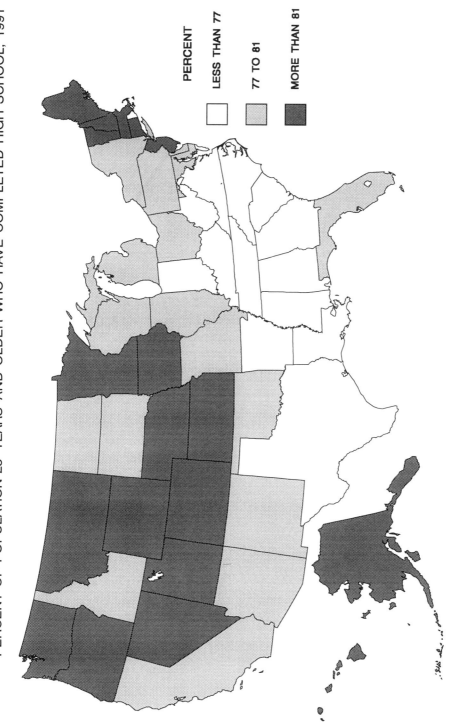

9.4 HIGH SCHOOL GRADUATES
PERCENT OF POPULATION 25 YEARS AND OLDER WHO HAVE COMPLETED HIGH SCHOOL, 1991

PERCENT

LESS THAN 77

77 TO 81

MORE THAN 81

Source: U.S. Bureau of the Census

9.5   PROJECTED CHANGE IN HIGH SCHOOL GRADUATES

After examining how both the problem of high school dropouts and the overall proportion of high school graduates in the population vary from state to state, it is appropriate to look at future variation. Will the number of American high school graduates increase or decrease in the immediate future, and will that change, whether it be increase or decrease, vary regionally? This question is important both in terms of labor supply and in terms of the ability of institutions of higher education to meet the demand. A 1993 publication of the Western Interstate Commission for Higher Education presented projections of high school graduates by state. Their demographic methodology involved birth rates, along with estimates of migration, mortality, non-promotion, and persistence in high school. The percentage change in the number of graduates from the 1991 school year to the 2002–2003 school year is mapped on the opposite page.

In the 1991–92 school year, there were a total of nearly 2,500,000 graduates in the United States, of which over 90 percent came from public schools and almost 10 percent from private schools. By 2002–2003, the number of graduates is projected to grow to slightly over 3,000,000, of which about 92 percent will be graduating from public schools and 8 percent from private. This national increase of about 21 percent in total number of graduates will not be equally shared throughout the country. The map shows that the states with projected growth of over 30 percent are all in the West, except for Florida (in the top five with a projected increase of 46%). Nevada has the highest growth rate (104%) and thus will double its high school graduates in little over a decade. Washington, Alaska, and Arizona all have growth rates of 47 or 48 percent.

East of the Mississippi, only a few states even fell into the middle category of 15 to 30 percent: Vermont, New Hampshire, Delaware, Maryland, Virginia, Georgia, and Wisconsin. Most were in the low category, with projected increases of 15 percent or less in high school graduates. The division into an "older" East and a "younger," growing West is apparent in this map.

The graph below shows the changes in actual numbers of high school graduates over the period covered by the map. From highs in the 1970s due to the famed baby boom cohorts, the number of graduates falls to a low in the mid-1990s, then begins to increase again as children of the baby-boomers (the baby boom "echo") reach college age.

HIGH SCHOOL GRADUATES
PROJECTED TO 2003

	PUBLIC	NONPUBLIC
1991–92	2,233,768	241,230
1992–93	2,266,900	239,650
1993–94	2,254,150	236,870
1994–95	2,341,250	240,790
1995–96	2,376,790	241,370
1996–97	2,453,170	242,300
1997–98	2,539,060	245,740
1998–99	2,598,190	244,480
1999–00	2,658,040	242,660
2000–01	2,679,940	238,100
2001–02	2,708,120	237,270
2002–03	2,765,370	238,300

Source: Western Interstate Commission for Higher Education, *High School Graduates, Projections by State 1992–2009*, 1993

9.5 PROJECTED CHANGE IN HIGH SCHOOL GRADUATES, 1992–2003

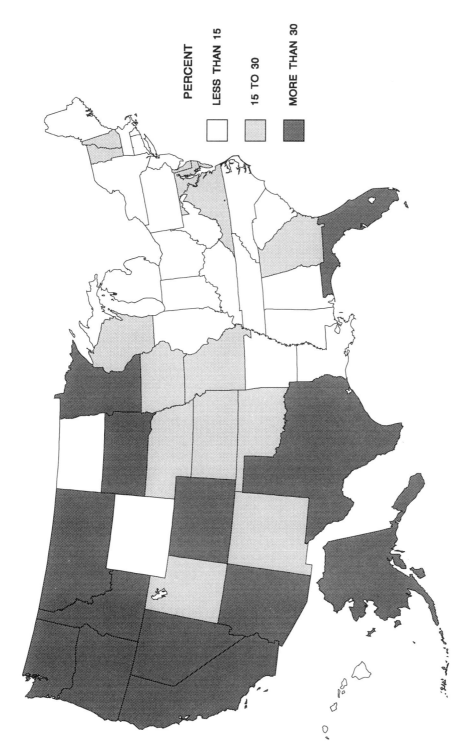

PERCENT

LESS THAN 15

15 TO 30

MORE THAN 30

Source: Western Interstate Commission for Higher Education in Chronicle

9.6   COST PER PUPIL

A map of expenditures per pupil seems appropriate in view of the debate over whether or not spending more money on schools will produce higher levels of achievement and fewer problems. The map shows that spending per pupil varies significantly from state to state; it may be compared with the maps of achievement (NAEP tests, proportion of high school graduates) and with the map of the dropout problem, as well as with various other maps such as income. A natural assumption is that cost per pupil varies with the overall wealth of the state and with differences in cost of living.

The graph below shows how average expenditures per pupil for the whole nation gradually increased over a period of two decades. In the school year 1992–93, the total national expenditures on education amounted to about $466 billion, of which $279 billion went to elementary and secondary schools and $187 billion for higher education. This amounted to somewhere between 7 and 8 percent of gross domestic product. In that year, 47 percent of school revenues came from local funding, 47 percent from the state, and 6 percent from the federal government. The large proportion coming from local and state sources helps to explain the great variation on the map.

Data on the map are for the 1991–92 school year, in which the national average expenditure per pupil was about $5,400. The range was from highs of $9,549 in the District of Columbia and $9,317 in New Jersey to lows of $3,040 in Utah and $3,245 in Mississippi. The northeast quadrant is the region of high spending. All of the states east of the Mississippi and north of the Ohio and Potomac rivers spend over $5,600 per pupil, except for Indiana, which falls into the middle category. Outside this region, the three states of Alaska ($8,450), Oregon ($5,913), and Wyoming are the only others in the high category. The low category (less than $4,800) comprises the tier of southern states, extending all the way from the Carolinas to Arizona, but it also includes Utah, Idaho, and the Dakotas. The middle category includes a large number of states in the spending category $4,800 to $5,600, rather close to the national average. They are mostly in the northern half of the country west of the Mississippi, but include Florida, Nevada and California, and Hawaii.

How is this money spent? About 88 percent of expenditures are for current expenses, and 12 percent for capital outlay and school debt. The lion's share of the current expenditures goes for instruction (55%), most of which is for teachers' salaries and benefits.

CURRENT EXPENDITURE PER PUPIL IN AVERAGE DAILY ATTENDANCE
1970–71 TO 1992–93

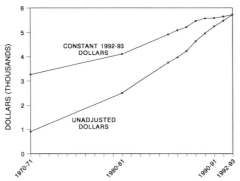

Source: National Center for Education Statistics, *Mini-Digest of Education Statistics 1993*, Table 23

144

9.6 COST PER PUPIL
EXPENDITURE PER PUPIL IN PUBLIC SCHOOLS, 1991–92

DOLLARS

LESS THAN 4,800

4,800 TO 5,600

MORE THAN 5,600

Source: National Center for Education Statistics

10

Higher Education

10.1 COLLEGE ENROLLMENT

Higher education enrollments in fall 1992 in all public and private colleges at both the undergraduate and graduate levels totaled more than 14,491,000. Enrollments have reached record levels in each of the seven years up to and including 1992. The boom is predicted to continue. The primary cause of this growth is the "baby boomlet," the wave of young people, children of the baby-boom generation, approaching age 18 who are graduating from high school. This phenomenon was discussed on Map 9.5, Projected High School Graduates. The wave of college-bound students should continue through the early years of the next decade. While the number of part-time students continues to grow (many of them older adults, particularly re-entry women), the baby boomlet will cause full-time enrollments to grow more rapidly. This is a reversal of trends over the past decade. The graph below shows these trends. Note that full-time enrollment will grow from approximately 8,300,000 in 1998 to 9,100,000 in 2004, while part-time enrollment will remain stable at 6,800,000 over the same period.

As the map shows, a few states have a relatively high proportion of college students compared to total population (more than 6%). Some of this variation is explained by regional differences among states in the percentage of young people who go on to college, just as there are regional differences among states in the proportion of high school graduates. There are also states with a large proportion of out-of-state students, such as New York and the New England states, in which higher education is an industry adding to the economic base of the region. Three New England states, Massachusetts, Rhode Island and Vermont, and a large bloc of western and southwestern states from Kansas and Nebraska to California stand out in the highest category of enrollment. Illinois also falls in this category. States in much of the South are in the lowest category, less than 5 percent college students to total population. With the exception of North Carolina in the intermediate category, and Alabama in the highest, all southern states east of Texas and south of Virginia fall in the lowest category. West Virginia, Nevada, Montana, Maine and New Jersey are outliers in the lowest category. The difference from the highest to lowest ranked state is substantial: Rhode Island, highest at 7.9 percent, has almost twice as many students to residents as Arkansas, the lowest state at 4.1 percent.

TOTAL PROJECTED ENROLLMENT IN HIGHER EDUCATION INSTITUTIONS, 1992–2004

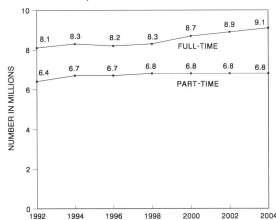

Source: National Center for Education Statistics, *Projections of Education Statistics to 2004*, NCES 93–256

148

10.1 COLLEGE ENROLLMENT
HIGHER EDUCATION ENROLLMENT AS A PERCENT OF POPULATION

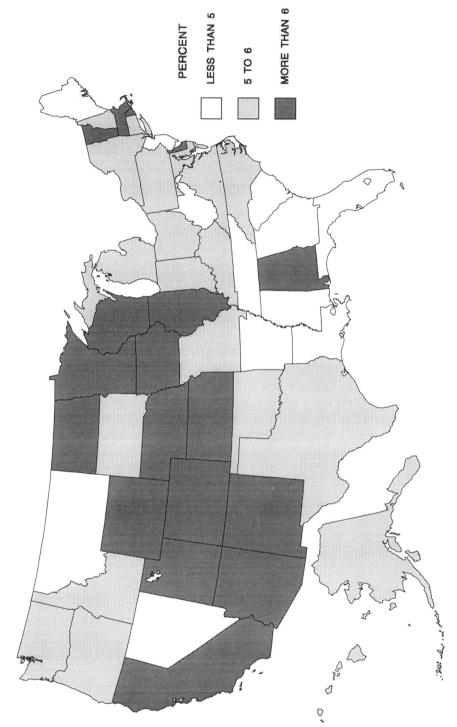

PERCENT

LESS THAN 5

5 TO 6

MORE THAN 6

Source: National Center for Education Statistics

149

10.2   TWO-YEAR COLLEGE ENROLLMENT

The map of two-year college enrollment shows data for all public and private junior and community colleges and two-year technical schools. Nationally, 45 percent of all higher education enrollment is in two-year colleges, a total of more than 5,650,000 students. Because of the low percentage of two-year enrollment in private junior colleges (about 11%), it is easy to lose sight of the fact that 53 percent of public college enrollment is at two-year schools. The range of enrollment in two-year schools is quite remarkable: from a high of 71 percent in California to a low of 1 percent in Arkansas. California alone, with almost 1,274,000 community college students, has almost one-quarter of the nation's public two-year enrollment. Other very large community college systems are Texas (396,000 students), Illinois (369,000) and Florida (323,000). In addition to these four states, seven others have more than 32 percent of their enrollment in two-year colleges: Wyoming, Arizona, Washington, Nevada, Oregon and Maryland. Private two-year enrollment is important in a few states, especially New York, Pennsylvania and Ohio. These three states combined have 40 percent of the nation's 250,000 private two-year college students.

The West and Southwest are the leading regions in two-year enrollments. Every state along the western and southwestern rim of the nation as well as Nevada and Wyoming have more than 48 percent of their students in two-year colleges. States in the low category, less than 32 percent, are located in New England (all states except Connecticut), the northern Great Plains and northern Rocky Mountain states, and a band of states in the eastern Midwest and the South from Missouri to Louisiana. Alaska is also in this category. With the exception of New England, which has many states with high enrollment per capita (thus two-year college enrollment is a relatively small proportion of total enrollment), many of the states in the low category are the more rural states. This reflects the tendency for much two-year college enrollment to be in urban areas convenient to part-time students. Generally, the most populous states with large urban areas not only have the largest numbers of students, but also a relatively larger proportion of their students enrolling in two-year colleges than do smaller, less urban, more rural states. Two states, Alaska and South Dakota, do not have public community colleges. States in the intermediate category, 32 percent to 48 percent, are clustered in four areas: the southeastern quadrant of the nation; the upper Midwest; a bloc of states in the southern Great Plains; and three states of the Megalopolis corridor: New York, New Jersey and Connecticut.

UNDERGRADUATE ENROLLMENT
PERCENT IN 4-YEAR AND 2-YEAR PUBLIC AND PRIVATE COLLEGES

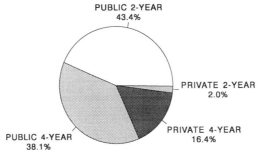

PUBLIC 2-YEAR
43.4%

PRIVATE 2-YEAR
2.0%

PRIVATE 4-YEAR
16.4%

PUBLIC 4-YEAR
38.1%

Source: National Center for Education Statistics, *Fall Enrollment, 1991*, IPEDS, 1993

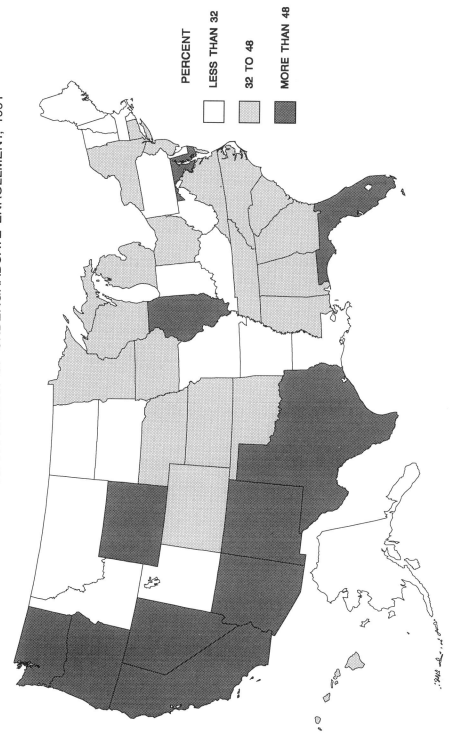

10.2 TWO-YEAR COLLEGE ENROLLMENT
TWO-YEAR ENROLLMENT AS A PERCENT OF UNDERGRADUATE ENROLLMENT, 1991

PERCENT

LESS THAN 32

32 TO 48

MORE THAN 48

Source: National Center for Education Statistics

10.3   MINORITY ENROLLMENT

Minority enrollment in the United States totaled 3,163,500 in 1992, about 22.5 percent of the nation's 14,500,000 college students. Minority enrollment includes African Americans, Hispanics, Asian/Pacific Islanders, Native Americans and non-resident aliens (more commonly called international students, who may be of any race or ethnicity).

The map shows a concentration of minority students around the southern rim of the nation and in states with large urban populations such as Illinois, New York, New Jersey and Maryland. As one might expect, this pattern is very close to that of minority population in general as shown on Map 5.1, Ethnic-Racial Diversity. The southern rim stands out in the highest category (more than 21% minority students) because of a number of minority groups: African Americans across the South and in California; Hispanics in California and the Southwest and Cubans in Florida. California also has a large proportion of Asian and Pacific Islander students. Other states in the highest category include Hawaii with its large Asian and Pacific Islander groups, and New York, New Jersey and Illinois with large numbers of all minority groups in their big urban areas. International students are very concentrated in large universities in major urban areas; California alone has 20 percent of international student enrollment.

States without large percentages of minorities, those less than 12 percent, tend to be located in the northern rim and in the interior. The northern New England states stand out as well as a large bloc of states in the upper Midwest and northern Great Plains. Utah, Oregon, Idaho and Wyoming also have few minority students, as do the Appalachian South states of Kentucky and West Virginia. States in the intermediate category tend to be those in an intermediate geographical position between the high and low groups of states. The differences in minority enrollment between states in the highest and lowest categories are quite striking: Hawaii has 69 percent minority student enrollment; northern New England and West Virginia have less than 6 percent.

African Americans make up about 44 percent of minority college enrollment, almost 1,400,000 students. Four states stand out: California with almost 140,000 African American students, New York (129,000), Illinois (94,000) and Texas (89,000). Combined, these four states have about one-third of the nation's black college students. Many African American students in the southern states attend some of the 177 historically black colleges and universities.

The nation's 954,000 Hispanic students (30% of minority enrollment) are concentrated in a few states where they represent a large proportion of enrollment. California alone has 315,000 Hispanic students (33% of the national total) and Texas has almost 169,000 (17.7%). Like African American students, many Hispanic students attend colleges identified by the Hispanic Association of Colleges and Universities as Hispanic-serving because at least 25 percent of the student body is Hispanic.

Native Americans also have 27 small (mostly two-year) colleges identified as "tribal colleges." These colleges are primarily located in Montana, the Dakotas, Arizona and a few other western states. California and Oklahoma are the two states with the largest share of the country's 119,000 Native American college students; the two states enroll 18 percent and 10 percent, respectively, of the student population. Native Americans make up about 4 percent of minority student enrollment.

Almost 697,000 college students are Asian or Pacific Islanders (22% of minority students). More than 40 percent are enrolled in California; the second largest group, 8 percent, attends college in New York. As a percentage of the student population, Hawaii ranks first with 59 percent of its college students among this minority group.

152

10.3 MINORITY ENROLLMENT
MINORITY ENROLLMENT AS A PERCENT OF ENROLLMENT, 1992

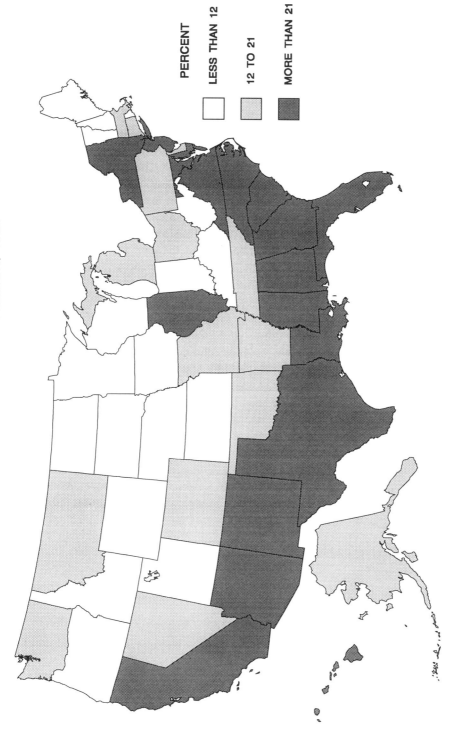

PERCENT

LESS THAN 12

12 TO 21

MORE THAN 21

Source: National Center for Education Statistics

153

10.4   COLLEGE GRADUATES

The proportion of the population 25 years of age and older that has completed four years of college or more varies greatly by state. In Colorado the figure is 32 percent, but in West Virginia it is slightly less than 12 percent.

A number of factors affect the distribution shown on the map. First are regional differences in attitude toward education and in financial ability to complete college. A comparison of this map with Map 9.3, High School Dropouts, and with Map 10.1, College Enrollment, shows that many of the same states with a large percentage of college graduates are also those states with low high school dropout rates and with a relatively large proportion of college enrollments. There is not necessarily a one-to-one correspondence, however, particularly with the college enrollment map, because some states such as New York and the New England states specialize in higher education and grant college degrees to many students who are not residents of their state. Migration is also a factor. In rural states with fewer big-city economic opportunities, the people most likely to leave are those with more education. Thus states such as Mississippi and West Virginia, long centers of out-migration, appear in the low category on this map partly for that reason. Urbanized states with growing metropolitan areas attract highly skilled and highly educated people who are college graduates. Thus many of the highly urbanized states are in the highest category on the map, unless, as in the case of Texas and Florida, states are also attracting large numbers of recent immigrants who do not hold college degrees.

In general, the West Coast and the northeastern coastal states (including Maryland) fall in the highest category, with more than 23 percent of their population 25 years and older holding college degrees. Illinois, Hawaii and Alaska and two western states, Colorado and Kansas, also fall in the high category. States in the lowest group, less than 19 percent college graduates, tend to be located in the eastern Midwest, adjacent Kentucky and West Virginia, and in most of the remainder of the South, except for Georgia and Florida, which are in the intermediate group. Iowa, Idaho, South Dakota and Nevada are the only other states in the lowest category. Most western states not already mentioned fall in the intermediate category. In addition to Georgia and Florida, as mentioned, of states east of the Mississippi River, Wisconsin, Maine, Virginia, Delaware and Rhode Island are the only states in the intermediate category. In general, with the exception of the Atlantic Coast states in the high and intermediate categories, there is an element of an east-west pattern to the map. This macro-pattern partly reflects the nation's general western migration trend, in which more educated people move West, leaving fewer college graduates living in the eastern states. Eastern states are exceptions because the urban centers of the Megalopolis corridor also attract migrants.

154

10.4 COLLEGE GRADUATES
PERCENT OF PERSONS 25 AND OLDER WHO HAVE COMPLETED COLLEGE, 1991

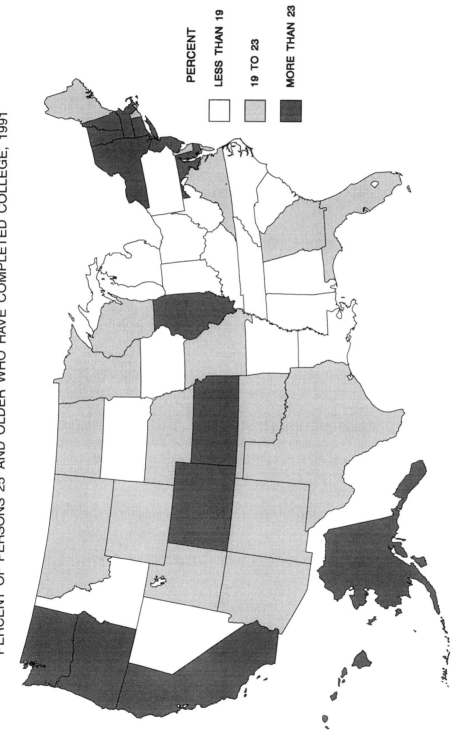

PERCENT

LESS THAN 19

19 TO 23

MORE THAN 23

Source: U.S. Bureau of the Census

10.5   IN-STATE TUITION

The ability to earn a college degree is in part a function of the cost of a college education. This map shows undergraduate tuition cost only for in-state students at public four-year colleges, in order to provide an easy basis for comparison among states. The variation in cost reflects regional cost of living differences, tuition charges at competing private colleges, and perhaps most important, the willingness of states to underwrite or subsidize in-state students out of general revenue funds. Perhaps the cost differential also partly reflects differences in quality of the educational experience through higher cost paid for better-qualified faculty or better or newer facilities.

In-state tuition at public four-year colleges rose 10 percent from 1991–92 averages, but is still a bargain compared to the national average tuition at private colleges of $10,393 in 1992–93. In addition to average tuition charges of $2,352, students at public colleges could expect to pay an average of $3,677 for room and board, for a total average college expense of slightly more than $6,000 for an in-state student. For comparison, room and board at private schools added, on average, another $4,735 for a total bill of $15,128 at private schools. Four-year tuition is substantially higher than the average of $1,018 for the same year at public community colleges. The highest average tuition at private colleges was $13,973 in Massachusetts; the lowest was $2,411 in Utah. Average community college tuition also varies greatly, from $209 in California to a high of $2,645 in Vermont.

The maps shows a distinct regional pattern. The northeastern quadrant of the country charges the highest tuition. Virginia and Delaware are the only two high tuition states outside the boundaries of this area and even they are neighbors to the region. Tuition in these high-cost states varies from just over $2,800 in Illinois to more than $5,300 in Vermont.

States charging the lowest tuition, less than $1,800, are located along the southern rim of the country from Arizona to North Carolina, overlapping into Nevada in the West and also Kentucky and West Virginia. (The states of the Deep South are an exception; a band from South Carolina to Louisiana falls in the intermediate category.) Alaska, Hawaii, Idaho and Wyoming are also in the low tuition category. States in the intermediate tuition category, $1,800 to $2,800, form a fairly solid bloc (with the exception of the low-tuition western states already mentioned) west of the Mississippi and north of Oklahoma. Wisconsin, Indiana, Maryland and the Deep South are the only states in the intermediate category that are located outside this bloc.

AVERAGE UNDERGRADUATE TUITION, ROOM, AND BOARD
PUBLIC INSTITUTIONS, IN-STATE RATES, 1965–92

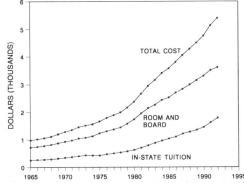

Source: National Center for Education Statistics, *Projections of Education Statistics to 2004*, NCES 93–256

156

10.5 IN-STATE TUITION
AVERAGE UNDERGRADUATE IN-STATE TUITION AT PUBLIC FOUR-YEAR COLLEGES, 1992–93

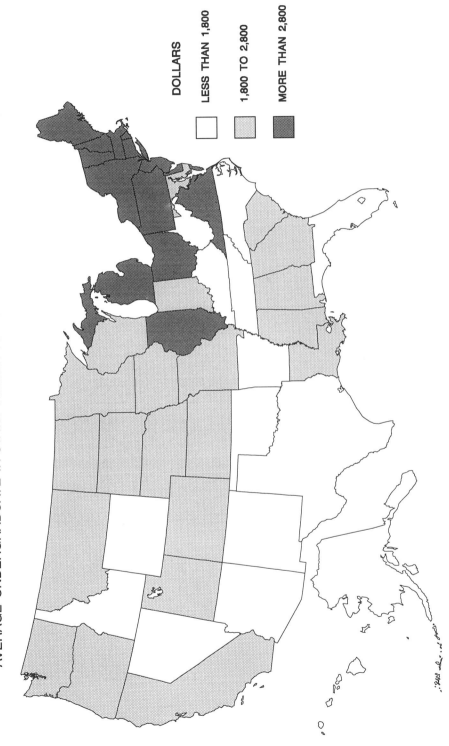

DOLLARS

LESS THAN 1,800

1,800 TO 2,800

MORE THAN 2,800

Source: National Center for Education Statistics

157

11

Crime and Violence

11.1   CRIME INDEX

The FBI's crime index includes both violent crime and property crime. Violent crime includes murder, non-negligent manslaughter, rape, robbery, and aggravated assault; property crime includes burglary, larceny-theft, and motor vehicle theft. On average in 1992, 5,660 crimes were reported per 100,000 inhabitants for the country as a whole. Most crime is property crime, which accounts for 4,903 incidents per 100,000 population compared to 758 incidents for violent crime. The graph below shows how the crime rate skyrocketed from 1960 to the early 1980s, slowed a bit, and appears to be on the increase again.

Areas with the highest crime rates, more than 5,800 per 100,000 population, are concentrated largely in the southern and western rims of the nation (excluding Mississippi and Alabama), but also including New York, Maryland and Hawaii. States with the lowest crime rates, less than 4,600, are concentrated in the northern half of the country, especially a large bloc from Idaho to Wisconsin. Northern New England and Rhode Island, a bloc of Middle Atlantic states extending inland to Kentucky, and Mississippi, are also in the lowest category. States with intermediate crime rates are located between the high and low areas, particularly in a band stretching from Kansas and Oklahoma to the eastern Midwest.

Why this pattern? One of the most important variables in explaining it is urbanization. (Compare with Map 1.3 showing Metropolitan Population.) The crime rate in metropolitan statistical areas in 1992 was 6,272 per 100,000; in rural areas, the rate was 2,026. Metropolitan areas are concentrations of people and property offering opportunity for crime. Metropolitan areas also contain concentrations of population most likely to commit crimes—the poor, unemployed, undereducated persons, many in the dense inner cities, and some who turn to crime to support drug use or because of family instability and lack of alternative economic opportunities. This map can be compared with Map 13.4, Children in Mother-Headed Households. Many suffering under these adverse conditions are African Americans, Hispanics and other urban minorities; much crime is inflicted upon members of their own groups. Age is also a factor; most crimes are committed by people under thirty (particularly young men) and the Sunbelt and West Coast distribution shown on the map undoubtedly reflects the relative youthfulness of the population in these states. The urban factor predominates, however, as shown by Mississippi, which has a large minority population, much poverty, a large proportion of female-headed households and a youthful population, and yet is ranked in the lowest crime index category. West Virginia, a relatively rural state, is the lowest-ranked state on the crime index.

CRIME RATE 1960–92: OFFENSES PER 100,000 INHABITANTS

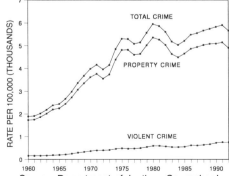

Source: Department of Justice, *Sourcebook of Criminal Justice Statistics, 1993*

160

11.1 CRIME INDEX
TOTAL CRIMES PER 100,000 POPULATION, 1992

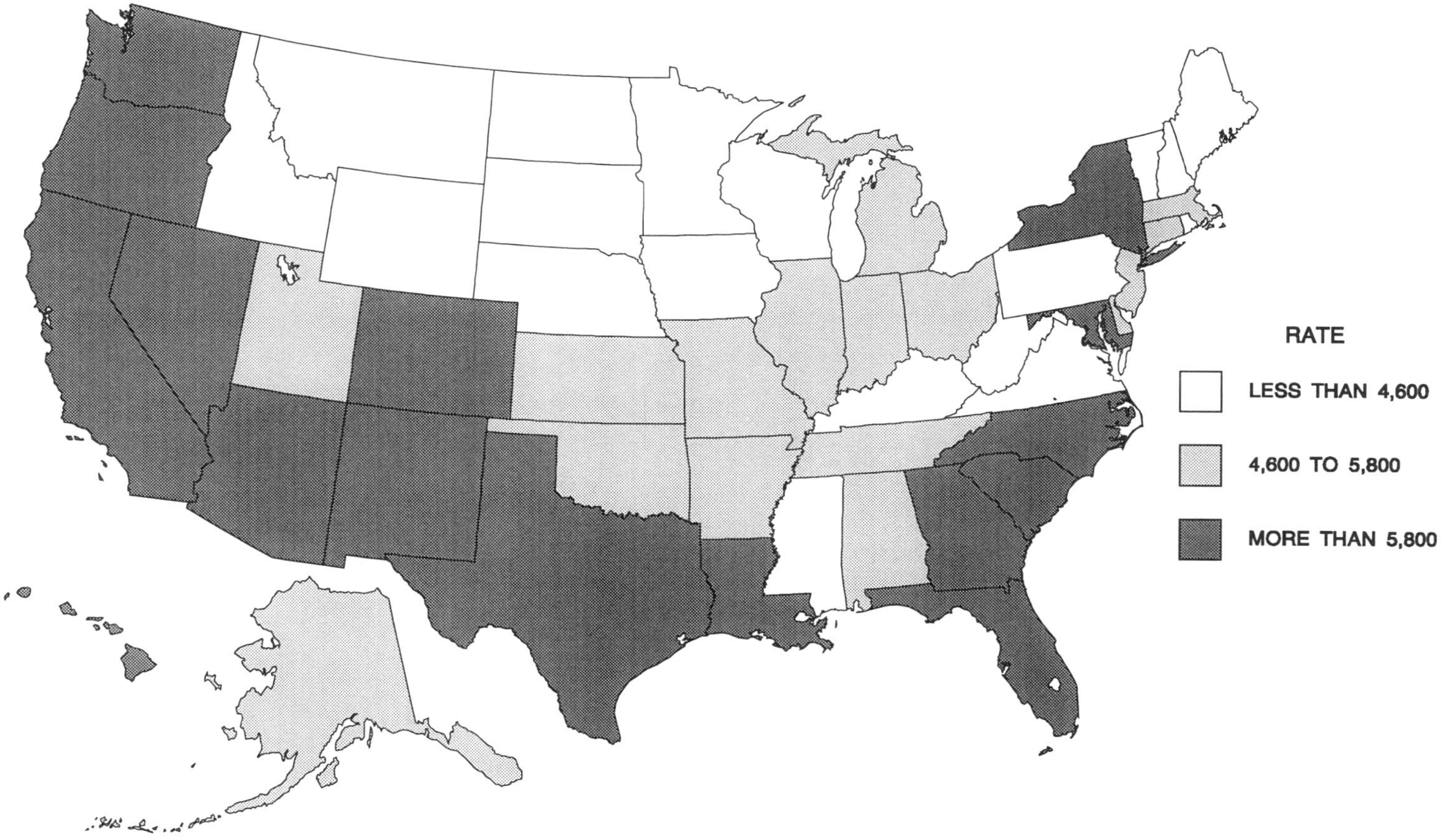

RATE

LESS THAN 4,600

4,600 TO 5,800

MORE THAN 5,800

Source: Federal Bureau of Investigation

11.2 POLICE

This map shows the distribution of full-time sworn law enforcement officers per 10,000 population. It includes state and local police, special police and sheriff officers. The national average is 24 officers per 10,000 residents but varies from a high of 38 per 10,000 in New York to 14 per 10,000 residents in West Virginia. Generally, states on the East Coast, particularly in the Northeast but also in Georgia and Florida, tend to have high ratios, more than 23 police officers per 10,000 residents. Illinois, Louisiana, Colorado, Wyoming and Hawaii are also in the highest group. States in the lowest category, with ratios less than 20, are concentrated in a few regional blocs: northern New England; the eastern Midwest, Kentucky and West Virginia; the northern interior from Minnesota and Iowa to Montana; Arkansas and Mississippi; Utah, and the Pacific Northwest in Washington, Oregon and Alaska. States in the intermediate category, with ratios from 20 to 23, are mostly in the southern half of the country, particularly the southwestern quadrant from Texas to California.

How does this map compare with the previous map, 11.1, showing the Crime Index? The most obvious correlation is found among blocs of relatively rural states that have both a low crime index and a low ratio of full-time police. The three states of northern New England, Kentucky and West Virginia, Mississippi, and a large bloc in the northern interior fall in this category. One caution in interpreting these data is that small police departments in rural areas often rely on part-time officers not counted by this index. At the other extreme, many states have high rates of crime and high levels of police per resident: New York, Maryland, Georgia, Florida, Colorado, Louisiana, and Hawaii are in this situation. One could argue from comparing the two maps that many states are underpoliced and need more police per resident to combat high rates of crime. There is no causal connection proven, however. Are crime rates low in Rhode Island and Wyoming because of the relatively high ratio of police or because of inherent demographic and sociological factors that give these states low crime rates anyway? The combination of high crime rates and high police ratios in seven states (notably Florida, the state with the highest crime rate) could be used to argue either way: "Additional policing doesn't help reduce crime," or, "Imagine how high the crime rates in these states would be without the high ratio of policing." The table below shows the number of police in ten of the nation's largest police departments.

LARGEST POLICE DEPARTMENTS, 1992

JURISDICTION	AGENCY	FULL-TIME SWORN OFFICERS
New York	New York City Police	28,812
Illinois	Chicago Police	12,605
California	Los Angeles County Sheriff	7,960
California	Los Angeles Police	7,900
Pennsylvania	Philadelphia Police	6,347
California	California Highway Patrol	6,062
District of Columbia	Washington Metropolitan Police	4,889
Illinois	Cook County Sheriff	4,801
New York	New York City Transit Police	4,409
Texas	Houston Police	4,262

Source: U.S. Department of Justice, *Census of Law Enforcement Agencies, 1992*

162

11.2 POLICE
FULL-TIME OFFICERS PER 10,000 POPULATION, 1992

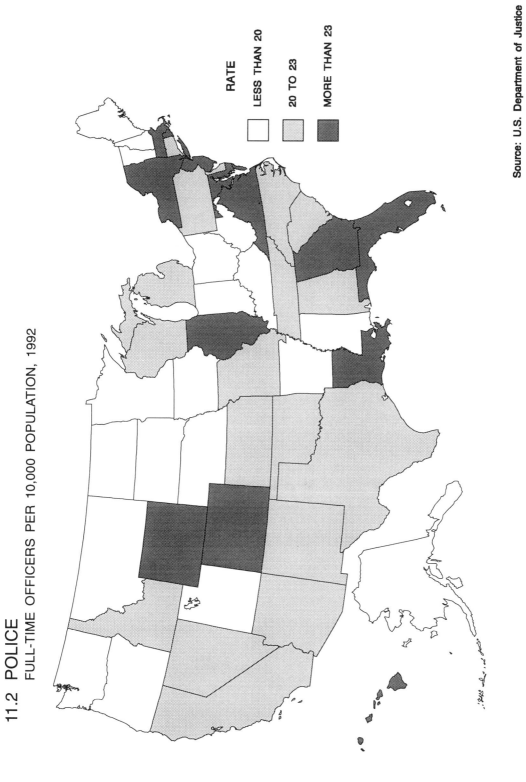

RATE

LESS THAN 20

20 TO 23

MORE THAN 23

Source: U.S. Department of Justice

11.3   INCARCERATION RATE

The third important factor (after the crime rate and the number of police) in any analysis of crime is the incarceration rate. The rate of adults incarcerated in institutions for crimes ranges from 5.8 per 1,000 population in Delaware to .8 in Minnesota. (The District of Columbia, an urban anomaly, actually has the highest rate at 17.6.)

Three large areas of the country stand out as having a high rate of incarceration. These include a cluster of states in the southwest: California, Nevada and Arizona. The second large bloc is in the South and Southeast ranging from Oklahoma and Missouri to South Carolina and Florida. In addition, a number of states scattered in the northeastern quadrant of the country have high ratios including Michigan, Ohio, Virginia, Maryland, Delaware, New York and Connecticut. States with the lowest incarceration rates are clustered in the northern United States from Washington to Wisconsin, in northern New England, West Virginia, and Tennessee.

It is reasonable to ask how the map of incarceration compares to the previous two maps of crime rate and rate of police per 10,000 population. The broadest generalization that can be made is one of the major themes of this atlas: that there are large regional differences in the nature of American society that persist despite the fact that migration, modernization and urbanization trends are promoting homogenization. Specifically, some regions such as northern New England, West Virginia, and the northern interior from Montana to Minnesota tend to be areas of low crime with low levels of policing and low incarceration rates. (Florida's crime rate is still double that of Minnesota's despite Florida's incarceration rate of four times that of Minnesota.) Other states such as New York, Maryland, Georgia and Florida tend to have a lot of crime despite much policing and a high incarceration rate. As with the comparison of crime rate and police, a comparison of incarceration rate and crime rate alone proves very little because there are few states at the extremes. One state, Washington, appears to need more incarcerations because it is the only state with both a low rate of incarceration and a high crime rate. Virginia and Mississippi are also anomalous because they are the only two states with high incarceration rates despite a low crime rate, which one could argue means a needlessly high rate of incarceration rate or, on the other hand, a low crime rate because of the high incarceration rate. In any case, the human impact of incarceration is illustrated in the table below, which gives the number of adult prisoners in the ten states with the largest prison populations.

STATES WITH THE LARGEST POPULATIONS OF ADULT PRISONERS, 1993

California	115,534
Texas	68,813
New York	63,743
Florida	50,603
Ohio	39,396
Michigan	38,115
Illinois	33,072
Georgia	26,711
Pennsylvania	25,598
North Carolina	21,277

Source: *Directory*, American Correctional Association, 1993

11.3 INCARCERATION RATE
ADULT INMATES PER 1,000 POPULATION, 1993

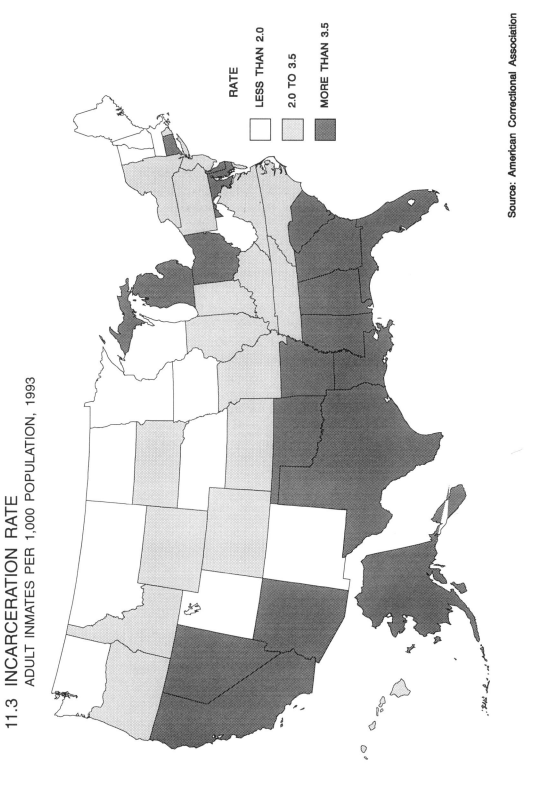

RATE

LESS THAN 2.0

2.0 TO 3.5

MORE THAN 3.5

Source: American Correctional Association

165

11.4   DRUNK DRIVING REPORT CARD

MADD, Mothers Against Drunk Driving, which produced the statistics used to compile this map, state that 45 percent of fatal highway crashes involve alcohol. In 1992 this meant 17,669 deaths and 1,200,00 injuries were alcohol-related. In its campaign to toughen state rules against drunk drivers, MADD rates each state on a scale of A+ to F in terms of its overall laws, regulations and penalties regarding drunk driving. In 1993 only one state, Illinois, rated a grade as high as A minus; Mississippi, the lowest ranked state, earned a D minus. On the map on the facing page, MADD's grading scale has been transformed into three categories representing high, low and medium grades.

The states earning the highest grades, B or higher, are scattered, but there is a tendency for them to be concentrated in two regions: the Southwest and West Coast, including Oregon, California, Arizona, New Mexico and Colorado, and a band of a few Midwest and East Coast states including Minnesota, Illinois, Ohio, Pennsylvania, New Jersey, Maryland and North Carolina. States ranked in the lowest category, C minus or lower, tended to be rural states, with a concentration in the southern states of Tennessee, Alabama, Mississippi, and Louisiana. Missouri and Oklahoma are also nearby. Other states in the low category are also rural, including Idaho, North Dakota, Wyoming, West Virginia and Vermont. Massachusetts is an anomaly. States in the intermediate category are scattered.

MADD has a number of policies it feels states must follow to show improvement in the war against drunk driving and to earn higher scores. These include passing laws to make it illegal for persons under the age of 21 to have any alcohol in their blood while driving; standardizing and tamper-proofing drivers' licenses that could be used as false identification; passing laws to revoke the license of anyone under 21 caught purchasing alcohol illegally; establishing more sobriety checkpoints on highways; requiring testing for drugs and alcohol in any crash involving a fatality or serious injury, and lowering the legal limit for blood alcohol from 0.1 to .08.

MADD feels the nation is making progress in combatting drunk driving; the overall national grade in 1993 was a B minus compared to a C in 1991. In the same two-year interval, the nation experienced a 20 percent reduction in alcohol-related auto fatalities.

166

11.4 DRUNK DRIVING REPORT CARD
MADD's EVALUATION OF STATES, 1993

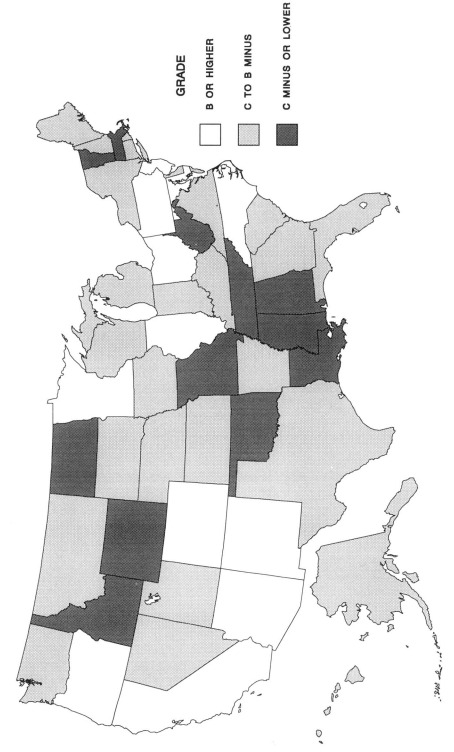

GRADE

☐ B OR HIGHER

▨ C TO B MINUS

■ C MINUS OR LOWER

Source: Mothers Against Drunk Driving

167

11.5   FIREARM AND MOTOR VEHICLE DEATHS

In early 1994, the Centers for Disease Control and Prevention made news with an astounding fact: in a few states, the number of deaths from firearms were now exceeding the number of deaths from auto fatalities. The six states first to achieve this not-so-honorable distinction are those shown with ratios above 1.0 on the map: California, Nevada, Texas, Louisiana, Virginia and New York. Nationally, the rate is 0.88, meaning that overall, a person is still more likely to die from an auto-related death than from a firearm-related death, but the death rates from the two causes are converging. The CDC notes that since 1968 motor vehicle-related deaths have decreased by 21 percent (to almost 55,000 in 1991) while firearm-related deaths have increased by 60 percent (to 38,000 in 1991).

A high ratio on the map may indicate a high proportion of firearm deaths or a low proportion of auto deaths; similarly a low ratio may indicate either a low rate of firearm deaths or a high rate of auto deaths. States with low ratios, less than .75, are concentrated in the Pacific Northwest, the northern Plains and upper Midwest states, the eastern half of New England, and a number of other states. States with high ratios are scattered. The distribution of auto deaths was dealt with in Map 8.4, Motor Vehicle Traffic Deaths. Two states, New York and California, which have a high rate of firearms to motor vehicle deaths, are in the lowest category of auto-related deaths. This means that their categorization on the facing map is due not so much to a high rate of firearm deaths as it is to a low rate of auto-related deaths. Louisiana, on the other hand, the only state which is in the highest category on both maps, has high rates of deaths in both categories.

Firearm deaths are unfortunately very concentrated among black males. As shown in the graph below, men have much higher rates than women for both firearm- and auto-related deaths. But while white males and African American males have almost identical death rates from auto-related causes, a black man is more than three times as likely to die from a firearm than is a white man, and about eighteen times more likely than a white woman. Rates in the very highest ranked states thus largely reflect urban violence, often in major metropolitan areas.

DEATH RATES FROM FIREARMS AND AUTOS
AGE-ADJUSTED RATES PER 100,000 POPULATION, 1991

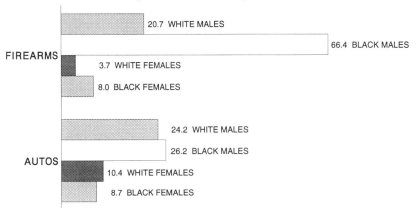

Source: Centers for Disease Control and Prevention, *MMWR*, January 28, 1994

168

11.5 FIREARM AND MOTOR VEHICLE DEATHS
RATIO OF FIREARM TO MOTOR VEHICLE DEATHS, 1991

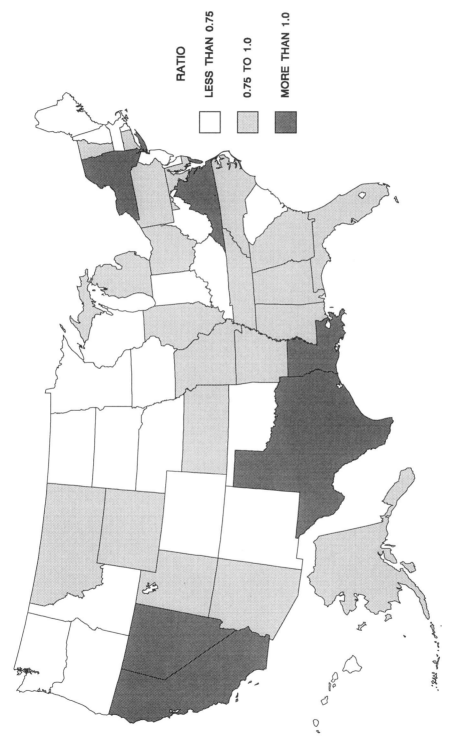

RATIO

LESS THAN 0.75

0.75 TO 1.0

MORE THAN 1.0

Source: Centers for Disease Control and Prevention

12

Status of Women

12.1   WOMEN IN POVERTY

The Population Reference Bureau (PRB), with the support of the Ford Foundation, analyzed and published data on women from the Public Use Microdata Sample of the 1990 census, data that would otherwise have been unavailable due to budget cuts. Particularly valuable is the fact that the sample data analyzed and published by PRB are broken down not only by state but by racial and ethnic origin. One section in the data analysis was concerned with how income and poverty are changing for women. During the 1980s, women who worked increased their annual earnings by about 20 percent, compared with 3 percent for men. More women were in the work force and were working longer hours.

Despite this gain, three-fifths of all adults living in poverty in 1990 were women. Poverty was a problem especially in the youngest and oldest age groups, as shown below. Each of these groups has its own particular problems; young women are often those heading single-parent families and caring for fatherless children. Older women, those over 65, and particularly those over 75, grew up in decades when most women married and husbands were the major earners. Women have greater life expectancy than men; thus many of these older women were widows, some without adequate means. The data show that 15 percent of all women over 65 in 1990 were living below the poverty line; this number rose to 36 percent for African American women. For whites, African Americans, Hispanics, and Native Americans, the percentage of women 18 and over living in poverty exceeded the percentage for men. Only among Asian Americans were the percentages equal.

The map shows regional variations in the percentage of women living in poverty; the major factors influencing differences were age composition and ethnic composition of the population. For the country as a whole, the percentage of women 18 and over living in poverty in 1990 was 13.2. This varied from highs of over 25 percent in Mississippi and nearly 24 percent in Louisiana to only 7 percent in Connecticut. In the high category (over 14%) are two regions, a large one extending across the southern part of the country and a northern cluster of three states, the Dakotas and Montana. The low category (less than 11.5 percent) includes the familiar bloc of states along the Atlantic Coast from New Hampshire to Virginia (in this case excluding New York). It also includes Minnesota and Wisconsin, Alaska and Hawaii, Washington, and Nevada. Many states in the interior of the country fall into the middle category.

WOMEN AND MEN IN POVERTY, BY AGE GROUP, 1990

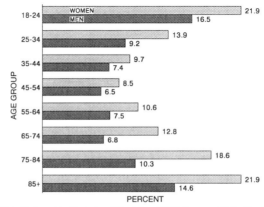

Source: Population Reference Bureau, *What the 1990 Census Tells Us About Women,* 1993, Figure 4

172

12.1 WOMEN IN POVERTY
PERCENT OF WOMEN AGE 18 AND OLDER LIVING IN POVERTY, 1990

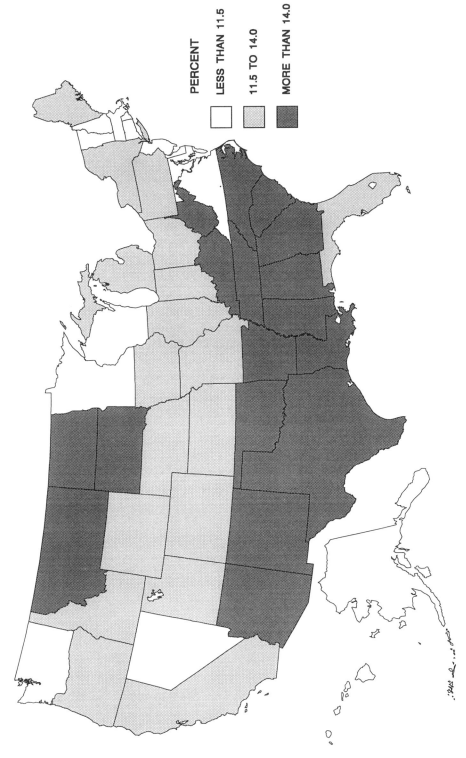

PERCENT

LESS THAN 11.5

11.5 TO 14.0

MORE THAN 14.0

Source: Population Reference Bureau

173

12.2 INCOME DISPARITY IN PROFESSIONAL OCCUPATIONS

There are many measures that may be used, and in fact have been used by researchers, to assess the status of women. Many of them compare women to men on various indicators, such as level of education. One issue or rallying cry that is agreed upon by almost all women, whether conservative housewives or radical feminists, is equal pay for equal work. We have selected income disparity between women and men as an indicator of women's status, and have mapped income disparity in a particular group of occupations, professional specialties.

This is a high status category that includes doctors, lawyers, teachers, and accountants, among others. Such occupations require higher education, usually graduate or professional degrees. By 1990, women made up the majority in this occupational group; they accounted for 53.7 percent of professionals, while men made up 46.3 percent. Only in two other categories did women make up more than half of all workers: administrative support (including clerical), in which they accounted for over 77 percent of all those employed, and service occupations, in which they accounted for about 58 percent. They were close to parity in sales (48%), and made up a substantial proportion of technical (45%) and managerial occupations (42%).

For the United States as a whole, women in professional jobs earned about three-fifths (59.1%) as much as men, as shown in the table below. Only in managerial and sales occupations was there a greater disparity between their incomes and those of men. There was also variation by state, from lows in North Dakota and Mississippi, where the average income of women professionals was only half that of men, to Alaska, where it was nearly three-fourths (72%). As noted on some other maps, however, there is a continuum of values from 50 percent to 64.9 percent, with only the District of Columbia (67.1%) and Alaska (72%) standing out at the top. Thus the division into the usual three categories is rather arbitrary.

Nonetheless, some generalizations can be made. Women tend to do better, that is, have incomes that more nearly approach equality with men, in the West and in the Northeast. They do least well in the South and in some northern interior states.

AVERAGE INCOME OF WOMEN AND MEN BY OCCUPATION
FULL-TIME YEAR-ROUND WORKERS, AGES 18–64, 1990

	MANAGERIAL	PROFESSIONAL SPECIALTY	TECHNICAL	SALES	ADMIN. SUPPORT (including clerical)
WOMEN	$28,900	$30,800	$24,600	$22,300	$19,900
MEN	$52,400	$52,100	$35,600	$41,200	$29,500
WOMEN'S INCOME AS % OF MEN'S	55.1%	59.1%	69.1%	54.1%	67.4%

	SERVICE	FARMING, FORESTRY, & FISHING	PRECISION, CRAFT, & REPAIR	OPERATORS, FABRICATORS, & LABORERS
WOMEN	$14,800	$14,100	$21,100	$16,700
MEN	$24,400	$22,900	$30,100	$25,500
WOMEN'S INCOME AS % OF MEN'S	60.6%	61.6%	70.0%	65.5%

Source: Population Reference Bureau, *What the 1990 Census Tells Us About Women*, 1993, State Table 20

174

12.2 INCOME DISPARITY IN PROFESSIONAL OCCUPATIONS
AVERAGE INCOME OF WOMEN COMPARED TO MEN, 1990

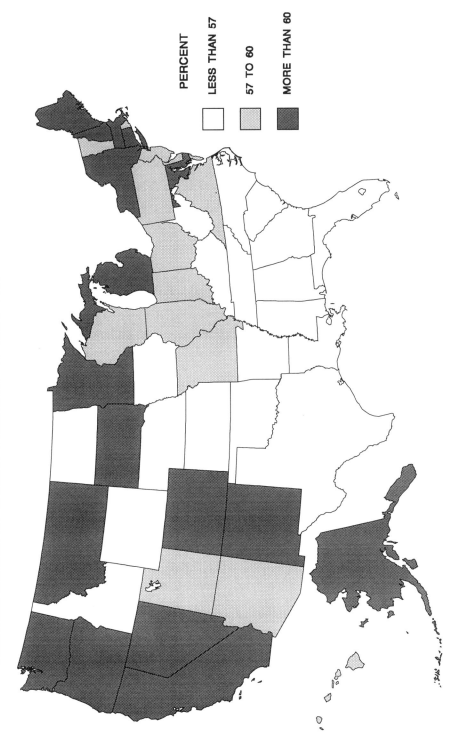

PERCENT

LESS THAN 57

57 TO 60

MORE THAN 60

Source: Population Reference Bureau

175

12.3   WOMEN IN STATE LEGISLATURES

An important aspect of women's status is political participation at all levels—local, state, and national. The presidential election year of 1992 was dubbed "The Year of the Woman" by the media because so many women ran for office and a goodly number of them won. Eleven women ran for the U.S. Senate and five were elected. In 1993, there were seven women in the Senate (five Democrats and two Republicans), making up 7 percent of senators. Both California senators were women, and Kansas, Maryland, Illinois, Washington, and Texas each had one. In the U.S. House of Representatives, 47 women were elected in 1992, making up 10.8 percent of members; 23 were incumbents and 24 were newly elected. Among these women were the first Mexican American woman and the first Puerto Rican woman to serve in the House, the first African American woman to serve from Georgia, and the first woman ever to serve from Virginia. At the national level, the gains for women in elected office were dramatic, and this was complemented by a number of appointments of women to cabinet posts and by the later appointment of the second woman to the Supreme Court.

The map depicts another aspect of women's increasing political clout, the percentage of women in state legislatures. Here women are better represented than at national levels, making up one-fifth (20.4%) of all state legislators in 1993. This may help to project women's participation at the national level into the future, as state offices provide a platform for running for national office.

· Once again, distinct regional patterns emerge. All the New England states, Maryland, three midwestern states (Minnesota, Wisconsin, and Illinois) and most of the western states (with Utah a notable exception) have a relatively high proportion of women legislators (more than 22%). The three highest states are all western: Washington (39.5%), Arizona (35.6%), Colorado (33.5%). The next three highest are in New England: Vermont (33.9%), New Hampshire (33.5%), and Maine (31.2%).

States with a low proportion of women as legislators (less than 16%) tend to be in the South, but there are some exceptions. All southern states are in the lowest category except Texas, Florida, Georgia, and North Carolina, all in the middle category. Maryland, sometimes regarded as a border state, is a distinct exception to the southern pattern; 23.4 percent of its state legislators are women. A few non-southern states have a low percentage of women legislators: Pennsylvania, New Jersey, and Iowa. Pennsylvania is a striking exception to the regional pattern; it ranks 45th in proportion of women in its legislature, only 9.9 percent. Utah is a distinct exception to the high percentages in the West, having only 13.5 percent, perhaps a reflection of the Mormon population with its distinctive cultural values.

Although no women won election as governors in 1992, three women elected in 1990 were still in office in 1993, in Kansas, Texas, and Oregon.

Also of interest is the fact that in 1993, 175 cities with populations over 30,000 had women mayors, making up 18 percent of all mayors of cities of this size, a significant increase from 1983, when the percentage was 8.8. In all, 33 states plus the District of Columbia had women mayors of cities in the over 30,000 category. California led with 53 women mayors.

12.3 WOMEN IN STATE LEGISLATURES
WOMEN AS A PERCENT OF LEGISLATORS, 1993

PERCENT

LESS THAN 16

16 TO 22

MORE THAN 22

Source: Congressional Quarterly

177

12.4 TEEN BIRTH RATE

After declining in the early 1980s, the teenage birth rate (number of births per 1,000 females age 15–19) began to rise. By 1991, the latest year for which data are available, it had risen to 62 for the country as a whole. This rate is far higher than the rate for European countries; most of them (except for Eastern Europe) have rates less than 25 per thousand. Why have the rates risen, despite mounting concern? Child Trends, Inc., a non-profit organization that publishes annual summaries of teenage births, has suggested that the declining use of abortion in some states, more difficult and more expensive access to contraceptive methods, worsening living conditions among inner-city populations, and immigration of new nationality groups with higher fertility norms are all involved.

The increasing rate is a matter of concern at all governmental levels, and it has an impact on numerous other topics treated in this atlas, such as welfare, education, poverty, women's status, and health costs. Teenage child-bearing limits options for both the mother and the baby. Many people concerned with the intractable problem of welfare reform think that the growing number of births to teenagers is at the heart of the problem. The Surgeon General, in a foreword to the Centers for Disease Control's latest summary on teenage pregnancy and child-bearing, stressed the medical, social, and economic impacts. Medically, babies born to young teens are more likely to be of low birth weight or have other problems, and there are adverse effects on the health of very young mothers. Socially, teen mothers are not only at a disadvantage in terms of completing their education and preparing for employment, but are also ill-prepared for parenting their babies. Economically, the cost to the country is enormous; one source estimates that the public costs related to teenage child-bearing in the period 1985 to 1990 (including Aid to Families with Dependent Children, Medicaid, and food stamps) totaled over $120 billion.

The map clearly shows that the Sunbelt is the teen baby belt. With the exception of Florida, the states that recorded more than 70 births per 1,000 teenage females cut a broad swath across the southern United States from Georgia and the Carolinas on the Atlantic Coast to California in the West. Alaska is the only state with a high teen birth rate outside this contiguous Sunbelt bloc. States with the highest teen birth rate are Mississippi (86), Arizona (81), Arkansas (80), New Mexico (80), and Texas (79). The map bears out observations made by data analysts that race and ethnicity are major factors influencing the teen birth rate. Child Trends, in its January 1994 fact sheet, reported that in 1991 the teen birth rate for Hispanics was 107 per 1,000, for non-Hispanic blacks was 118, and for non-Hispanic whites was 43. These differences, which are affected by cultural values and by low incomes among minorities, are reflected on the map. Also, the close correlation between this map and the map of the school dropout rate (Map 9.3) is obvious. Young women who drop out of school are more likely to have babies, and young women who have babies are more likely to drop out of school.

States with comparatively low teen birth rates (less than 55 births per 1000 females age 15–19) are concentrated in two regions. One is the East Coast region from Maine to Virginia (Delaware is an exception with a somewhat higher rate), and the other is a large bloc of eleven states extending westward from Wisconsin to Washington and dipping south to include Utah. The lowest rates are in New Hampshire (33), North Dakota (36), Minnesota (37), and Massachusetts (38).

178

12.4 TEEN BIRTH RATE
BIRTHS PER 1,000 FEMALES AGE 15–19, 1991

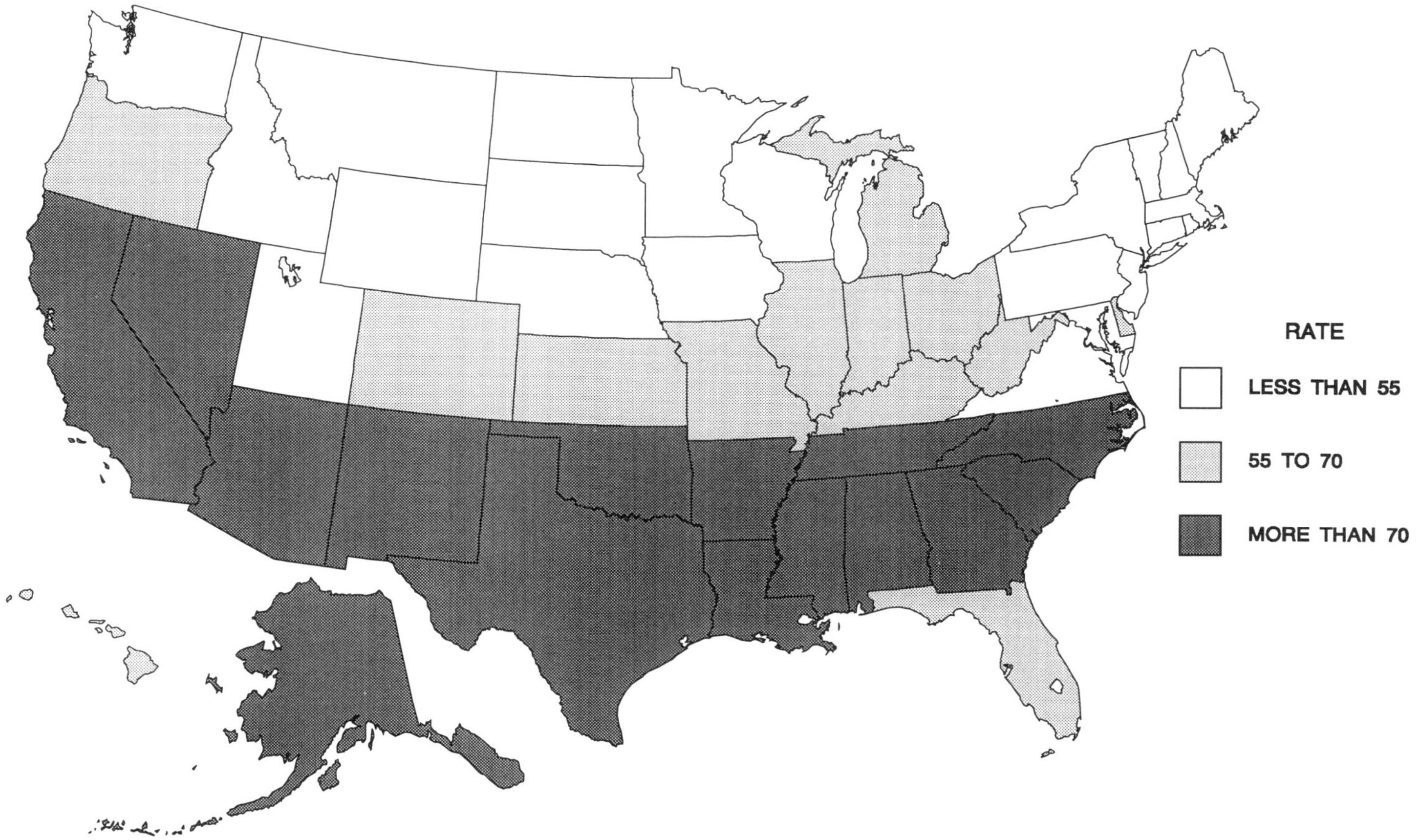

RATE

LESS THAN 55

55 TO 70

MORE THAN 70

Source: Child Trends, Inc.

12.5 NON-MARITAL BIRTHS TO TEENS

Compounding the problems associated with teenage child-bearing is the fact that many of these births are out of wedlock. Child Trends, Inc. reported that the total number of non-marital births to American women of all ages in 1991 was 1,213,800, of which 531,591 were to teenage mothers. At the national level, 69 percent of all teenage births were non-marital. Over the last three decades, the number of babies born to married teenage mothers has steadily declined, while the number born to unmarried teenage mothers has steadily increased.

This constitutes a major problem for American society. Two groups have been frequently compared by officials and journalists. The first group included young people who finished high school, got married, and reached age 20 before having their first child; the second included those who did not meet these criteria. Only a small percentage of the children of the first group were living in poverty, compared to a much larger percentage for the second group. Although different segments of the American social and political spectrum may have different views about the meaning of "family values," there seems little doubt that non-marital teen parenthood and dropping out of school is a recipe for disaster for the children and a problem for the society as a whole. Aid to Families with Dependent Children (AFDC) payments go disproportionately to teen mothers (over half of all payments in 1990), and unmarried teen mothers are especially likely to be in the poverty group. It is a self-perpetuating problem, as daughters born to teenage mothers are more likely to become teen mothers themselves.

The map showing the percentage of non-marital teenage births is very different from the preceding one of the teen birth rate. Some of the highest rates of births out of wedlock occur in states that ranked relatively low in the overall teen birth rate. One possible explanation lies in the high rates of non-marital births in the inner cities of the northern industrial belt, where living conditions have deteriorated, with a decreasing sense of community, and a breakdown of traditional family and religious values. There may also be another influence in that a high percentage of Catholic population means fewer abortions.

In 1991, over 90 percent of all teenage births were non-marital in such cities as Milwaukee, Minneapolis, Philadelphia, Pittsburgh, Washington, Boston, and Gary. The same is true for Atlanta and New Orleans, yet the state percentages of non-marital births in Georgia and Louisiana were in the 60s and 70s. In these states, there are sizeable rural populations, where teenage marriage is common. The percentages on the map range from a low of only 39 percent in Texas to highs of 86 and 85 percent in Massachusetts and Rhode Island.

NON-MARITAL BIRTHS
BIRTHS TO FEMALES UNDER AGE 20, BY MARITAL STATUS, 1960–91

Source: Child Trends, Inc., *Facts at a Glance*, January 1994

12.5 NON-MARITAL BIRTHS TO TEENS
MOTHERS UNDER AGE 20: PERCENT NON-MARITAL BIRTHS, 1991

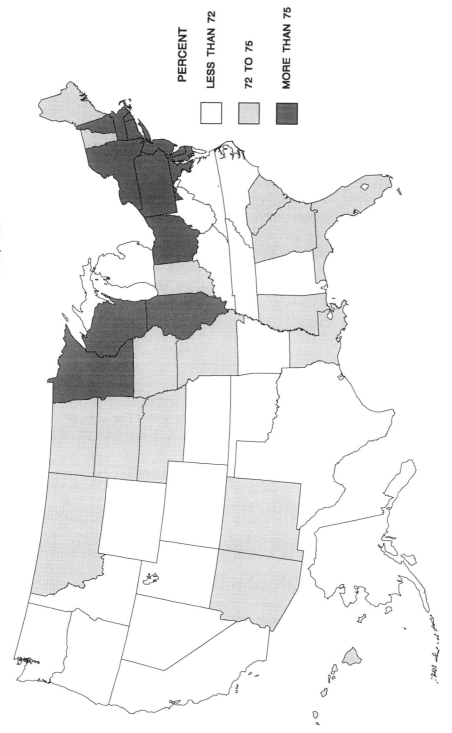

PERCENT

LESS THAN 72

72 TO 75

MORE THAN 75

Source: Child Trends, Inc.

181

12.6   ABORTION

Abortion is one of the most controversial subjects in American politics, and one that polarizes different elements of American society; it is one topic on which there seems to be little middle ground. Although it engages all members of the society, it is generally considered to be a women's issue, and we treat it here in the chapter on status of women.

Abortion is not only a controversial topic, but it is a difficult topic for data analysis. There are two major sources of abortion data at state and national levels. One is the Centers for Disease Control and Prevention (CDC), which compiles data collected by state health departments and regularly publishes and analyzes them in special CDC Surveillance Summaries. The other is the Alan Guttmacher Institute in New York (AGI), a not-for-profit corporation for reproductive health research, policy analysis and public education. The Guttmacher Institute regularly conducts surveys of all known abortion providers in the United States and collects data on abortions. Of the two, the Guttmacher Institute is considered to have the more reliable and complete data sets, due to the data collection methods.

Both sources have been used as background; the map is based on the latest available Guttmacher figures (Henshaw and Van Vort, 1994). Also extremely helpful is the detailed analysis of spatial patterns in abortion published by geographer Patricia Gober (1994). Gober's analysis, based on earlier figures from AGI, utilized a supply and demand model. In it, supply variables measure accessibility and include percentage of metropolitan population, state funding for poor women, and laws that place restrictions on abortion (parental notification, mandatory counseling, and waiting periods). The demand variables are demographic, relating to the composition of the population, and include race (blacks have higher rates), religion (Jews are generally pro-choice; Catholics are generally less tolerant of abortion), income (associated also with education), and population stability (abortion rates are usually lower in more stable regions with less population turnover).

The map shows that abortion rates were higher in the Megalopolis belt of the East Coast, in Michigan and Illinois, Georgia and Florida, and in three Pacific states (Hawaii, Washington, and California) and two adjacent states, Nevada and Arizona. The highest rates were found in New York (46.2) and Hawaii (46.0). There is a dramatic range from this high to the lowest rate (4.3) in Wyoming. Other very low rates were found in South Dakota (6.8), Idaho (7.2), West Virginia (7.7) and Utah (9.3). From these highs and lows, some of the influences that cause the abortion rate to vary from state to state may be inferred. Metropolitan influence is the dominant one, confirmed by both Gober and AGI. In 1992, 1,528,900 abortions were reported in the AGI survey, and of them only 23,000 (1.5%) were in non-metropolitan counties. The influence of religion, working through the political culture, is far less obvious, but can be seen in states in the low category, such as Utah and Idaho with their distinctive Mormon cultural milieu, or Louisiana with its distinctive division into Catholic and Baptist regions, both conservative. In the District of Columbia (not shown on the map), the rate in 1992 was 138 abortions per 1000 women aged 15–44, three times as high as that of the highest states. The District is not only totally metropolitan, but it provides services to a much larger metropolitan area. It is also heavily minority in its population composition, politically liberal, and its residential stability is low.

182

12.6 ABORTION
ABORTIONS PER 1,000 WOMEN AGE 15–44, 1992

RATE

LESS THAN 14.7

14.7 TO 23.9

MORE THAN 23.9

Source: Alan Guttmacher Institute

183

13

Children

13.1   CHILDREN

This section on children begins with the most important variable: where are America's children? Children are defined as those under eighteen years of age. As shown in the chart below, nationally, 25.9 percent of the American population falls in this category, far outnumbering the population of seniors. The population of children is further subdivided into those under five years old, 7.6 percent, and those between 5 and 18, 18.3 percent.

The variation in the percentage of children among the states is significant; 36 percent of Utah's population are children, but in Massachusetts only 23 percent. The east-west component of the map is the dominant trend. All of the East Coast states, with the exception of South Carolina and Georgia, fall in the lowest category, less than 25.3 percent. Vermont, West Virginia and Tennessee join the coastal states with the fewest children. The western half of the nation has the largest proportion of children, more than 26.8 percent. In the Great Plains and West, only a few states are not in the highest category, and those few are in the intermediate category: Hawaii, Washington, Oregon, Nevada, Colorado and Oklahoma. Mississippi is the only state in the high category that lies east of the Mississippi River. The intermediate category, states with 25.3 percent to 26.8 percent, occupy an intermediate position on the map as well. These states are primarily located in the Midwest and central interior and in a band in the Deep South from Alabama to South Carolina.

A number of factors influence the patterns shown on this map. The birth rate is the most important, and comparison with Map 2.6 shows a correspondence. (For example, there are no states with a high birth rate that have a low proportion of children.) Migration is another factor. In the general trend of east to west migration, younger people in their child-bearing years are the primary migrants. The East Coast, therefore, has lost many people in the 18 to 44 year age group, leaving behind a population that not only does not have a lot of children, but also has a relatively high percentage of older people and seniors. The best example of the boom in population due to in-migration is the still frontier state of Alaska, second highest with 31.6 percent of its population in the child age range. Cultural factors play a role as well. Utah's Mormons believe in having large families and Utah has the largest proportion of children of all the states. Many states with recent immigration have high birth rates and consequently a large proportion of children. For example, many of the states with significant Hispanic population are in the high category. Income is another important variable. "The rich get rich and the poor have children," run the ancient lyrics. Generally the wealthier states of the Northeast, which also have higher levels of educational attainment, show this influence.

AGE DISTRIBUTION OF THE POPULATION, 1990

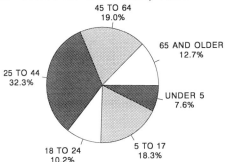

Source: U.S. Bureau of the Census

186

13.1 CHILDREN
PERCENT OF POPULATION UNDER AGE 18, 1992

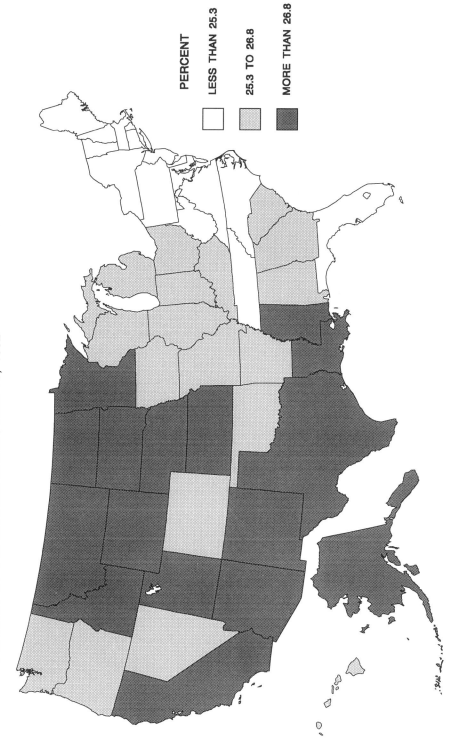

PERCENT

LESS THAN 25.3

25.3 TO 26.8

MORE THAN 26.8

Source: U.S. Bureau of the Census

187

13.2   THE CHANGING CHILD POPULATION

The previous map showed the distribution of children (those under 18) as of 1990. How has the child population changed since the Census of 1980? This map shows many of the east-west elements we saw on the previous map but with some differences. First, the rate of change of the child population is much more dramatic than simply the proportion of the population that is made up of children. The change in the population under 18 varies from an increase of 36.6 percent in Nevada to a decrease of 20.6 percent in West Virginia. Most of the states of the Rockies, the Southwest, and the Pacific Coast, including Alaska and Hawaii, fall in the highest category, with increases of at least 0.1 percent, although many of these states had increases of over 10 percent.

The relative youthfulness of the western states is a major factor, although that alone cannot account for increases of more than 20 percent experienced by several states. As was discussed on Map 13.1, Children, the general historic pattern of east to west migration plays a major role in this distribution as people in their child-bearing years (and the children they bring with them) are the primary group of migrants. Almost all the western states experienced a large proportion of in-migration from 1980 to 1990, but especially Nevada and Alaska, the two states with the highest increase in child population. East of the Mississippi, the four states in the highest category also have a large proportion of in-migration: New Hampshire, Virginia, Georgia and Florida. To the migration trend is added the influence of immigrant groups and cultural influences that result in higher birth rates among western populations such as Hispanics (compare this map with Map 5.3, Hispanic Population), Mormons, and Native Americans.

States in the lowest category of increase in child population (actually a decrease of at least 8.9%) are clustered in the Northeast and much of the Midwest. These are the older, densely urbanized states (sometimes called the Rustbelt) that have experienced a great deal of out-migration. The out-migrants are again parents in their child-bearing years and their children, leaving behind an older population. The phenomenon becomes circular—the states with the lowest proportion of children will have the fewest children in the next generation because their populations are getting older and stabilizing. States in the intermediate category, those with decreases of 0.1 percent to 8.8 percent, are found throughout the South except where in-migration is occurring, as in Florida, Georgia, Virginia and Texas. The northern Great Plains and northern Rocky Mountain states are another cluster in this category, as are Maine and Vermont.

Of all the maps in this atlas, this map stands out as one extremely important to public policy makers. Imagine the impact of a 30 percent growth in the child population over ten years as Nevada and Alaska have experienced. Consider the impact on hospital delivery rooms and on the need for pediatricians. Given that schools represent the largest percentage of local government spending, consider the cost of building schools and hiring teachers for a 30 percent increase in school-age children. In a few years this growth in numbers will impact the public colleges of these states. Also states must find employment for these young people as they enter the labor force. Law enforcement officials must deal with the impact that such increases in the child population may unfortunately bring when youths enter their late teens and early twenties.

13.2 THE CHANGING CHILD POPULATION
CHANGE IN PERCENT OF POPULATION UNDER AGE 18, 1980–90

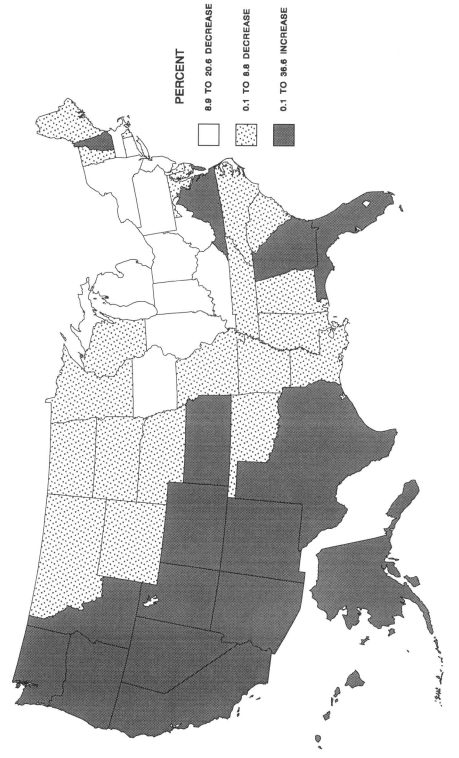

PERCENT

☐ 8.9 TO 20.6 DECREASE

▦ 0.1 TO 8.8 DECREASE

■ 0.1 TO 36.6 INCREASE

Source: Center for Study of Social Policy

189

13.3   HUNGRY CHILDREN

A number of problems affect the lives of children, our most precious natural resource. The next three maps look at three of these problems: hunger, children living in mother-headed households, and children who do not speak English at home. The Center on Hunger, Poverty and Nutrition Policy at Tufts University estimates that 18.3 percent of America's children were hungry in 1991. The Center defines a hungry child as one who repeatedly during the course of a year does not consume enough nutrients. Even mild levels of malnutrition in children can impede their physical development and affect their ability to study and learn in school. Data are estimated from census reports and statistics from food assistance programs.

The national figure of 18.3 percent varies greatly among the states, from a dramatic high of 34.3 percent in Mississippi to a relative low of 7.2 percent in New Hampshire. The South stands out as the area of the country with the largest proportion of hungry children, more than 21 percent. This band of southern states extends west to Arizona and New Mexico and north to the Appalachian South states of Kentucky and West Virginia. States with the smallest proportion of hungry children, less than 15 percent, and those in the intermediate category, 15 percent to 21 percent, are scattered on the map north of the Sunbelt. With the exception of New York and Pennsylvania, the band of states from New England to Virginia have few hungry children. Minnesota, Wisconsin and Iowa in the upper Midwest form another distinct cluster of states in the lowest category.

Income is one of the primary determining factors in the distribution of hungry children. There is a close correlation between this map and Map 4.1, Household Income. Unfortunately, because of the connection between minority populations and lower income, this also means that many hungry children are minority children. Compare this map with the distribution of minority populations shown on Maps 5.2, 5.3 and 5.5. Many African American children face hunger in South Carolina and the band of southern states from Alabama to Texas. Many Hispanic children are hungry in Texas, New Mexico and Arizona, and Native American children in states such as Oklahoma, New Mexico and Arizona. Poverty is not confined to minority populations, however; poor hungry white children in Appalachia make West Virginia and Kentucky the fourth and sixth worst states in terms of the proportion of hungry children. The table below shows estimated numbers and percent of hungry children.

TEN STATES WITH THE LARGEST NUMBER OF HUNGRY CHILDREN, 1991

STATE	RANK	NUMBER	PERCENT OF CHILDREN
California	1	1,442,000	18.2%
Texas	2	1,231,000	24.6%
New York	3	845,000	19.2%
Florida	4	552,000	18.7%
Illinois	5	524,000	17.2%
Ohio	6	523,000	18.0%
Mississippi	7	475,000	18.6%
Pennsylvania	8	455,000	15.8%
Louisiana	9	407,000	31.9%
Georgia	10	363,000	20.3%

Source: Tufts University Center on Hunger, Poverty and Nutrition Policy

13.3 HUNGRY CHILDREN
PERCENT OF CHILDREN WHO ARE HUNGRY, 1991

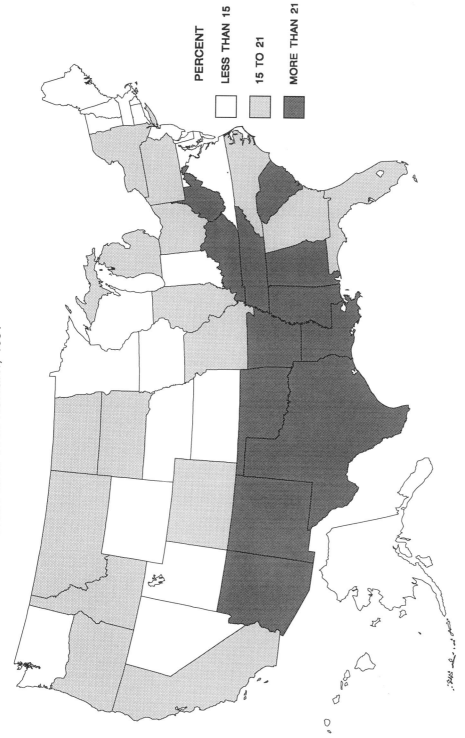

PERCENT

LESS THAN 15

15 TO 21

MORE THAN 21

Source: Tufts University Center on Hunger, Poverty, and Nutrition Policy

13.4   CHILDREN IN MOTHER-HEADED HOUSEHOLDS

The map of the distribution of children living in mother-headed households shows distinct regional patterns. First, all of the states in the highest category, with more than 16.5 percent living in mother-headed households, lie east of the Mississippi, with the exception of Louisiana just west of that river. Within this eastern concentration, the states are further divided into two regions: the southeastern quadrant of the country and a number of northern old industrial states scattered from Illinois to southern New England. Maryland falls in an intermediate position between the two groups. The states with the lowest proportion of children living in homes headed by mothers, less than 14 percent, are concentrated in a large western bloc from Minnesota and Iowa in the East to Idaho and Utah in the West. In addition Alaska, Hawaii, New Hampshire and West Virginia fall in the lowest category. States in the intermediate category are located along the West Coast and in southwestern United States and in between the two eastern regions described above. The variation from the highest to lowest state is 2:1; the state with the lowest proportion of mother-headed households is Utah, only 10.1 percent; the highest is Mississippi, at 22.2 percent.

What causes the distribution of mother-headed families to vary among states? The fact that Mississippi and Utah are the highest and lowest states gives a clue that cultural factors are at work. Mississippi is the state with the largest proportion of African Americans. Utah has the highest percentage of Mormon population, known for its family-centered culture. The chart below shows that the living arrangements of children vary greatly by ethnic and racial group. While 77 percent of white children live with both parents, only 65 percent of Hispanic children do so, and only 36 percent of African American children. Most African American children (54%) live with their mother only. A number of factors have taken their toll on African American families. These include the long history of family disruption caused by slavery; the traditional pattern of out-migration from the South where the males often left families behind in their search for work in northern cities, and more recently, the heavy toll of unemployment, poverty, drugs and violence that has continued to impact African American families much more than other cultural groups in the United States.

The distribution of the states with the highest category of children living in mother-headed households thus bears a close resemblance to the map of African American population distribution, Map 5.2. Similarly, the intermediate category found throughout the Southwest and West Coast shows a close similarity to Map 5.3, the Hispanic population. This map also corresponds somewhat with the maps of household income and proportion of hungry children.

LIVING ARRANGEMENTS OF CHILDREN UNDER 18, 1992

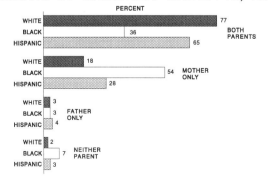

Source: *Statistical Abstract*

13.4 CHILDREN IN MOTHER-HEADED HOUSEHOLDS
PERCENT OF CHILDREN LIVING WITH THEIR MOTHERS, 1990

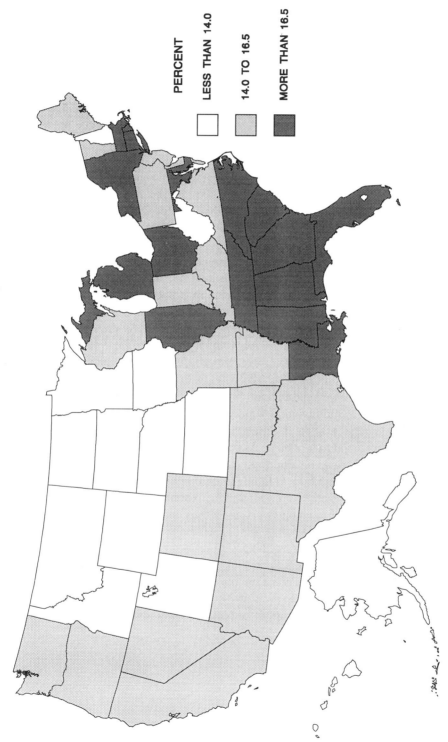

PERCENT

LESS THAN 14.0

14.0 TO 16.5

MORE THAN 16.5

Source: Center for the Study of Social Policy

13.5   CHILDREN WHO DO NOT SPEAK ENGLISH AT HOME

Of America's 45,342,000 children aged 5–17 in 1990, 6,323,000 did not speak English at home. This means that about 14 percent of the nation's children who are old enough to speak begin life with an exciting diversity of cultural heritage, but also somewhat handicapped in terms of their ability to do well at school and later in the larger society. All statistics in this section refer to non-speakers of English at home; many persons, including children, may have varying degrees of abilities to speak English outside the home but choose not to do so at home. The Bureau of the Census estimates that 1,763,000 children (about 4% of America's children, but 29% of those who use a language other than English at home) live in linguistic isolation; that is, they live in families where adults do not speak English inside or outside the home. Spanish is by far the primary language of non-English speakers, more than ten times the number of the next largest group, French.

The map shows great differences among regions of the country in terms of the proportion of children who do not speak English at home. The map bears a close resemblance to Map 3.5, the Foreign-Born Population, and to Map 3.6, Naturalized Citizens. The states in the highest category, more than 14 percent, are those experiencing a great deal of immigration: California and a band of southwestern states reaching to Texas, Florida, Illinois, and a cluster of northeastern states. California has the highest rate, a phenomenal 35 percent, but four other states have more than 20 percent, all with large Spanish-speaking populations: New Mexico, Texas, New York, and Arizona. States in the intermediate category, 5 percent to 14 percent, are, for the most part, adjacent to the core immigrant states in the Northeast, West and Southwest. States with the fewest children who do not speak English at home, less than 5 percent, are located throughout most of the South, in the northern Great Plains, in parts of the Midwest, and in northern New England. South Dakota, West Virginia and Kentucky fall below 3 percent.

As noted in the discussion of Map 3.5, Foreign-Born Population, the different language groups are not evenly scattered throughout the nation. Big cities attract (and keep, since not all non-English speakers are immigrants) the largest populations of non-English speakers. Illinois shows on the map largely because of Chicago, and Florida because of Miami and other large cities. Spanish-speaking children may be Mexican in Texas, Mexican and Central American in California, Cuban in Florida, and Puerto Rican and Dominican in New York. French speakers, the second largest group, range from Haitians in Florida to French-Canadians in the Northeast. German, Italian and Polish speakers are found in the Northeast and California but also in almost all large cities throughout the nation because of their large numbers and the persistence of immigration from Italy, Poland and the various German-speaking countries. Children who are speakers of various Asian languages (Chinese, Tagalog, Korean, Vietnamese, Japanese) live in large metropolitan areas of both East and West Coasts and Honolulu. The Tagalog speakers from the Philippines, because of a long-standing special employment on U.S. naval vessels, are concentrated in big navy cities, such as Norfolk, San Diego and Honolulu. Portuguese are also quite concentrated in a few areas of southern New England, northern California and Hawaii.

13.5 CHILDREN WHO DO NOT SPEAK ENGLISH AT HOME
PERCENT OF CHILDREN AGE 5–17 WHO DO NOT SPEAK ENGLISH, 1990

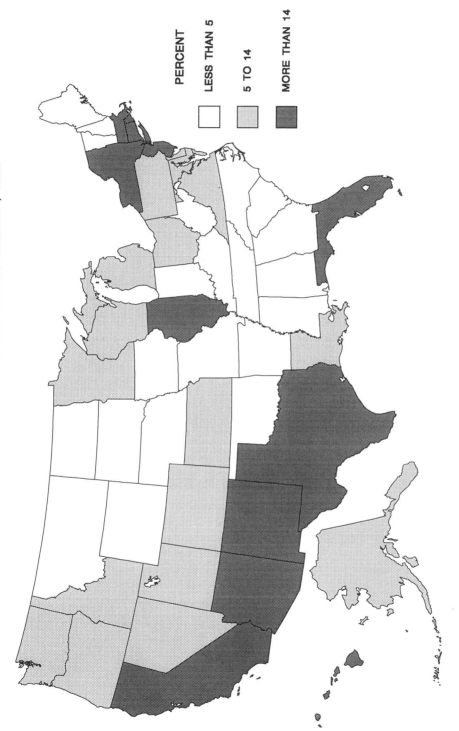

PERCENT

☐ LESS THAN 5

▨ 5 TO 14

■ MORE THAN 14

Source: Center for the Study of Social Policy

195

13.6 CHILD WELL-BEING

This map shows a measure of child well-being compiled by the Annie E. Casey Foundation. In its 1994 publication, *Kids Count Data Book: State Profiles of Child Well-Being*, the foundation used ten measures to assess the condition of children by creating a composite index to rank the states. The ten measures included several variables that are mapped in this atlas. The measures are (1) percent low-birth-weight babies born, (2) infant mortality rate, (3) child death rate, (4) percent of all births that are to single teens, (5) juvenile violent crime arrest rate, (6) percent graduating from high school on time, (7) percent of teens not in school and not in the labor force, (8) teen violent death rate, (9) percent of children in poverty, and (10) percent of children in single-parent families.

This map shows the Casey Foundation's measures as ranks rather than as scores since the foundation's emphasis was on ranks. The states are divided into the top third, middle third and bottom third. States in the upper third of ranks are largely in the northern half of the country, especially the six New England states, and (with the exception of South Dakota) in a solid band from Wisconsin west to the Pacific Northwest and Utah. The five highest-ranked states in order are New Hampshire, North Dakota, Vermont, Minnesota and Nebraska. States in the lower third are mostly located in the eastern half of the country. The South forms a solid bloc of states ranking low on child well-being, from Arkansas and Louisiana, north to Kentucky, and east along the South Atlantic Coast from North Carolina to Florida. Three large northern urban-industrial states are also in the lowest category: New York, Illinois and Michigan. Arizona and New Mexico are the only western states in the low category. States in the middle third (ranks 18 to 35) occupy locations in between those states in the high and low categories. There is a large cluster in the eastern Midwest and Middle Atlantic region; in Texas and states to the north; California, Nevada, Alaska and Hawaii.

The reasons for this pattern are based on the ten separate variables chosen for the composite map by the Casey Foundation. Relationships can be seen with any of the maps in this atlas, which map the same or similar measures used by the foundation. In a larger sense, the composite map of child well-being is explained by the map of household income (Map 4.1) and by the maps of the distributions of minorities, especially African Americans (5.2), Hispanics (5.3) and Native Americans (5.5). The higher unemployment rates, lower income and lower educational attainment of America's minority populations, combined with the many factors that have caused cultural and social disruption in these groups, result in low values on these important measures of child well-being. Thus, the southern bloc on the map largely (but not totally, as there are many poor southern whites) reflects conditions among the South's African American population, and in the case of Florida, among poor immigrants. New Mexico's and Arizona's ranks reflect conditions mainly among their Hispanic and Native American child populations. New York, Illinois and Michigan show the inner-city conditions of African American, Hispanic and immigrant children in metropolises such as Chicago, Detroit and New York City. Hawaii and Alaska's intermediate rank most likely reflects the condition of native Hawaiians and Alaskan Native Americans. Similarly, the different ranking of North Dakota (2nd) and South Dakota (19th) is largely due to the latter's larger Native American population.

196

13.6 CHILD WELL-BEING
CASEY FOUNDATION RANK, 1994

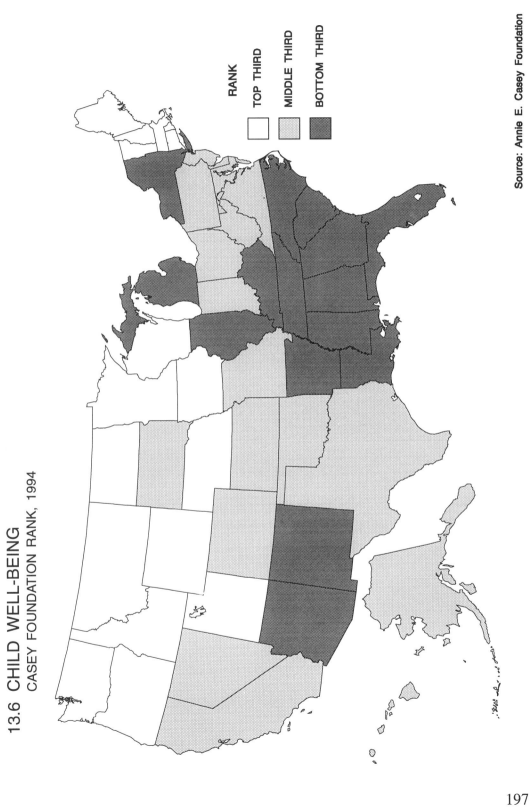

RANK

TOP THIRD

MIDDLE THIRD

BOTTOM THIRD

Source: Annie E. Casey Foundation

14

Senior Citizens

14.1 SENIOR CITIZENS

The 1990 census counted more than 31 million persons over 65, making up 12.6 percent of the population. Thus one in eight citizens falls into the category of "the elderly," or "senior citizens," or "older adults." It is projected that by the year 2010 this age group will increase to a total of over 39 million people. Our nation is aging in the same demographic process observed in all industrialized, urbanized, highly developed countries. In Japan, the percentage is about the same as in the United States, in Europe as a whole it is slightly higher, and in Sweden it rises to 18 percent.

Within the United States, the age structure of the population varies from state to state. Overall, the percentages of people over 65 fall within a range from about 10 to 15 percent, but there are a few extremes at both ends of the spectrum. Florida, a magnet for retirees, ranked highest at 18.3 percent, about the same as Sweden. Alaska, attractive to young pioneers, had a dramatic low 4.1 percent, which is more like that of some developing countries. Utah, noted for its high birth rate, was next lowest with 8.7 percent. The pattern shown on the map is one of three regions of older populations. There is the Megalopolitan region of the Northeast, which extends southwestward to include West Virginia. Vermont and New Hampshire are exceptions to this regional pattern. Then there is a very large interior region of farming and ranching states, including the western states of the Midwest and some Plains and Mountain states. In this region Minnesota stands out as an exception with a somewhat lower percentage of older adults. Finally, there is the region of the Pacific Northwest. Smaller proportions of elderly are generally characteristic of the Sunbelt, with its youthful population. Exceptions are Florida and Arizona, which are retirement meccas.

Although differences in birth rates affect the age structure of the population, the demographic process that has particularly influenced these regional differences in the elderly population of the United States is age-selective migration. In some cases, particularly in the interior states of the country, it is out-migration of the young, leaving an older population; this is called aging in place. In other cases, including Sunbelt states and with Florida as the prototypical example, it is in-migration of the elderly, who are attracted by the climate and other retirement amenities. Arizona ia a good example of a state where both high birth rates and high in-migration rates of older people are important in the age structure of the population.

MARITAL STATUS
PERSONS 65 YEARS AND OLDER, 1992

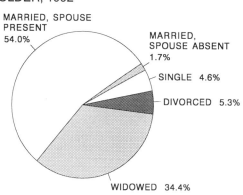

MARRIED, SPOUSE
PRESENT
54.0%

MARRIED,
SPOUSE ABSENT
1.7%

SINGLE 4.6%

DIVORCED 5.3%

WIDOWED 34.4%

Source: *Statistical Abstract of the United States*, 1993, Table 48

14.1 SENIOR CITIZENS
PERCENT OF POPULATION 65 AND OLDER, 1990

PERCENT

LESS THAN 11.5

11.5 TO 13.0

MORE THAN 13.0

Source: U.S. Bureau of the Census

14.2 PROJECTED GROWTH IN ELDERLY POPULATION

This map shows the projected growth rate in the population 65 and over for the two decades from 1990 to 2010. The pattern is quite different from the preceding map. It is in the very regions that now have youthful populations that the rate of growth of the senior citizens will be greatest, as these same youthful populations age in place. Thus the Sunbelt states in both the southeastern and southwestern parts of the country will have the greatest increases in the proportion of older Americans. This is also be true of the two non-contiguous Pacific states, Hawaii and Alaska. This means that two prominent retirement states, Florida and Arizona, which have a large growth potential due to the inclusion of considerable minority populations, will have even larger proportions of elderly in 2010 than they do today. A considerable number of northern and interior states will concurrently show slow rates of growth of the elderly population, and in some states it will actually decrease.

The range in the projected growth rate of the over-65 population is dramatic. The highest growth rates are projected for Alaska and Hawaii, both around 80 percent. Arizona (75%) and Florida (65%) come next. At the other extreme are the five states in which the elderly population will decrease: Wyoming (minus 17%), West Virginia (minus 10%), North Dakota (minus 10%), Iowa (minus 8%), and Montana (minus 3%).

Within the over-65 group, the growth of the over-85 population, sometimes referred to as the oldest old, will be marked. While the projected 1990–2010 growth rate for the total U.S. population over 65 is 26 percent, the projected rate for the over-85 group is over 98 percent, meaning that this group will almost double for the country as a whole. In many states, the over-85 population will more than double, with the most striking increases in Hawaii (237%), Arizona (205%), and Florida (182%). Regional variations in growth rates are shown below.

POPULATION 65 YEARS AND OVER FOR REGIONS, BY AGE: 1990 & 2010

	PERSONS 65 YEARS AND OVER			PERSONS 85 YEARS AND OVER		
	NUMBER		PERCENT CHANGE, 1990 TO 2010	NUMBER		PERCENT CHANGE, 1990 TO 2010
	1990	2010		1990	2010	
United States	**31,242**	**39,362**	**26.0**	**3,080**	**6,115**	**98.5**
Northeast	6,995	7,709	10.2	710	1,266	78.4
New England	1,770	2,023	14.3	194	351	80.7
Middle Atlantic	5,225	5,687	8.8	516	915	77.5
Midwest	7,749	8,356	7.8	840	1,409	67.8
East North Central	5,299	5,683	7.2	539	940	74.5
West North Central	2,450	2,672	9.1	301	469	55.7
South	10,724	15,083	40.6	992	2,229	124.7
South Atlantic	5,834	8,932	53.1	515	1,313	155.0
East South Central	1,930	2,395	24.1	186	362	94.7
West South Central	2,960	3,756	26.9	291	554	90.3
West	5,773	8,214	42.3	538	1,211	124.9
Mountain	1,524	2,147	40.9	133	305	130.2
Pacific	4,250	6,068	42.8	406	906	123.2

Source: U.S. Bureau of the Census, *Sixty-five Plus in America*, May 1993, Table 5-4

14.2 PROJECTED GROWTH IN ELDERLY POPULATION
CHANGE IN POPULATION 65 AND OLDER, 1990–2010

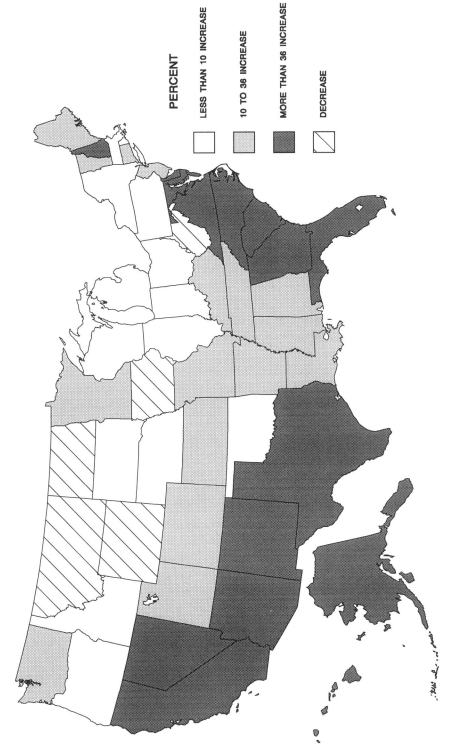

PERCENT

LESS THAN 10 INCREASE

10 TO 36 INCREASE

MORE THAN 36 INCREASE

DECREASE

Source: U.S. Bureau of the Census

203

14.3   AARP MEMBERSHIP

The American Association of Retired Persons is a huge organization having over 33 million members at the beginning of 1994. Its membership makes up just over half of the total population of the United States age 50 or more. Its political clout is great at all levels, and from its national headquarters in Washington it wields considerable influence on federal legislation. It is particularly active in advocating control of health care costs and protecting retirement benefits. AARP is a symbol of the growing numbers of older citizens and of their political strength.

How has this organization attracted so many members and gained such influence? It was founded in 1958 as an outgrowth of the National Retired Teachers Association. AARP's purposes were to improve the lives of older people through service, advocacy, education, and volunteer efforts. In terms of these aims today, AARP provides a whole array of services for its members, who in 1994 paid only $8 in annual dues. One of the best known is the pharmacy service; the organization provides a complete prescription drug service to its members, a very important service to the elderly. Another service is insurance, ranging from group health insurance to automobile insurance to mobile home insurance. Other services range from free help with tax forms (using volunteers) to travel discounts on rental cars and motels to low-interest VISA cards. AARP provides information to its members through two major publications, the bimonthly magazine *Modern Maturity* and a monthly news bulletin; these keep members apprised of the organization's advocacy efforts and feature articles of interest to seniors. AARP promotes volunteerism and supports research on aging.

The map shows the percentage of the population age 50 and older who were members of AARP (including NRTA, which now makes up a small division within the organization) at the end of 1993. For an organization with such a large membership nationwide, there is a rather surprising range among the states. The highest percentage is found in New Hampshire, where 67 percent of persons 50 and over belong to AARP. Neighboring Vermont is not far behind, with 65 percent, and Delaware falls in between the two with 66 percent. These states all have small populations, but some large population states, such as Michigan and New Jersey, are also near the top of the list. At the bottom of the list are Alabama and Hawaii, with slightly less than 36 percent.

There is no clear regional pattern in terms of the states where a large proportion of the older population has chosen to join this organization. Fourteen states and the District of Columbia make up the top category, where over 54 percent of people over 50 are members, and these states are widely scattered. They include a belt of seven northeast coast states, a bloc of interior states formed by Kansas, Colorado and Wyoming, and the individual states of Arizona, Michigan, Oregon, and Alaska.

A regional pattern is more distinguishable in the low category (less than 48%), where there is a large southern region extending from the Carolinas to Oklahoma. Also there is a regional grouping of low percentages in the Dakotas, Nebraska, and Iowa. California, Utah and Hawaii complete this category. Since the major attractions of AARP for most people are its features relating to health (group health insurance with some long-term care provisions, relatively inexpensive prescription service) and its advocacy of retirement benefits, membership in these states may be low because of less need for these services. Hawaii has a statewide health plan, California has generally good benefits, and Utah has the long tradition of self-help associated with the Mormon church. In the southern bloc, the reasons for lower membership are probably very different; there is a large minority population whose members may be underinformed and ill-equipped to pay even modest costs for services.

204

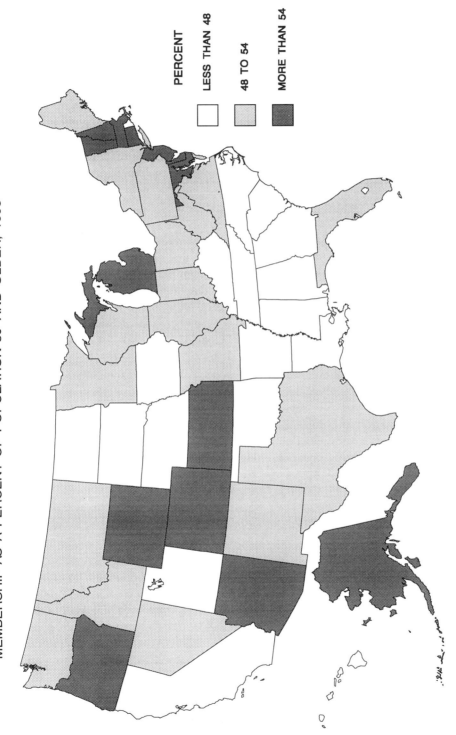

14.3 AARP MEMBERSHIP
MEMBERSHIP AS A PERCENT OF POPULATION 50 AND OLDER, 1993

PERCENT

LESS THAN 48

48 TO 54

MORE THAN 54

Source: American Association of Retired Persons

14.4   RETIREMENT FACILITIES

Housing the senior citizens in a country with increasing proportions of elderly has become big business, as is witnessed by the entry into the field of such giants as Marriott and Hyatt. Retirement facilities range from large developments of single-family luxury homes to small boarding homes for a few elderly persons. At grass roots level, it may be a small neighborhood business, tending to the needs of the many older people who are not affluent.

Our map depicts the approximate number of retirement facilities in each state, estimates derived from the annually published *Directory of Retirement Facilities*. There are three caveats to the map. One is that the listing of facilities may be incomplete (although the best available) and that it contains only names and addresses for many facilities. The second is that the range in services and in number of elderly served is so great that small boarding homes are counted equally with luxurious retirement complexes. Third, this listing of retirement facilities takes no account of the thousands of retirees who simply go on living in their own homes, buy another home in a different state, or rent an individual apartment. These limitations apply to all states, however, so the map gives some idea of how the states vary in terms of the facilities available for seniors.

The directory from which the map was drawn gives four general categories of retirement facilities: congregate care, assisted living, independent living, and continuing care. Nursing homes are not included in the listing, except as nursing home care is included within a few "continuing care" facilities. Congregate care means that there are private living quarters (rooms or apartments) in a building devoted to the elderly, with shared living spaces and a central dining area. Assisted living is a term applied to state-licensed facilities for those who need some help in daily living (including part-time nursing assistance) but not the total care of a nursing home. Independent living is a broad category covering various living units for people who can take care of themselves; the housing may be apartments, condominiums, mobile homes, or single-family homes. Some may include subsidized housing, while others are very expensive. What they have in common is that they are designated for seniors, often with a minimum age limit. A continuing care (or life care) facility is a fourth type; it provides, on a contractual basis and usually with a substantial entry fee, services for the remainder of the resident's life.

The map shows that the number of facilities does not simply vary with the size of population. Three states stand out as having a large number of facilities: California, Pennsylvania and Florida. If the number of facilities corresponded to the size of population, California would be first, followed by New York and Texas. The attractions of climate, cost of living differentials, state tax laws, and availability of medical services all enter into the pattern, as well as personal choices.

More detail for a retirement city in Florida, St. Petersburg, presents the complexity of retirement facilities. The 1994 directory listed over 160 names of facilities in St. Petersburg; of these 31 were only names and addresses. Congregate care facilities were most numerous and mostly small, serving 5 to 20 people, though a few were large, with over 100 units. Assisted living facilities numbered 33, and independent living facilities 30. Only 5 listed themselves as having continuing care. Independent living facilities were large, typically having 200 or more units. They included many mobile homes (actually, manufactured housing, for most are not truly mobile once in place). These facilities do not, of course, include retirees who live scattered throughout the St. Petersburg area in individual houses, apartments, or mobile homes not specifically designated for seniors.

206

14.4 RETIREMENT FACILITIES
NUMBER OF FACILITIES, 1993

NUMBER

62 (DELAWARE)

377 (TEXAS)

2,342 (PENNSYLVANIA)

(1992 DATA FOR OKLAHOMA)

Source: *Directory of Retirement Facilities, 1994*, HCIA, Inc., 1993

14.5   NURSING HOME RESIDENTS

A nursing home is a residence that is staffed and equipped to provide long-term care for the chronically ill, infirm, or disabled. It differs from a retirement residence that provides "assisted living," and from a hospital, or a hospice. Although people of all ages may sometimes have need for nursing home care, the vast majority of residents are elderly people. Most are over 75, and many are women.

Providing long-term care for the elderly and for others who need care for a long-term illness is recognized as one of the big problems in the American health care system. Medicare does not provide for such care, although Medicaid does. Long-term medical care can wipe out the savings of the elderly; it is one of the possibilities that many senior citizens fear most.

The dimensions of the problem vary along with the proportion of elderly in the population. The map is one of the most clearly regionalized ones, for there is a single region in which the percentages of the population in nursing homes in 1990 are relatively high. This nine-state region in the northern interior includes the western and northern Midwest, adjacent Plains states, and Montana. The tiny state of Rhode Island in southern New England also falls into this category. The large interior region corresponds closely to a large region with a high proportion of older population shown on Map 14.1. The maps do not correspond precisely, however; a large proportion of senior citizens, particularly those who have the energy and means to move to retirement destinations such as Florida and Arizona, are younger seniors who are healthy. The correspondence is with the large aging-in-place region, where the proportion of really elderly people, over 85, is high. Demographer Cynthia Taeuber, in the census publication *Sixty-Five Plus in America*, has suggested that out-migration of the young from this region means that a smaller number of family members are there to help care for the elderly, hence higher rates of institutionalization. In contrast, the percent of the population in nursing homes is low in most of the West, including Alaska and Hawaii, five Deep South states (South Carolina, Georgia, Florida, Alabama and Mississippi), and several states in the Middle Atlantic area (New Jersey, Maryland and Virginia). New Jersey, Florida, Arizona and Oregon are interesting cases; they have low percentages of nursing home patients yet high percentages over 65.

The percentages on this map are tiny, ranging from 0.2 percent in Alaska up to 1.3 percent in Iowa and the Dakotas. The total number of people in nursing homes in 1990 was 1.8 million; this had increased by 24 percent since 1980. The projected growth in the oldest elderly, discussed in 14.2, suggests that nursing home care will continue to be a high priority of health care reform.

PROPORTION OF ELDERLY IN NURSING HOMES, 1990

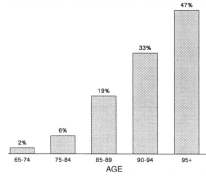

Source: Census Press Release, June 28, 1993; CB93-117

14.5 NURSING HOME RESIDENTS
PERCENT OF POPULATION, 1990

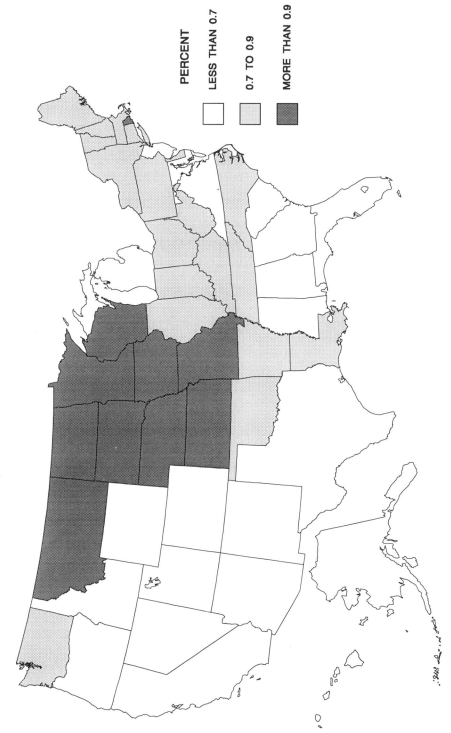

PERCENT

LESS THAN 0.7

0.7 TO 0.9

MORE THAN 0.9

Source: U.S. Bureau of the Census

209

15

Politics and Religion

15.1   LEADING DENOMINATIONS

The last few maps in this atlas deal with religion and politics, two very important aspects of American society that are also useful background for some of the other maps. In turn, some of the other maps are background for understanding how people vote. The association between religion and politics is a big topic in the 1990s. It is paradoxical that in a country that has been built on the separation of church and state, one cannot understand the political patterns without understanding the religious patterns, and sometimes vice versa. Religious convictions and strong political expressions of them exist about many of the topics presented in the maps: abortion, teenage pregnancy, birth rate, AIDS, crime rates, and perhaps many more.

Because of the emphasis on the separation of church and state, the census does not collect information on religion. The map is based on data in *Churches and Church Membership in the United States 1990*, the result of a voluntary decennial effort to collect and publish religious data by state and county. The map is generalized from the large and detailed map of the United States by county that accompanies that volume.

In the second part of the twentieth century, membership has declined in most of the structured mainstream Protestant churches, those with centralized church administration and a governing hierarchy. These include Lutherans, Methodists, Presbyterians, Episcopalians, and the United Church of Christ. Meanwhile the Southern Baptists, the Mormons, and the many groups variously described as fundamentalist, born-again, or Pentecostal have been growing. The Roman Catholics have lost active members in many cities and areas, but continue to gain adherents through the flow of Hispanic immigrants; they remain the most numerous group in the country. Non-denominational Christian churches are rapidly increasing.

With these changes taking place, can a broad regional grouping still be discerned? In 1990 the traditional religious regions associated with migration and with ancestry and ethnic groups were still apparent, though with some changes in outline over the years. The most notable changes of the past few decades were the expansion of the Mormon region from its solid Utah core into surrounding states, the solidification of a very large Southern Baptist region, and the fact that formerly large and solid Catholic regions were somewhat frayed around the edges. The map shows five regions where a single denomination is a major factor in regional identity—Catholics in the Northeast and Southwest, Southern Baptists in the South, Lutherans in the northern Midwest and Plains, and Mormons (adherents of the Church of Latter-Day Saints) in the Utah-centered region. In addition, separating these regions is a transition zone in which the numerous denominations mix and mingle. In this zone no single denomination is generally dominant over a large area, although they may be dominant in individual counties or cities.

All the major regions on the map, as well as the many sub-regions that cannot be depicted at this scale, are associated with past patterns of migration and ethnicity. In the northern Catholic region, early Irish and German immigrants were later joined by Italians, Poles, French Canadians, and others. In the southwestern Catholic region, the character was first set by very early Spanish settlers and continues to be reinforced by large numbers of Mexican immigrants today. The Lutheran region derives its character from nineteenth-century immigration of Germans and Scandinavians. Catholics are also numerous in this region, as many German immigrants were Catholic. In the South, early white immigration was primarily of the British nationalities—Scots, Irish, Scotch-Irish, and English. The very large African American population of these states is dominantly Baptist, often belonging to the various churches grouped as "Black Baptists."

15.1 LEADING RELIGIOUS DENOMINATIONS, 1990

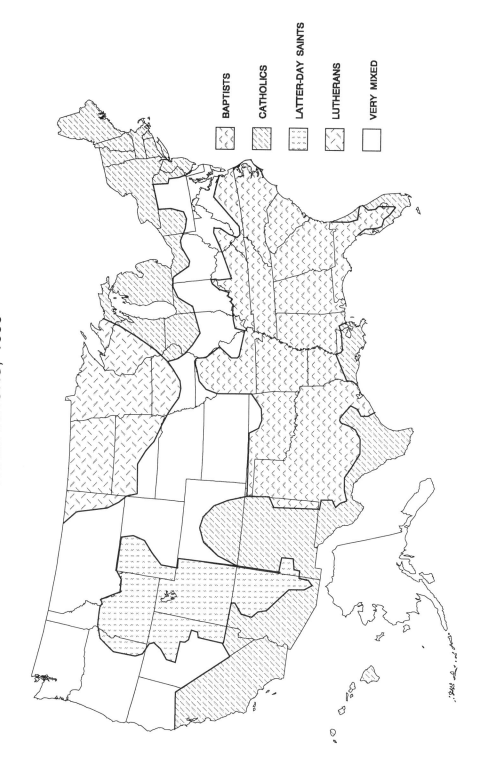

BAPTISTS

CATHOLICS

LATTER-DAY SAINTS

LUTHERANS

VERY MIXED

Source: Generalized from *Churches and Church Membership in the U.S., 1990*

15.2   POPULATION WITH NO RELIGIOUS IDENTIFICATION

This map looks at a different aspect of religion in the United States—the proportion of the population that answered "none" to the question "What is your religion?" This was the prime question in the National Survey of Religious Identification, a massive sample study conducted under the auspices of the City University of New York (Kosmin and Lachman, 1993). A telephone survey of 113,000 carefully selected households collected information not only about religious identification, but about related social variables such as marital status, ethnicity, education, and political party preference. These data, believed to have a very low sampling error, were inferred to the larger populations of the 48 contiguous states. The regional patterns on Map 15.1 are confirmed, but an interesting new dimension emerges when the percentage of respondents reporting no religious identification is mapped. For example, there is a striking resemblance between the pattern on this map and Map 6.9, Suicide.

Although the proportion of such persons in the overall population is about 7.5 percent, the range among the states is considerable. Oregon has the highest proportion of non-religious population, over 17 percent, and neighboring Washington has the second highest, 14 percent. These states are far removed from the established core areas of the various denominations, having been settled late and by a great variety of migrants bringing a diversity of religions. At the opposite pole is North Dakota, where only 1.6 percent of the respondents to this survey claimed no religious identification. North Dakota, according to the survey, had 36.5 percent Lutherans and 30.1 percent Catholics. It has had little recent in-migration to dilute the traditional religious composition.

The West stands out on the map as the region where the non-religious proportions are largest; in ten states, 10 percent or more of the population claimed no religious identification. The line that divides the states of the Great Plains from the mountain states seems also to be a dividing line between the more settled, more religious populations of the East and the pioneering, free-spirited, rugged individualists of the West. The exception to this rule is Utah, where the population is largely Mormon (Church of Latter-Day Saints) and the proportion of non-religious persons drops to 8.5 percent. Only two states outside this western region are in the high category, both in northern New England—Vermont and Maine. Though on the opposite side of the continent, these, too, are states with strong traditions of rugged individualism. The states in the low category are also regionalized. The South, recognized as the Bible Belt, has a low percentage of non-believers. So do several states that are all or partly in the Lutheran core area (the Dakotas, Minnesota, and Iowa). Kansas has a lower percentage than its neighbors, and the three states of Pennsylvania, New Jersey, and Connecticut also have low percentages.

The other data from this National Survey of Religious Identification allow for some broad generalizations regarding the religious makeup of the United States as a country. These state data confirm the patterns on Map 15.1. About 87 percent of U.S. adults are Christian. Of these the leading groups are Roman Catholic (26%), Baptist (19%), "Protestant" (10%), Methodists (8%), and Lutherans (5%). About 2 percent are Jewish, 2 percent "other." The last category was chiefly made up by recent Asian immigrants, mostly adherents of Islam, Hinduism, and Buddhism. According to the survey, Utah was by far the most religiously homogeneous state, with 70 percent of its population Mormon. Rhode Island was 61 percent Roman Catholic, while Massachusetts was 54 percent and Connecticut was 50 percent. There were three states that were more than 50 percent Baptist (Mississippi, Alabama and Georgia). Three states were over 30 percent Lutheran (North Dakota, South Dakota and Minnesota).

214

15.2 POPULATION WITH NO RELIGIOUS IDENTIFICATION, 1990

PERCENT

☐ LESS THAN 6.5

▨ 6.5 TO 9.9

▩ MORE THAN 9.9

▨ DATA NOT AVAILABLE

Source: *The National Survey of Religious Identification*

15.3 POLITICAL AFFILIATION

The outcome of recent presidential elections (1960 and later) has been mapped as an important measure of political affiliation. During the nine elections examined since 1960, Republican candidates won five times and Democrats won four times; therefore, the data on the map are expressed in terms of number of times states voted for the Republican candidate.

Twenty states voted for Republicans at least six times; many of these voted Republican seven or eight times, or in the case of Arizona, which voted for home-state candidate Goldwater in 1964, nine times. These core Republican states fill most of the West from the Great Plains to the Pacific and include Alaska. Oregon, New Mexico and Nevada are the only three western states not firmly in the Republican lineup. Even highly coveted California with its 54 electoral votes in 1992 has only voted for two Democrats in the time span of this map: Johnson in 1964 and Clinton in 1992. In the eastern half of the nation, three southern states, Virginia, South Carolina and Florida, back Republicans, as well as two New England states, Vermont and New Hampshire. Indiana rounds out the Republican states.

Ten states lean toward Democrats, although often only by a margin of 5:4 over the last nine elections. These ten states are shown as having voted Republican less than five times in recent elections. The largest cluster is in the northeastern quadrant, comprised of Pennsylvania, New York, Massachusetts, Rhode Island, Maryland, the District of Columbia and West Virginia. Hawaii and two southern states, Georgia and Arkansas (home states of Carter and Clinton, respectively) and Minnesota (home state of candidates Humphrey and Mondale) round out the Democratic camp.

The remaining twenty states are not toss-up states; rather they also lean toward the Republicans, but not as strongly as those in the first category. All voted Republican five or six times in the nine elections. Mississippi and Alabama fall in this category because of their votes for conservative third party candidates in 1960 and 1968. These twenty states are primarily in the South and Midwest, although three northeastern states are included (Maine, Connecticut and New Jersey), and four western states (Washington, Oregon, Nevada, New Mexico). Presidential elections are uphill battles for Democratic candidates: in terms of electoral votes as of 1992, the Republican-leaning states account for 178 relatively safe votes, while the Democratic-leaning states account for 120 electoral votes. The chart below shows the presidential and vice-presidential candidates for the nine elections and the popular and electoral votes.

PRESIDENTIAL ELECTION RESULTS, 1960–92

YEAR	DEMOMCRATIC CANDIDATES	PERCENT POPULATION VOTE	ELECTORAL VOTES	REPUBLICAN CANDIDATES	PERCENT POPULATION VOTE	ELECTORAL VOTES
1992	*Clinton/Gore	43.0%	370	Bush/Quayle	37.4%	168
1988	Dukakis/Bentsen	45.6%	111	*Bush/Quayle	53.4%	426
1984	Mondale/Ferraro	40.6%	13	*Reagan/Bush	58.8%	525
1980	Carter/Mondale	41.0%	49	*Reagan/Bush	50.7%	489
1976	*Carter/Mondale	50.1%	297	Ford/Dole	48.0%	240
1972	McGovern/Shriver	37.5%	17	*Nixon/Agnew	60.7%	520
1968	Humphrey/Muskie	42.7%	191	*Nixon/Agnew	43.4%	301
1964	*Johnson/Humphrey	61.1%	486	Goldwater/Miller	38.5%	52
1960	*Kennedy/Johnson	49.7%	303	Nixon/Lodge	49.5%	219

*Elected

Source: Congressional Quarterly, *America Votes 20*, 1993

15.3 POLITICAL AFFILIATION
PARTY VOTING IN PRESIDENTIAL ELECTIONS, 1960–92

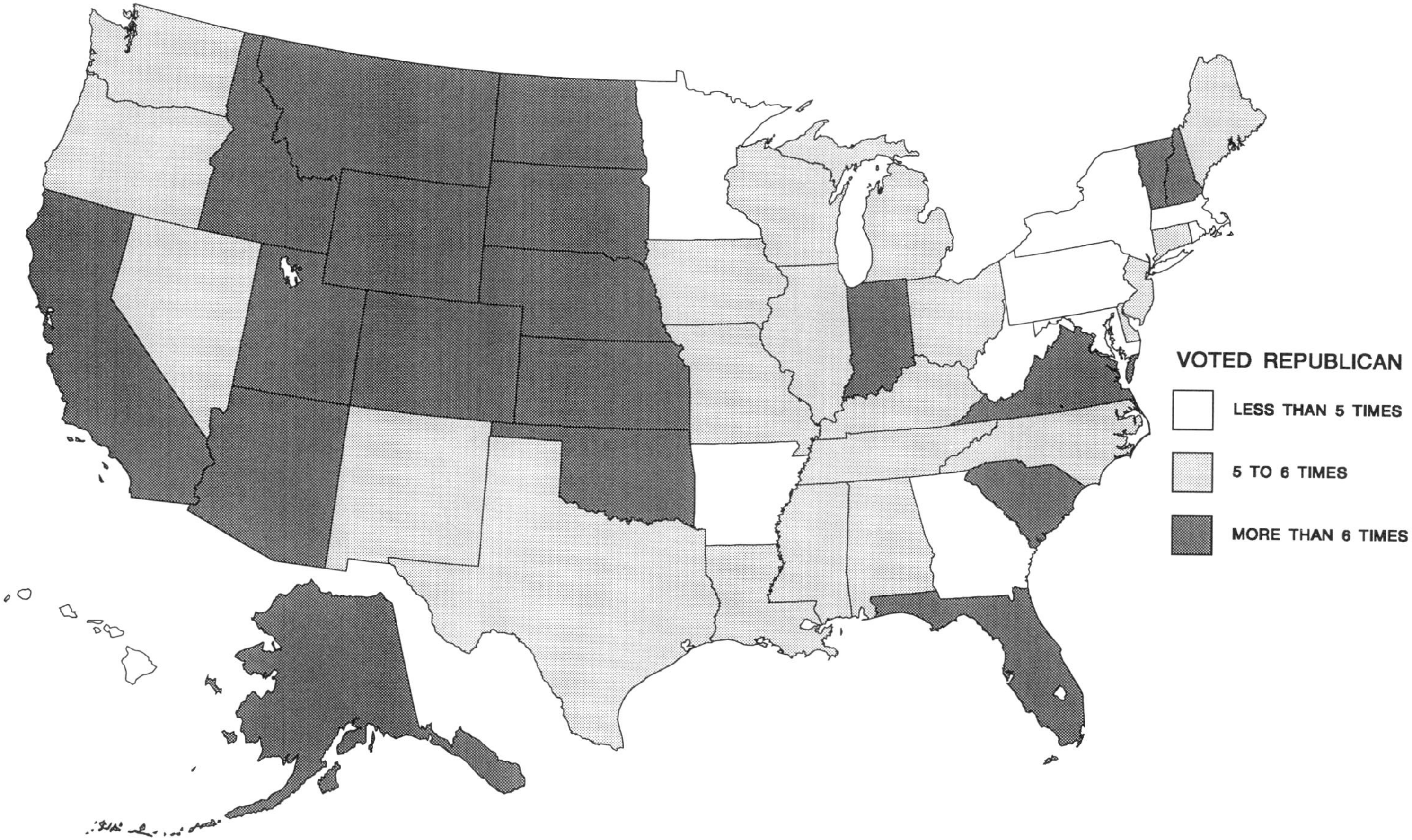

VOTED REPUBLICAN

LESS THAN 5 TIMES

5 TO 6 TIMES

MORE THAN 6 TIMES

Source: *America Votes 20*, Congressional Quarterly

217

15.4   VOTER TURNOUT

Participation in the democratic process by voting is an important measure of societal well-being. We chose voter turnout (percent of voting age population who voted) in the 1992 presidential election as one measure of participation. The more commonly used measure, percent of registered voters who voted, is less significant because it misses the huge number of people who are so uninvolved politically that they do not register. The results from any single election, however, must be treated with caution; election day weather can be a factor, and the home states of particular candidates can come into play (as in Arkansas where less than one percent fewer voters would have landed President Clinton's home state in the lowest turnout category).

The most marked regional pattern on the map is that of the northwestern interior half of the nation—a huge bloc stretching from Oregon to Michigan and from Utah to Missouri where more than 61 percent of the voting-age population voted. Alaska and four New England states (all but Massachusetts and Rhode Island) were the only other states in this category. Maine had the highest figure, 72 percent; Minnesota and Montana were the only other states above 70 percent turnout.

States with low voter turnout were concentrated in the southeastern corner of the country, in Texas and New Mexico, and in California and Nevada. New York and Hawaii were the only other states in the lowest category. The percentage of voting age population who voted ranged as low as 41.9 percent in Hawaii. South Carolina, Georgia, California and Texas were the only other states below 50 percent. Those states in the intermediate category (53% to 61%) were scattered, but with a large bloc in the eastern Midwest, and a secondary cluster made up of Oklahoma, Arkansas and Louisiana.

The overall pattern is partly explained by the well-known association of voting with income and levels of educational attainment, as can be seen by comparison with Map 4.1, Household Income, and Map 10.4, College Graduates. A related map is 3.5, Foreign-Born, because those states with a large number of foreign-born also are usually home to recent immigrants ineligible yet to vote. California, Texas, Florida and New York are the primary examples, but relatively large immigrant populations are probably also a factor that kept percentages lower in Massachusetts, Rhode Island and Illinois.

As 1992 was a presidential election year, voter turnout was higher than in non-presidential election years. The graph below shows that about 60 percent of the voting-age population votes in years of a presidential election; only about 45 percent votes in off-years. These figures have been remarkably consistent since 1978.

PERCENT OF VOTING AGE POPULATION WHO REPORTED VOTING, 1978–92

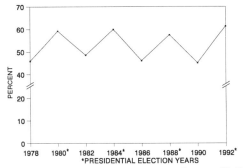

Source: *Statistical Abstract,* 1993, Table 454

218

15.4 VOTER TURNOUT: 1992 PRESIDENTIAL ELECTION
PERCENT OF VOTING AGE POPULATION WHO VOTED

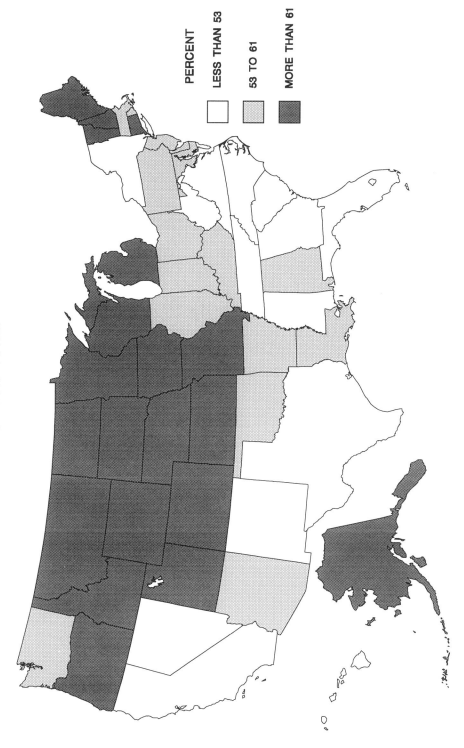

PERCENT

LESS THAN 53

53 TO 61

MORE THAN 61

Source: *America Votes 20, Congressional Quarterly*

16

Summary and Conclusions

We conclude with a brief summary of each chapter, a composite ranking of the states based on seventeen important measures of social well-being, and reflections on the persistence of regional variables in the social well-being of the United States.

MAJOR FINDINGS

In keeping with our three goals, the summary and conclusions are divided into three parts: a summary of the findings in each chapter, a composite map of seventeen selected indicators and an analysis of the map, and a commentary on the regional findings.

1. City and Countryside

There are several major generalizations about population distribution in the United States that are useful in interpreting all of the maps. The population is heavily concentrated along the two coasts, and the eastern half of the country is more densely populated than the western. Furthermore, the American population is very urbanized, with about four-fifths of the total population living in metropolitan areas. Many socioeconomic characteristics are affected by metropolitan residence. The maps often reflect the presence of the area that has come to be called Megalopolis, a string of cities and urban counties extending from the New Hampshire coast to the Northern Virginia suburbs of Washington, DC. Similarly, California is largely metropolitan. Nonetheless, there are still areas where over one-third of the population is rural, notably northern New England, the Southeast, and a large bloc of states in the northern Great Plains and Rockies. Within the rural category, the farm and non-farm mix varies from region to region; the largest proportions of farming population are found in the Midwest and West.

2. Demographics

The range of birth rates among the states is quite small, the major influences on the birth rate being the age composition of the population and various cultural factors such as ethnicity, religion, and education. Similarly, death rates vary chiefly due to differences in the proportion of elderly in the state populations, being higher in the interior of the country and in Florida. The infant mortality rate, one of the best indicators of quality of life in international comparisons, varies slightly within the United States; the South and parts of the Midwest have higher rates. Higher infant mortality largely reflects lower income and lower educational attainment, which are in turn associated with nutrition and accessibility to medical care.

Marriage and divorce rates have been relatively stable in the United States in the past decade, with the divorce rate just about half the marriage rate. Marriage rates do not show a pronounced regional pattern; divorce rates, however, are generally higher in the South and West. The map of the sex ratio (males per 100 females) is the most dramatically regional map in the demographic series, with higher sex ratios in the West.

3. Population, Migration, Mobility and Change

American society is in constant transition and the magnitude of change can be startling. Just

222

in the thirteen years between 1980 and 1993, the United States added more than 31 million to its population, a figure larger than the populations of all but thirty of the world's 190 nations. While the bulk of that growth was concentrated in California, Texas and Florida, large relative increases occurred in more than half of the remaining states. Americans are known for their great mobility and the maps show that millions of Americans are unfazed by migration over great distances, particularly to regional magnets in California and Florida. The eastern half of the nation has greater residential stability than the western half as migrants tend to move from east to west. Foreigners continue to arrive in the United States in a massive wave of immigration particularly from Mexico, Central America and the Caribbean, and the Pacific Rim. These new arrivals concentrate in a few states, especially California, Texas, Florida and Illinois, but also in New York and adjacent areas of New Jersey and southern New England.

4. Poverty versus Affluence

America's highest household incomes are concentrated in the two coasts with distinct regions of much lower income throughout much of the South and the western interior. The poverty map parallels fairly closely the distribution of lower incomes, just as the map of life insurance in force parallels the distribution of higher-income areas. Interestingly, the maps of unemployment rate and the change in the poverty rate indicate scattered pockets of improving and worsening state economies without much regional pattern. The federal government's role in the economy, as measured by the per capita flow of federal dollars, appears to be one of redistributing wealth from wealthier areas to poorer ones, particularly from some of the high-income states of both coasts to the South and interior West.

5. Racial-Ethnic Diversity

The first map in this section is the map of racial-ethnic diversity based on *USA TODAY*'s diversity index, a statistical index "based on the chance that two randomly selected people in a particular area are different from each other racially or ethnically." The map shows a pattern in which a southern rim of states from California all the way to Virginia and Maryland has high values on the diversity index. The other four maps each depict one of the racial-ethnic minorities reported by the U.S. Census. By using a combination of choropleth and proportional circle techniques, the maps display both percentages and actual numbers.

States with high percentages of African Americans are in the South and in several industrial states of the Northeast whose cities attracted large numbers of black migrants from the South. Both California and Texas have large numbers of blacks, though their percentage in the total population is not so high. The Hispanic map presents quite a different pattern, with concentrations in the states bordering Mexico from California to Texas, in Florida, and in large metropolitan areas of the North, especially New York and Chicago. The Asian and Pacific Islander population, only about seven million in 1990, is growing. The largest numbers are found in California and New York. Hawaii is in a class by itself, where this population makes up a majority. By far the smallest of the ethnic groups is the Native American population, and it is highly concentrated. More than half of all Native Americans live in just six states: Oklahoma, California, Arizona, New Mexico, Alaska and Washington.

6. Health and Disease

A measure of overall health compiled by Northwestern National Life Insurance shows great regional variation among states in death rates from disease and in general measures of socio-economic well-being. The northeastern quadrant of the nation and the Northwest fare much better than the Sunbelt states, especially the Deep South, and parts of the interior of the nation. An examination of the distribution of major threats from cardiovascular disease, cancer and stroke, the three leading killers of Americans, shows patterns related primarily to the underlying age distribution of the population. The patterns of these three diseases are also related to the distribution of racial and ethnic groups who are predisposed in some cases to certain diseases, or relatively immune to others. The maps of two sex-specific forms of cancer, breast cancer and prostate cancer, are age-adjusted and show concentrations perhaps related to environmental pollution in older urban-industrial states but also to the African American population, which is more severely affected in both cases. Because of these underlying factors, the eastern half of the nation, particularly the South, is more severely affected by the diseases we examined. The maps of two communicable diseases, tuberculosis and AIDS, show that certain spatially concentrated populations are disproportionately affected. New immigrants in crowded living conditions are vulnerable to tuberculosis; homosexual males, particularly those in inner cities are likely to be victims of AIDS. The distribution of suicides reverses the overall regional pattern with a primary concentration in the western half of the country.

7. Health Care and Costs

Physicians tend to be concentrated in metropolitan areas. Low ratios of physicians to population are found in some sparsely populated western states and in some southern states. Health Maintenance Organizations also thrive in metropolitan areas. Although the complete immunization of children is a high priority, we are far from achieving that goal. The proportion of children who had received one important immunization, MMR (measles, mumps, rubella), was mapped. New England, New York, and scattered other states had the highest percentages. The percentage of people not covered by health insurance varies among the states, for there are 50 different approaches to health care. There is a wide range from Hawaii, which has a state health care system in place, to Texas, where over one-fifth of the population was without insurance in 1990–92. The map showing lack of access to primary medical practitioners shows two regions where high proportions of the population are not served: the Deep South and some states in the northern Plains and Rockies.

Data that adequately display variations in health care cost are difficult to identify. One map on this topic, Hospital Expenditures, reveals that average daily costs per patient to community hospitals are higher in the West and Southwest, plus Florida and a few small states in the Northeast. The map of Medicare payments per enrollee has no regional pattern; high levels of benefit payments appear in some states of the Northeast, as well as some in the South and Southwest. Similarly, there is little regional pattern on the map showing the percentage of the population eligible for Medicaid. A closer correspondence with poverty rates would be expected, but the many state options do not allow complete comparability from state to state. The final map shows Medicaid expenditures in terms of average cost per recipient in 1992. The highest average payments to health care vendors (physicians, hospitals, and other services) were in the states of the Northeast, plus Indiana, Wisconsin, Minnesota, North Dakota, and Nevada.

224

8. Lifestyle Risks

The population of the western half of the nation, perhaps in part because of its relative youthfulness, has many healthier habits than that of the eastern half. The dominant trend on several of the maps of lifestyle risks suggests that those in western states engage in more leisure-time physical activity, smoke less, and are less frequently overweight. On the other hand, the east-west split is reversed on other aspects of lifestyle risks. Westerners suffer higher auto death rates probably because of the higher death rates in rural areas. They are also less likely to use seat belts. On all the measures discussed so far, the east-west division is a broad generalization: a few northeastern states tend to be like the West in having healthier lifestyle characteristics; and the southern states, particularly the Deep South, as well as the Midwest, tend to have populations indulging in riskier behavior. On the map of drug use, while the West shows the highest usage of marijuana and cocaine, the northeastern Megalopolis states are not far behind; the most distinctive division is between the two coasts on one hand and the South and the western and central interior states on the other. Similarly, homelessness is closely correlated with the denser urban populations of states along the Atlantic and Pacific. These states have many of the nation's major metropolitan areas. The map showing homelessness, which is not necessarily a lifestyle choice, is based on data from a single-night Census Bureau count that must be interpreted with caution.

9. Education K–12

Education is one of the most important topics in this atlas; raising levels of performance and school completion would improve any number of other social indicators, such as poverty rates, infant mortality rates, unemployment rates, and teen pregnancy rates, among others. We looked at five indicators, beginning with preschool. Head Start, a generally successful program, varies according to state and local interest as well as by need; two-thirds of children enrolled are minorities.

A map of fourth grade reading and math proficiency, by region, used results from the National Assessment of Educational Progress. In both subjects the Northeast scored highest, followed by the Central Region, West, and South. Lowering the incidence of high school dropouts has been a major priority, and the rate has fallen for both whites and blacks, but remains high for Hispanics. A map of the dropout rate shows that the Sunbelt is the dropout belt. The percentage of high school graduates in the population was high in New England, New Jersey, and many states in the northwestern quadrant of the country, plus Hawaii and Alaska.

Looking to the future, states with a large projected change in high school graduates include many states of the West, as well as Florida. A map of cost per pupil shows that highest spending per pupil occurs in the Northeast, as well as in Alaska, Oregon, and Wyoming. The lowest amounts per pupil are spent in a tier of southern states from the Carolinas to Arizona, in Utah and Idaho, and in the Dakotas.

10. Higher Education

Almost 14,500,000 Americans are enrolled in college. Naturally, the states with the largest population have the greatest enrollments, so a measure of enrollment per capita was used. Just as there are differences among states in the proportions of high school graduates, there are regional differences in college enrollment per capita. Some states with high enrollment per capita, such as New England and New York, specialize in college education almost as an industry. In general, enrollment per capita is higher in the Northeast and West Coast than in the interior and the South. Two-year college enrollment varies strikingly, with many western and southwestern states having more than half of their college enrollment in two-year colleges. Minority enrollment patterns largely follow the distribution of the nation's minority population, particularly the African American, Hispanic and Asian populations. There are large proportions of minority college students in the Sunbelt states and in a few states with large urban minority populations. Also located in the Northeast and on the West Coast are the states with the largest proportions of adults who have completed college; the lowest percentages are in the South and some interior states. In-state tuition at public colleges is highest in the Northeast and lowest along the southern rim of the country.

11. Crime

The FBI's crime rate index, which maps both violent and property crime, is highest in the Sunbelt and in several states with very urbanized populations; it is lowest in interior states, particularly rural states. Poverty and single parent families are often associated with high crime rates, and urban areas offer greater opportunities for crime. High ratios of full-time police officers per capita are concentrated in the Northeast and in other states outside that region with high crime rates. Rural states tend to have both low crime rates and small numbers of police per capita. As the nation's prison population approaches 1,000,000 people, a handful of states account for a large proportion of incarcerations; these are mainly in the Southwest, parts of the South and Southeast, and in a few urbanized states of the Northeast. Many rural states have a low proportion of incarcerated adults, low ratios of police per capita, and yet low crime rates. Some states, such as Florida, have high ratios of incarceration and police and yet still have high crime rates. Mothers Against Drunk Driving has rated state policies regulating one particular crime, driving while intoxicated. These data were mapped without evidence of any strong regional patterns. The comparison of deaths from firearms with deaths from auto accidents is a complex map; it shows that higher rates of auto deaths per capita are associated with rural states, while firearm deaths appear concentrated in states with large proportions of African American males.

12. Status of Women

Six indicators of the status of women were examined. In 1990, three-fifths of all adults living in poverty were women, and poverty was especially a problem for the youngest and oldest women. Ethnic composition strongly influenced the map, showing high poverty rates for women in the tier of southern states, but also in the Dakotas and Montana. Income disparity was mapped for the professional occupations; women do better in the West and Northeast, and they do least well in the South and a few states of the northern interior. The percentage of women in state legislatures is an index of the increasing role of women in politics. New England and most western states, plus Minnesota, Illinois, and Wisconsin, have a relatively high proportion of women legislators. Women are poorly represented in state legislatures in the South, and in Pennsylvania, New Jersey, Iowa, and Utah.

The last three maps are on topics that are often examined in the context of women's reproductive health: teen birth rates, non-marital births to teens, and abortion. While the Sunbelt is the teen baby belt, the map of non-marital births to teens does not match it. Some of the highest rates of non-marital births occur in the northern industrial belt. Abortion is a topic that is not only controversial, but a difficult one for data collection. The map confirms that high abortion rates are associated with metropolitan populations.

13. Children

The dominant pattern on the map of proportion of children in the population is that of an east-west split. The states west of the Mississippi have a younger population due to migration patterns and higher birth rates associated with that younger population. This is particularly evident among some groups such as Hispanics and Mormons. This pattern also reflects the older age pattern of the eastern half of the country. The change in the proportion of children follows a similar pattern of greatest growth in the West, and to some extent the Sunbelt in general, with substantial declines in the proportion of children in the Northeast and Midwest. The maps of hungry children and children in mother-headed households show a good deal of correspondence, particularly in the concentration of these children in the Sunbelt states, especially the Southeast, and in a few urbanized states of the Northeast. Children who do not speak English at home are concentrated in the states with large Hispanic populations and/or large foreign-born populations. These areas include California, the Southwest, Texas, Florida, and a few states such as New York and Illinois that have very culturally diverse populations. As expected from the preceding maps, the Annie E. Casey Foundation's index of child well-being shows a distinct band of states with the best conditions for children across the northern tier of the country (with exceptions such as New York and Michigan) and the worst conditions concentrated in the South.

14. Senior Citizens

Senior citizens make up an increasing proportion of our population, a proportion that will continue to grow. In most states, the percentage of persons over 65 falls within a range of about 10 to 15 percent, but the proportion in individual states varies with birth rates and with age-selective migration. Florida, a retirement magnet, has the largest proportion, while Alaska and Utah have low percentages. However, states that now have low percentages of elderly will see that proportion increase as their populations age.

Senior citizens have growing political clout, as we are reminded by a map showing the percentages of AARP membership among the over-50 population; these proportions are impressive, ranging from 36 to 67 percent. A map of retirement facilities, using proportional circles, shows that the number of facilities does not simply vary with size of population. Though California, the largest population state, is first, it is followed by Pennsylvania and Florida. The distribution of nursing home residents shows that the problem of providing care for the chronically ill and infirm varies with the proportion of elderly in the population. Most residents of nursing homes are elderly; most are over 75 and many are women.

15. Politics and Religion

The map of major religious denominations shows five regions where a single denomination is a major factor in regional identity. Catholics predominate in the Northeast and Southwest, Southern Baptists in the South, Lutherans in the northern Midwest and Plains, and Mormons in a large region centered around Utah. A large transition zone separates these regions where the numerous denominations mingle. Persons without religious affiliation are concentrated in the western half of the nation and in a few states in northern New England. There is an interesting correspondence between this map and the map of suicide. Political party preference as expressed in presidential elections from 1960 to 1992 shows that Republicans captured most of the presidential vote and that a distinct regional core of support for Republican presidential candidates covers most of the West and much of the South. Only a few states, mainly in the Northeast and Minnesota, consistently tend toward Democratic presidential candidates. The remaining states frequently switch their allegiance between parties. The map of voter turnout shows a striking north-south division of the nation, as states with the largest percentages of voting age population who actually vote are concentrated in a band across the northern half of the country. Much lower voter turnout is found in the Sunbelt states, particularly those states that have large percentages of low-income minority populations and residents who do not speak English.

COMPOSITE MAP

Another way of summarizing the data presented in this atlas is to create a composite map combining some of the most important indices measuring social well-being by state. This is a common practice; in fact, several such composite measures are used on maps in this atlas. The FBI's Crime Index (Map 11.1), which combines violent crime and property crime, is one simple example. The Annie E. Casey Foundation's map of Child Well-Being (Map 13.6) is more complex, combining many social, demographic and economic measures of child welfare. We choose to use both of these composite rankings in our composite map. To the extent that this means that a few measures are "double-counted" (income and poverty, for example, are used in the Casey Foundation's index), we believe that these measures are rightfully given slight additional weight in the rankings. Another method was used by Northwestern National Life (Map 6.1), where extra weight was assigned to some key variables.

Our index makes no claim to be a scientific measure of the "health" of American society, but rather is an index that can be useful in calling attention to the relative standing among states on a limited number of important variables. Such an index is but one way of ranking the states. We encourage readers to use the maps and the tables in the Appendix to experiment and to devise other composite rankings based on variables they consider critical. The methodology is simple. The 50 states and the District of Columbia were ranked on the basis of the 17 variables we selected as most important. A grand total of scores (ranks) was calculated and then divided by 17 (or 16 in a few cases where data were not available for a particular state) to give an overall rank. The 51 states were then divided simply into thirds.

The 17 variables we chose as important indicators of social well-being were infant mortality rate, divorce rate, household income, unemployment rate, proportion of persons below the poverty line, suicide rate, proportion of people without health insurance, proportion of persons lacking access to primary medical practitioners, percentage of smokers, high school dropout rate, proportion of women in state legislatures, proportion of adults who are college graduates, cost of in-state tuition, crime rate, proportion of non-marital births to teens, the Casey Foundation's index of child well-being, and the proportion of the voting age population who actually voted in the 1992 presidential election.

When the individual state scores were calculated and ranked, no state came close to a

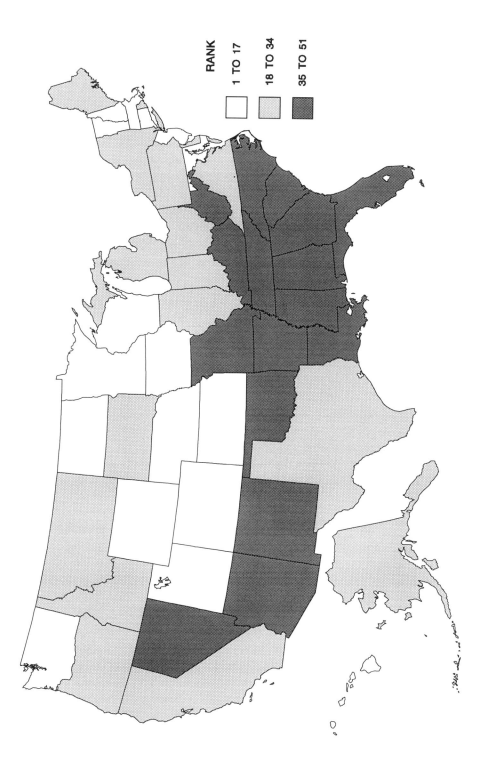

16.1 COMPOSITE RANKING

RANK

1 TO 17

18 TO 34

35 TO 51

229

"perfect score" of 1.0 (number one ranking on all 17 factors), but Hawaii was closest to the top with a score of 12.9 and was considerably ahead of the second-ranked state, Connecticut, which scored 14.4. Nebraska, Minnesota, New Hampshire and Vermont also ranked high, all with scores below 16.0. Fortunately, no state fell anywhere near the mathematically lowest possible score of 51.0 (number 51 ranking on all 17 variables). Louisiana was ranked 51st with a score of 39.2, followed by neighbors Mississippi (38.6) and Alabama (36.8). South Carolina, Florida and Tennessee were the other states with composite scores of over 35.

The regional pattern of state rankings is not unexpected based on the patterns of many individual maps. A number of the states in the highest third of ranks (1 to 17) are concentrated in the Northeast, many in the Megalopolis corridor. Four New England states are here, all except Maine and Rhode Island (although these two ranked 18th and 19th respectively, just missing the top category). New Jersey and Maryland are also in this cluster. A very large bloc of the highest-ranked states is located in the northern and western interior from Wisconsin to North Dakota and from Iowa to Utah. Wyoming, Colorado, Nebraska and Kansas are also in this grouping. The only other states in the top category are highest-ranked Hawaii and Washington State. Many of these states were named over and over again in the map analysis as being favorably ranked in the top cluster of measures such as income, child well-being, voter turnout, educational variables, health and lifestyle risks.

States in the lower third (ranks 35–51) form a broad band of mostly Sunbelt states; in fact, almost all the Sunbelt states are here except for California and Texas, which were ranked in the intermediate category. Many of the states in this group have large proportions of minority population. We have noted often in this atlas the well-known but unfortunate status of America's minorities on measures associated with income, education and, in many cases, health and lifestyle risks. The Sunbelt has emerged as the "teen baby belt" on some maps and the "dropout belt" on others, so it is not surprising to see this distinct regional pattern once again. All the southern states are in the low third group except Maryland, the only southern state in the top third, and Virginia, California and Texas, all in the intermediate category. In addition, three states neighboring on the South, West Virginia, Kentucky and Missouri, are also in this group; all the lower third of states are in this contiguous bloc. The District of Columbia also ranks with this group.

The remaining states are in the intermediate third (ranks 18–34). They too form relatively contiguous groupings. The group with the largest number of states is located in the eastern Midwest and Middle Atlantic stretching from New York, Pennsylvania and Delaware to Illinois. A second large bloc is comprised of a number of western states from California north to Oregon and inland to Idaho, Montana and South Dakota. Two New England states, Maine and Rhode Island, are in this category as well as Alaska, and, as noted, Texas and California.

Interestingly, as Map 16.2 shows in cartogram format, many of the nation's most populous states fall in this intermediate category. Perhaps this could be anticipated given that the middle third represents a kind of "average" or median category. It includes California, New York, Texas, Pennsylvania, Illinois, Ohio, Michigan; in fact all the ten most populous states are here except for Florida and North Carolina, which fall in the lowest third, and New Jersey, which falls in the highest third. Of the nation's 258 million people, just about half (51%) live in states ranked in the intermediate category; about 21 percent live in the states ranked 1–17 (top third), and about 28 percent live in the states and the District of Columbia in ranks 35–51 (lowest third). Thus, the majority of the area of Map 16.2 is in the intermediate category; a smaller area in the lowest category; and the smallest area in the highest category.

16.2 COMPOSITE INDEX WEIGHTED BY POPULATION

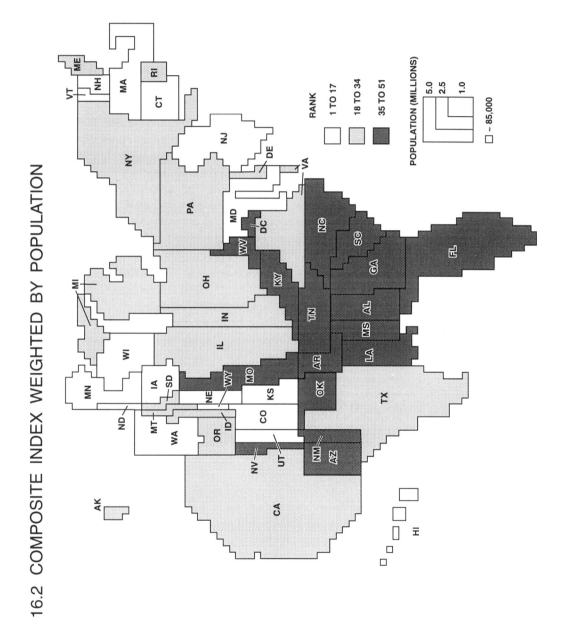

231

THE PERSISTENCE OF REGIONS

Our third aim in this atlas was to examine the persistence of traditional cultural regions and to look for the emergence of new ones. The maps provided plenty of evidence for both. Cultural regions exist, and they may be defined by various combinations of demographic and socio-economic criteria. Long-established regions such as New England, the South, and the Pacific Coast appeared on many maps. They are influenced by regional economies, physical geography, resource endowment, and by the history of population migrations. The boundaries of these regions are not fixed, however; they vary with the specific criteria that are used, and they are really transitional zones, not sharp boundaries. What may be called the South in one case may shrink to the Southeast in another, and the Midwest may sometimes be a unit, sometimes divided into eastern and western portions.

A good example of changing regionalizations may be found in New England. On many maps, New England still appeared as a unit made up of six states; examples include 10.5, In-State Tuition, and 12.3, Women in State Legislatures. However, New England has also traditionally been subdivided into two sub-regions, northern New England (Maine, New Hampshire, Vermont) and southern New England (Massachusetts, Connecticut, Rhode Island). Sometimes these regions also appeared, as on 5.1, Racial-Ethnic Diversity. But on many maps New Hampshire assumed an identity more akin to that of Massachusetts than its neighbors to the east and west, as is true on 4.1, Household Income, and 4.2, Unemployment. This shift in New Hampshire's sub-regional alignment is occurring due to the in-migration of population from the south, particularly the spillover of the Boston metropolitan area into southern New Hampshire. Portsmouth, NH, has often been cited as the northern end of Megalopolis. What is happening is that New Hampshire can itself be divided into smaller intrastate regions. The southern part is becoming more and more metropolitan, while the northern part retains the more rural and small-town character. The larger numbers of people in the southern part make their weight felt in the overall socioeconomic characteristics of the state.

Another example of changing regionalization has to do with the Midwest, a frequently used name but an elusive region. Only recently the U.S. Census Bureau adopted the name Midwest for a region formerly designated as Central. In our atlas maps, however, it has become apparent that the Midwest census region is frequently divided. Illinois and the states east of it are often in the same data category as the Northeast region, while Indiana often joins the South. These are not new phenomena, but somewhat more surprising is the fact that the western parts of the Midwest are, on many maps, in the same categories as the northern Plains states and northern Rockies. Does this represent an extension of traditional midwestern characteristics into the northern Plains and Rockies, which might be a logical result of population movement? The migration maps (3.2 and 3.3) tend to support this.

Closely related to the interest in regionalization is the situation of individual states. Florida seldom goes with its neighbors in the South, but is often in the same category as the Northeast; it has changed due to in-migration from the Northeast and immigration from Latin America. Utah is often distinctive in its western region, and the distinctiveness can usually be attributed to its homogeneity in religion, as the center of a Mormon cultural region. Idaho, growing more similar to Utah in religion and associated cultural traits, is sometimes like Utah on a particular social indicator, but in other cases more like its neighbors to the east and west.

Virginia is also a distinctive state. Once considered part of the traditional South, it is changing. The state that once contained the capital of the Confederacy now appears on many maps to be part of the new northeastern coastal Megalopolis region that has emerged in the second half of the twentieth century. Again, it is migration that is at work, particularly in Northern

Virginia, where a significant proportion of the state's population is concentrated. Virginia is becoming more Megalopolitan, but there is still enough of the rural South in this large state to keep it in the middle category on many measures of social well-being and on the composite map. Also, because Virginia is changing and is different from its western neighbors, West Virginia and Kentucky, it seems to accentuate their similarity to other states of the South, as appears on many maps and is confirmed on the composite map.

In fact, every state is distinctive in some ways, but we will cite only a few more examples. The non-contiguous states, Alaska and Hawaii, are unique, due to their location and history. Even adjacent states sharing a common history and a common name may differ in many respects, as do North and South Dakota, North and South Carolina, Virginia and West Virginia. Washington and Oregon, so often lumped together in the past, show up differently on many measures and on the composite map.

The uniqueness of the American system is demonstrated, even as we try to look at the persistence of regions. Fifty states, fifty sets of laws, fifty educational systems—they are bound to perpetuate both state and regional patterns. Yet, superimposed, is the federal system with its laws and institutions. Not only do all states have the Presidency, the Congress, and the Supreme Court, but they also have many small agencies and programs that affect the everyday life of the society. A few examples of these include Social Security and Medicare, the Immigration and Naturalization Service, and various federal welfare programs such as Aid to Families with Dependent Children. There is a vast diversity among the states on almost all social and demographic indicators, yet the federal system provides the national structure within which the identities of states and regions may still flourish.

Appendix of Tables

Table 1.1
1992 Population (in thousands)

Alabama (22)	4,136	Kentucky (24)	3,755	North Dakota (47)	636
Alaska (49)	587	Louisiana (21)	4,287	Ohio (7)	11,016
Arizona (23)	3,832	Maine (39)	1,235	Oklahoma (28)	3,212
Arkansas (33)	2,399	Maryland (19)	4,908	Oregon (29)	2,977
California (1)	30,867	Massachusetts (13)	5,998	Pennsylvania (5)	12,009
Colorado (26)	3,470	Michigan (8)	9,437	Rhode Island (43)	1,005
Connecticut (27)	3,281	Minnesota (20)	4,480	South Carolina (25)	3,603
Delaware (46)	689	Mississippi (31)	2,614	South Dakota (45)	711
D.C. (48)	589	Missouri (15)	5,193	Tennessee (17)	5,024
Florida (4)	13,488	Montana (44)	824	Texas (3)	17,656
Georgia (11)	6,751	Nebraska (36)	1,606	Utah (34)	1,813
Hawaii (40)	1,160	Nevada (38)	1,327	Vermont (50)	570
Idaho (42)	1,067	New Hampshire (41)	1,111	Virginia (12)	6,377
Illinois (6)	11,631	New Jersey (9)	7,789	Washington (16)	5,136
Indiana (14)	5,662	New Mexico (37)	1,581	West Virginia (35)	1,812
Iowa (30)	2,812	New York (2)	18,119	Wisconsin (18)	5,007
Kansas (32)	2,523	North Carolina (10)	6,843	Wyoming (51)	466

Source: U.S. Bureau of the Census, *State Population Estimates by Age and Sex: 1980 to 1992*

Table 1.2
Metropolitan Statistical Areas (No table: printed from Atlas*GIS data files.)

Table 1.3
Metropolitan Population
Percent in metropolitan areas, 1990

Alabama (30)	67.1	Kentucky (39)	47.6	North Dakota (44)	40.3
Alaska (43)	41.1	Louisiana (23)	73.5	Ohio (19)	81.4
Arizona (11)	84.7	Maine (45)	36.1	Oklahoma (34)	59.4
Arkansas (40)	44.2	Maryland (8)	92.8	Oregon (25)	69.8
California (3)	96.8	Massachusetts (4)	96.2	Pennsylvania (10)	84.9
Colorado (18)	81.5	Michigan (17)	82.8	Rhode Island (6)	93.5
Connecticut (5)	95.7	Minnesota (27)	68.8	South Carolina (26)	69.5
Delaware (15)	83.0	Mississippi (47)	30.1	South Dakota (46)	31.7
D.C. (1)	100.0	Missouri (28)	68.2	Tennessee (32)	65.5
Florida (7)	92.9	Montana (51)	23.9	Texas (14)	83.4
Georgia (31)	66.9	Nebraska (38)	49.9	Utah (20)	77.5
Hawaii (22)	75.5	Nevada (12)	84.4	Vermont (50)	26.9
Idaho (49)	29.4	New Hampshire (34)	59.4	Virginia (21)	77.1
Illinois (13)	83.8	New Jersey (1)	100.0	Washington (16)	82.9
Indiana (24)	71.5	New Mexico (36)	55.6	West Virginia (42)	41.7
Iowa (41)	43.2	New York (9)	91.8	Wisconsin (29)	68.1
Kansas (37)	53.8	North Carolina (33)	65.2	Wyoming (48)	29.6

Source: U.S. Bureau of the Census, *Statistical Abstract of the United States: 1993*, Table 41

Table 1.4
Rural Population
Percent living in rural areas, 1990

Alabama (14)	39.6	Kentucky (8)	48.2	North Dakota (6)	49.6
Alaska (22)	32.5	Louisiana (24)	31.9	Ohio (34)	25.9
Arizona (46)	12.5	Maine (3)	55.4	Oklahoma (23)	32.3
Arkansas (11)	46.5	Maryland (38)	18.7	Oregon (30)	29.5
California (50)	7.4	Massachusetts (40)	15.7	Pennsylvania (26)	31.1
Colorado (39)	17.6	Michigan (30)	29.5	Rhode Island (44)	14.0
Connecticut (36)	20.9	Minnesota (29)	30.1	South Carolina (12)	45.4
Delaware (32)	27.0	Mississippi (4)	52.9	South Dakota (5)	50.0
D.C. (51)	0.0	Missouri (25)	31.3	Tennessee (16)	39.1
Florida (43)	15.2	Montana (9)	47.5	Texas (37)	19.7
Georgia (17)	36.8	Nebraska (21)	33.9	Utah (45)	13.0
Hawaii (48)	11.0	Nevada (47)	11.7	Vermont (1)	67.8
Idaho (13)	42.6	New Hampshire (7)	49.0	Virginia (28)	30.6
Illinois (42)	15.4	New Jersey (49)	10.6	Washington (35)	23.6
Indiana (18)	35.1	New Mexico (32)	27.0	West Virginia (2)	63.9
Iowa (15)	39.4	New York (40)	15.7	Wisconsin (20)	34.3
Kansas (27)	30.9	North Carolina (10)	46.7	Wyoming (19)	35.0

Source: U.S. Bureau of the Census, *Statistical Abstract of the United States: 1993*, Table 37

Table 1.5
Rural Farm and Rural Non-Farm Population, 1991
(Numbers in thousands)

	U.S.		Northeast		Midwest	
Total Rural Population	67,962		11,713		17,844	
Farm Population	4,632	(6.8%)	258	(2%)	2,285	(13%)
Non-Farm Population	63,330	(93.2%)	11,455	(98%)	15,559	(87%)

	South		West	
Total Rural Population	29,622		8,782	
Farm Population	1,371	(5%)	719	(8%)
Non-Farm Population	28,251	(95%)	8,063	(92%)

Source: Dacquel and Dahmann, *Current Population Reports, P20-472, 1993*, Tables 1 and 2

Table 2.1
Birth Rate
Live births per 1,000 population, 1992

Alabama (25)	15.2	Kentucky (38)	14.4	North Dakota (43)	14.0
Alaska (2)	19.9	Louisiana (10)	16.7	Ohio (23)	15.3
Arizona (6)	17.4	Maine (50)	12.7	Oklahoma (27)	14.9
Arkansas (34)	14.6	Maryland (20)	15.5	Oregon (43)	14.0
California (3)	19.5	Massachusetts (30)	14.7	Pennsylvania (47)	13.8
Colorado (18)	15.7	Michigan (30)	14.7	Rhode Island (30)	14.7
Connecticut (38)	14.4	Minnesota (34)	14.6	South Carolina (18)	15.7
Delaware (16)	15.8	Mississippi (11)	16.6	South Dakota (15)	15.9
D.C. (8)	17.1	Missouri (37)	14.5	Tennessee (30)	14.7
Florida (40)	14.3	Montana (43)	14.0	Texas (4)	18.4
Georgia (12)	16.5	Nebraska (40)	14.3	Utah (1)	20.6
Hawaii (7)	17.2	Nevada (9)	16.8	Vermont (49)	13.4
Idaho (14)	16.4	New Hampshire (42)	14.1	Virginia (23)	15.3
Illinois (12)	16.5	New Jersey (21)	15.4	Washington (21)	15.4
Indiana (29)	14.8	New Mexico (5)	18.0	West Virginia (51)	12.2
Iowa (48)	13.6	New York (16)	15.8	Wisconsin (43)	14.0
Kansas (27)	14.9	North Carolina (26)	15.1	Wyoming (34)	14.6

Source: National Center for Health Statisitcs, *Monthly Vital Statistics*, Vol. 41, No. 13. 1993. Table 1

Table 2.2
Death Rate
Deaths per 1,000 persons of all ages, 1992

Alabama (9)	9.6	Kentucky (12)	9.4	North Dakota (16)	9.1
Alaska (51)	3.8	Louisiana (24)	8.7	Ohio (20)	9.0
Arizona (35)	8.0	Maine (22)	8.8	Oklahoma (11)	9.5
Arkansas (3)	10.5	Maryland (39)	7.7	Oregon (24)	8.7
California (47)	7.0	Massachusetts (16)	9.1	Pennsylvania (5)	10.3
Colorado (48)	6.5	Michigan (32)	8.4	Rhode Island (12)	9.4
Connecticut (29)	8.6	Minnesota (37)	7.8	South Carolina (31)	8.5
Delaware (29)	8.6	Mississippi (6)	9.7	South Dakota (6)	9.7
D.C. (1)	11.2	Missouri (6)	9.7	Tennessee (12)	9.4
Florida (4)	10.4	Montana (24)	8.7	Texas (43)	7.4
Georgia (36)	7.9	Nebraska (15)	9.2	Utah (50)	5.5
Hawaii (49)	6.0	Nevada (41)	7.6	Vermont (33)	8.3
Idaho (41)	7.6	New Hampshire (39)	7.7	Virginia (37)	7.8
Illinois (24)	8.7	New Jersey (16)	9.1	Washington (44)	7.3
Indiana (21)	8.9	New Mexico (44)	7.3	West Virginia (2)	11.1
Iowa (9)	9.6	New York (16)	9.1	Wisconsin (33)	8.3
Kansas (22)	8.8	North Carolina (24)	8.7	Wyoming (46)	7.2

Source: National Center for Health Statistics, *Monthly Vital Statistics*, Vol. 41, No. 13, 1993, Table 3

Table 2.3

Infant Mortality
Deaths of infants under one year of age per 1,000 live births, 1992

State	Rate	State	Rate	State	Rate
Alabama (3)	10.8	Kentucky (22)	8.7	North Dakota (34)	7.8
Alaska (26)	8.5	Louisiana (12)	9.6	Ohio (22)	8.7
Arizona (26)	8.5	Maine (50)	5.7	Oklahoma (16)	9.2
Arkansas (10)	9.8	Maryland (20)	8.9	Oregon (38)	7.4
California (42)	6.9	Massachusetts (43)	6.8	Pennsylvania (24)	8.6
Colorado (39)	7.3	Michigan (4)	10.5	Rhode Island (33)	7.9
Connecticut (37)	7.5	Minnesota (41)	7.0	South Carolina (4)	10.5
Delaware (11)	9.7	Mississippi (2)	11.6	South Dakota (8)	10.0
D.C. (1)	18.6	Missouri (19)	9.0	Tennessee (13)	9.5
Florida (17)	9.1	Montana (26)	8.5	Texas (36)	7.7
Georgia (6)	10.4	Nebraska (45)	6.7	Utah (48)	6.2
Hawaii (46)	6.6	Nevada (46)	6.6	Vermont (43)	6.8
Idaho (32)	8.2	New Hampshire (51)	5.4	Virginia (15)	9.4
Illinois (8)	10.0	New Jersey (24)	8.6	Washington (48)	6.2
Indiana (13)	9.5	New Mexico (31)	8.3	West Virginia (17)	9.1
Iowa (34)	7.8	New York (26)	8.5	Wisconsin (40)	7.1
Kansas (30)	8.4	North Carolina (7)	10.2	Wyoming (21)	8.8

Source: National Center for Health Statistics, *Monthly Vital Statistics*, Vol. 41, No. 13, 1993, Table 3

Table 2.4

Marriage Rate
Marriages per 1,000 population, 1992

State	Rate	State	Rate	State	Rate
Alabama (16)	9.8	Kentucky (7)	13.3	North Dakota (39)	7.6
Alaska (16)	9.8	Louisiana (32)	8.3	Ohio (31)	8.4
Arizona (19)	9.5	Maine (21)	9.1	Oklahoma (15)	9.9
Arkansas (2)	15.6	Maryland (22)	9.0	Oregon (33)	8.2
California (40)	7.5	Massachusetts (47)	7.0	Pennsylvania (50)	6.7
Colorado (18)	9.7	Michigan (40)	7.5	Rhode Island (43)	7.3
Connecticut (24)	8.8	Minnesota (45)	7.2	South Carolina (4)	14.8
Delaware (43)	7.3	Mississippi (27)	8.7	South Dakota (10)	10.6
D.C. (50)	6.7	Missouri (27)	8.7	Tennessee (5)	14.1
Florida (14)	10.2	Montana (24)	8.8	Texas (12)	10.4
Georgia (20)	9.4	Nebraska (35)	8.0	Utah (8)	11.0
Hawaii (3)	15.2	Nevada (1)	86.1	Vermont (12)	10.4
Idaho (6)	13.5	New Hampshire (37)	7.9	Virginia (9)	10.9
Illinois (35)	8.0	New Jersey (46)	7.1	Washington (24)	8.8
Indiana (23)	8.9	New Mexico (33)	8.2	West Virginia (49)	6.8
Iowa (37)	7.9	New York (29)	8.6	Wisconsin (42)	7.4
Kansas (29)	8.6	North Carolina (47)	7.0	Wyoming (11)	10.5

Source: National Center for Health Statistics, *Monthly Vital Statistics*, Vol. 41, No. 3, 1993, Table 2

Table 2.5

Divorce Rate

Divorces per 1,000 population, 1992

Alabama (7)	6.5	Kentucky (8)	6.4	North Dakota (41)	3.6
Alaska (9)	6.3	Louisiana	no data	Ohio (26)	4.9
Arizona (6)	6.7	Maine (29)	4.8	Oklahoma (3)	7.3
Arkansas (2)	7.7	Maryland (41)	3.6	Oregon (19)	5.3
California (33)	4.3*	Massachusetts (49)	2.8	Pennsylvania (45)	3.3
Colorado (15)	5.6	Michigan (35)	4.2	Rhode Island (41)	3.6
Connecticut (47)	3.1	Minnesota (41)	3.6	South Carolina (32)	4.4
Delaware (26)	4.9	Mississippi (15)	5.6	South Dakota (36)	4.1
D.C. (31)	4.5	Missouri (26)	4.9	Tennessee (5)	6.8
Florida (11)	6.2	Montana (22)	5.2	Texas (15)	5.6
Georgia (13)	5.9	Nebraska (36)	4.1	Utah (19)	5.3
Hawaii (33)	4.3	Nevada (1)	11.1*	Vermont (22)	5.2
Idaho (9)	6.3	New Hampshire (25)	5.0	Virginia (30)	4.7
Illinois (39)	3.7	New Jersey (45)	3.3	Washington (14)	5.7
Indiana	no data	New Mexico (11)	6.2	West Virginia (18)	5.4
Iowa (38)	3.9	New York (47)	3.1	Wisconsin (39)	3.7
Kansas (22)	5.2	North Carolina (19)	5.3	Wyoming (4)	6.9

Source: National Center for Health Statistics, *Monthly Vital Statistics*, Vol. 41, No. 13, 1993, Table 2
*1990 data

Table 2.6

Sex Ratio

Males per 100 females, 1992

Alabama (49)	92.19	Kentucky (34)	94.06	North Dakota (7)	99.37
Alaska (1)	111.91	Louisiana (43)	92.93	Ohio (40)	93.21
Arizona (12)	97.63	Maine (25)	95.10	Oklahoma (24)	95.14
Arkansas (41)	93.16	Maryland (30)	94.45	Oregon (15)	97.02
California (5)	100.29	Massachusetts (45)	92.65	Pennsylvania (48)	92.28
Colorado (11)	98.34	Michigan (28)	94.58	Rhode Island (46)	92.53
Connecticut (35)	94.03	Minnesota (18)	96.54	South Carolina (36)	94.02
Delaware (27)	94.63	Mississippi (50)	91.64	South Dakota (16)	96.95
D.C. (51)	87.86	Missouri (39)	93.26	Tennessee (42)	93.01
Florida (37)	93.96	Montana (10)	98.55	Texas (13)	97.15
Georgia (29)	94.50	Nebraska (23)	95.38	Utah (8)	98.90
Hawaii (3)	103.15	Nevada (2)	103.84	Vermont (20)	96.21
Idaho (6)	99.44	New Hampshire (22)	95.94	Virginia (19)	96.25
Illinois (26)	94.69	New Jersey (38)	93.61	Washington (9)	98.68
Indiana (32)	94.34	New Mexico (14)	97.13	West Virginia (44)	92.77
Iowa (33)	94.33	New York (47)	92.40	Wisconsin (21)	96.12
Kansas (17)	96.57	North Carolina (31)	94.35	Wyoming (4)	100.86

Source: Calculated from 1990 Census data

Table 3.1

Population Change

Percent change 1980–93

State	%	State	%	State	%
Alabama (25)	7.5	Kentucky (39)	3.5	North Dakota (48)	-2.8
Alaska (3)	49.0	Louisiana (45)	2.1	Ohio (41)	2.7
Arizona (4)	44.9	Maine (24)	10.1	Oklahoma (29)	6.8
Arkansas (32)	6.0	Maryland (17)	17.7	Oregon (20)	15.2
California (7)	31.9	Massachusetts (35)	4.8	Pennsylvania (46)	1.6
Colorado (11)	23.4	Michigan (44)	2.3	Rhode Island (33)	5.6
Connecticut (34)	5.4	Minnesota (23)	10.8	South Carolina (18)	16.7
Delaware (16)	17.8	Mississippi (35)	4.8	South Dakota (39)	3.5
D.C. (51)	-9.4	Missouri (31)	6.4	Tennessee (22)	11.1
Florida (5)	40.4	Montana (30)	6.6	Texas (9)	26.7
Georgia (10)	26.6	Nebraska (42)	2.4	Utah (8)	27.3
Hawaii (13)	21.5	Nevada (1)	73.6	Vermont (21)	12.7
Idaho (19)	16.4	New Hampshire (12)	22.1	Virginia (14)	21.4
Illinois (42)	2.4	New Jersey (28)	7.0	Washington (2)	51.4
Indiana (37)	4.1	New Mexico (6)	39.5	West Virginia (50)	-6.7
Iowa (49)	-3.4	New York (38)	3.6	Wisconsin (26)	7.1
Kansas (26)	7.1	North Carolina (15)	18.1	Wyoming (47)	0.0

Source: U.S. Bureau of the Census, No. 28

Table 3.2

Where Were Residents Born?

Residents of Alabama born in Georgia	127,076
Residents of Alaska born in California	38,334
Residents of Arizona born in California	226,117
Residents of Arkansas born in Texas	100,761
Residents of California born in New York	763,900
Residents of Colorado born in California	131,525
Residents of Connecticut born in New York	308,943
Residents of Delaware born in Pennsylvania	91,154
Residents of District of Columbia born in Virginia	37,435
Residents of Florida born in New York	1,270,667
Residents of Georgia born in Alabama	220,771
Residents of Hawaii born in California	61,277
Residents of Idaho born in California	72,904
Residents of Illinois born in Michigan	129,005
Residents of Indiana born in Kentucky	265,189
Residents of Iowa born in Illinois	92,836
Residents of Kansas born in Missouri	232,720
Residents of Kentucky born in Ohio	156,481
Residents of Louisiana born in Texas	137,685

Table 3.2 (cont.)

Residents of Maine born in Massachusetts	87,080
Residents of Maryland born in Pennsylvania	260,531
Residents of Massachusetts born in New York	256,125
Residents of Michigan born in Ohio	224,458
Residents of Minnesota born in Wisconsin	165,633
Residents of Mississippi born in Tennessee	88,451
Residents of Missouri born in Illinois	214,758
Residents of Montana born in North Dakota	39,035
Residents of Nebraska born in Iowa	89,050
Residents of Nevada born in California	184,184
Residents of New Hampshire born in Massachusetts	268,133
Residents of New Jersey born in New York	902,851
Residents of New Mexico born in Texas	136,140
Residents of New York born in Pennsylvania	354,636
Residents of North Carolina born in Virginia	202,121
Residents of North Dakota born in Minnesota	56,606
Residents of Ohio born in Pennsylvania	337,730
Residents of Oklahoma born in Texas	206,499
Residents of Oregon born in California	312,069
Residents of Pennsylvania born in New York	352,691
Residents of Rhode Island born in Massachusetts	92,794
Residents of South Carolina born in North Carolina	173,471
Residents of South Dakota born in Minnesota	36,869
Residents of Tennessee born in Mississippi	136,095
Residents of Texas born in Louisiana	396,818
Residents of Utah born in California	95,443
Residents of Vermont born in New York	47,826
Residents of Virginia born in North Carolina	240,237
Residents of Washington born in California	343,857
Residents of West Virginia born in Ohio	81,636
Residents of Wisconsin born in Illinois	252,582
Residents of Wyoming born in Colorado	24,064

Source: Kristin A. Hansen, *Selected Place of Birth and Migration Statistics for States*, U.S. Bureau of Census, 1990

Table 3.3

Where Did Former Residents Go?
Number of out-migrants between states, 1985 to 1990

Moved from Alabama to Florida	253,606
Moved from Alaska to Washington	28,994
Moved from Arizona to California	217,947
Moved from Arkansas to California	214,700
Moved from California to Washington	343,857
Moved from Colorado to California	231,257

Moved from Connecticut to Florida	143,516
Moved from Delaware to Maryland	33,602
Moved from District of Columbia to Maryland	455,991
Moved from Florida to Georgia	203,155
Moved from Georgia to Florida	435,529
Moved from Hawaii to California	132,151
Moved from Idaho to Washington	100,258
Moved from Illinois to California	647,875
Moved from Indiana to Florida	232,619
Moved from Iowa to California	237,559
Moved from Kansas to California	199,272
Moved from Kentucky to Ohio	327,636
Moved from Louisiana to Texas	396,818
Moved from Maine to Massachusetts	55,211
Moved from Maryland to Virginia	127,440
Moved from Massachusetts to Florida	279,902
Moved from Michigan to California	369,447
Moved from Minnesota to California	244,538
Moved from Mississippi to Illinois	226,140
Moved from Missouri to California	297,844
Moved from Montana to Washington	94,364
Moved from Nebraska to California	169,466
Moved from Nevada to California	64,460
Moved from New Hampshire to Massachusetts	50,946
Moved from New Jersey to Florida	374,887
Moved from New Mexico to California	129,719
Moved from New York to Florida	1,270,667
Moved from North Carolina to Virginia	240,237
Moved from North Dakota to Minnesota	118,145
Moved from Ohio to Florida	519,668
Moved from Oklahoma to Texas	378,207
Moved from Oregon to Washington	207,994
Moved from Pennsylvania to New Jersey	601,139
Moved from Rhode Island to Massachusetts	85,613
Moved from South Carolina to North Carolina	187,806
Moved from South Dakota to California	86,256
Moved from Tennessee to Georgia	155,756
Moved from Texas to California	702,191
Moved from Utah to California	145,072
Moved from Vermont to New York	32,767
Moved from Virginia to North Carolina	202,121
Moved from Washington to California	274,765
Moved from West Virginia to Ohio	324,988
Moved from Wisconsin to California	190,855
Moved from Wyoming to California	42,350

Source: Kristin A. Hansen, *Selected Place of Birth and Migration Statistics for States*, U.S. Bureau of Census, 1990

Table 3.4
Population Stability
Percent of population age five and older who lived in the same house in 1990 as in 1985

Alabama (12)	57.3	Kentucky (16)	56.7	North Dakota (12)	57.3
Alaska (50)	40.6	Louisiana (5)	59.3	Ohio (9)	57.6
Arizona (49)	43.1	Maine (19)	55.6	Oklahoma (32)	52.1
Arkansas (24)	54.3	Maryland (31)	52.4	Oregon (44)	46.1
California (48)	44.4	Massachusetts (7)	58.4	Pennsylvania (2)	63.4
Colorado (46)	45.2	Michigan (15)	56.9	Rhode Island (10)	57.4
Connecticut (10)	57.4	Minnesota (22)	55.5	South Carolina (19)	55.6
Delaware (28)	53.8	Mississippi (6)	59.2	South Dakota (22)	55.5
D.C. (29)	53.5	Missouri (24)	54.3	Tennessee (27)	54.0
Florida (47)	44.9	Montana (33)	52.0	Texas (42)	49.2
Georgia (41)	49.4	Nebraska (17)	55.9	Utah (30)	52.7
Hawaii (37)	50.9	Nevada (51)	34.7	Vermont (34)	51.9
Idaho (39)	50.5	New Hampshire (38)	50.7	Virginia (43)	49.1
Illinois (18)	55.7	New Jersey (4)	60.1	Washington (45)	45.9
Indiana (19)	55.6	New Mexico (35)	51.8	West Virginia (1)	64.2
Iowa (8)	58.2	New York (3)	62.0	Wisconsin (12)	57.3
Kansas (36)	51.7	North Carolina (24)	54.3	Wyoming (40)	49.5

Source: U.S. Bureau of the Census, Table 4, 1990 CPH-L-121

Table 3.5
Foreign-Born
Percent of total population, 1990

Alabama (46)	1.1	Kentucky (49)	0.9	North Dakota (43)	1.5
Alaska (19)	4.5	Louisiana (34)	2.1	Ohio (33)	2.4
Arizona (13)	7.6	Maine (27)	3.0	Oklahoma (34)	2.1
Arkansas (46)	1.1	Maryland (14)	6.6	Oregon (18)	4.9
California (1)	21.7	Massachusetts (7)	9.5	Pennsylvania (25)	3.1
Colorado (20)	4.3	Michigan (21)	3.8	Rhode Island (7)	9.5
Connecticut (11)	8.5	Minnesota (30)	2.6	South Carolina (44)	1.4
Delaware (24)	3.3	Mississippi (51)	0.8	South Dakota (46)	1.1
D.C. (6)	9.7	Missouri (41)	1.6	Tennessee (45)	1.2
Florida (4)	12.9	Montana (37)	1.7	Texas (9)	9.0
Georgia (29)	2.7	Nebraska (36)	1.8	Utah (23)	3.4
Hawaii (3)	14.7	Nevada (10)	8.7	Vermont (25)	3.1
Idaho (28)	2.9	New Hampshire (22)	3.7	Virginia (17)	5.0
Illinois (12)	8.3	New Jersey (5)	12.5	Washington (14)	6.6
Indiana (37)	1.7	New Mexico (16)	5.3	West Virginia (49)	0.9
Iowa (41)	1.6	New York (2)	15.9	Wisconsin (31)	2.5
Kansas (31)	2.5	North Carolina (37)	1.7	Wyoming (37)	1.7

Source: *1993 County and City Extra, Annual Metro, City and County Data Book*, Lanham, MD: Bernan Press, 1993

244

Table 3.6

Naturalized Citizens
Number of persons naturalized, 1992

State	Number	State	Number	State	Number
Alabama (35)	598	Kentucky (36)	567	North Dakota (49)	119
Alaska (30)	793	Louisiana (21)	1,709	Ohio (15)	2,669
Arizona (14)	3,037	Maine (39)	400	Oklahoma (29)	876
Arkansas (40)	380	Maryland (10)	4,620	Oregon (19)	1,994
California (1)	52,411	Massachusetts (7)	7,381	Pennsylvania (13)	3,839
Colorado (24)	1,402	Michigan (16)	2,616	Rhode Island (26)	1,043
Connecticut (8)	5,070	Minnesota (20)	1,850	South Carolina (33)	670
Delaware (44)	289	Mississippi (43)	315	South Dakota (50)	62
D.C. (31)	786	Missouri (23)	1,453	Tennessee (27)	979
Florida (3)	21,129	Montana (48)	127	Texas (4)	17,631
Georgia (17)	2,299	Nebraska (38)	432	Utah (34)	649
Hawaii (11)	4,475	Nevada (22)	1,533	Vermont (45)	219
Idaho (46)	208	New Hampshire (42)	357	Virginia (9)	4,662
Illinois (6)	10,891	New Jersey (5)	16,598	Washington (12)	4,307
Indiana (25)	1,323	New Mexico (37)	495	West Virginia (47)	137
Iowa (41)	374	New York (2)	43,447	Wisconsin (32)	681
Kansas (28)	911	North Carolina (18)	2,172	Wyoming (51)	50

Source: INS, Statistics Division, Demography Statistics Branch, Table 50

Table 4.1

Household Income
Three-year average of median income, 1990–92

Alabama (45)	$25,348	Kentucky (47)	$24,882	North Dakota (40)	$26,965
Alaska (2)	41,996	Louisiana (46)	25,197	Ohio (23)	31,461
Arizona (25)	30,875	Maine (30)	29,298	Oklahoma (43)	25,922
Arkansas (49)	24,164	Maryland (6)	39,021	Oregon (22)	31,548
California (9)	35,195	Massachusetts (8)	37,419	Pennsylvania (26)	30,800
Colorado (15)	32,718	Michigan (17)	32,522	Rhode Island (18)	32,239
Connecticut (1)	42,069	Minnesota (21)	31,740	South Carolina (33)	28,934
Delaware (11)	34,124	Mississippi (51)	20,769	South Dakota (42)	26,036
D.C. (28)	30,182	Missouri (35)	28,532	Tennessee (48)	24,593
Florida (37)	28,058	Montana (44)	25,756	Texas (32)	29,050
Georgia (34)	28,835	Nebraska (29)	30,039	Utah (20)	31,883
Hawaii (3)	40,773	Nevada (12)	33,443	Vermont (19)	32,081
Idaho (39)	27,283	New Hampshire (5)	40,188	Virginia (7)	37,699
Illinois (13)	33,161	New Jersey (4)	40,687	Washington (10)	34,509
Indiana (36)	28,491	New Mexico (41)	26,792	West Virginia (50)	22,636
Iowa (31)	29,195	New York (16)	32,639	Wisconsin (14)	32,817
Kansas (24)	30,913	North Carolina (38)	27,920	Wyoming (27)	30,642

Source: U.S. Bureau of the Census, *Money Income of Households, Families, and Persons in the United States: 1992*, Table C

Table 4.2

Unemployment
Average annual unemployment rate, percent, 1993

Alabama (8)	7.5	Kentucky (26)	6.2	North Dakota (46)	4.3
Alaska (7)	7.6	Louisiana (12)	7.4	Ohio (23)	6.5
Arizona (26)	6.2	Maine (4)	7.9	Oklahoma (32)	6.0
Arkansas (26)	6.2	Maryland (26)	6.2	Oregon (15)	7.2
California (2)	9.2	Massachusetts (21)	6.9	Pennsylvania (17)	7.0
Colorado (40)	5.2	Michigan (17)	7.0	Rhode Island (5)	7.7
Connecticut (26)	6.2	Minnesota (41)	5.1	South Carolina (8)	7.5
Delaware (38)	5.3	Mississippi (25)	6.3	South Dakota (50)	3.5
D.C. (3)	8.5	Missouri (24)	6.4	Tennessee (35)	5.7
Florida (17)	7.0	Montana (32)	6.0	Texas (17)	7.0
Georgia (34)	5.8	Nebraska (51)	2.6	Utah (49)	3.9
Hawaii (47)	4.2	Nevada (15)	7.2	Vermont (36)	5.4
Idaho (31)	6.1	New Hampshire (22)	6.6	Virginia (42)	5.0
Illinois (12)	7.4	New Jersey (12)	7.4	Washington (8)	7.5
Indiana (38)	5.3	New Mexico (8)	7.5	West Virginia (1)	10.8
Iowa (48)	4.0	New York (5)	7.7	Wisconsin (45)	4.7
Kansas (42)	5.0	North Carolina (44)	4.9	Wyoming (36)	5.4

Source: Department of Labor, Bureau of Labor Statistics, 1993

Table 4.3

Federal Funds Per Capita

Net flow of federal funds, 1989–91

Alabama (7)	$1,261	Kentucky (16)	$ 822	North Dakota (3)	$1,715
Alaska (12)	1,069	Louisiana (20)	744	Ohio (37)	-155
Arizona (18)	766	Maine (22)	600	Oklahoma (21)	697
Arkansas (17)	798	Maryland (14)	1,033	Oregon (35)	-137
California (40)	-411	Massachusetts (31)	26	Pennsylvania (34)	-129
Colorado (19)	751	Michigan (44)	-855	Rhode Island (29)	60
Connecticut (48)	-1,374	Minnesota (41)	-449	South Carolina (15)	1,000
Delaware (49)	-1,475	Mississippi (4)	1,602	South Dakota (6)	1,296
D.C.	no data	Missouri (8)	1,232	Tennessee (23)	541
Florida (30)	43	Montana (5)	1,349	Texas (32)	-29
Georgia (33)	-99	Nebraska (25)	407	Utah (9)	1,122
Hawaii (13)	1,043	Nevada (43)	-579	Vermont (39)	-395
Idaho (10)	1,086	New Hampshire (47)	-1,345	Virginia (2)	1,741
Illinois (46)	-1,219	New Jersey (50)	-2,107	Washington (27)	208
Indiana (38)	-341	New Mexico (1)	2,942	West Virginia (11)	1,081
Iowa (26)	219	New York (45)	-888	Wisconsin (42)	-500
Kansas (28)	202	North Carolina (36)	-148	Wyoming (24)	515

Source: Advisory Commission on Intergovernmental Relations, Table 31

Table 4.4

Poverty

Three-year average percentage of persons below the poverty line, 1990–92

Alabama (7)	18.4	Kentucky (6)	18.6	North Dakota (27)	13.4
Alaska (36)	11.1	Louisiana (2)	22.3	Ohio (29)	12.4
Arizona (20)	14.5	Maine (25)	13.5	Oklahoma (11)	17.0
Arkansas (8)	18.1	Maryland (40)	10.2	Oregon (32)	11.3
California (14)	15.1	Massachusetts (37)	10.6	Pennsylvania (34)	11.2
Colorado (31)	11.6	Michigan (23)	14.0	Rhode Island (43)	10.0
Connecticut (49)	8.0	Minnesota (28)	12.6	South Carolina (9)	17.2
Delaware (51)	7.3	Mississippi (1)	24.6	South Dakota (23)	14.0
D.C. (4)	20.0	Missouri (18)	14.6	Tennessee (13)	16.5
Florida (16)	15.0	Montana (14)	15.1	Texas (10)	17.1
Georgia (12)	16.9	Nebraska (43)	10.0	Utah (41)	10.1
Hawaii (46)	9.9	Nevada (30)	11.9	Vermont (32)	11.3
Idaho (18)	14.6	New Hampshire (50)	7.4	Virginia (41)	10.1
Illinois (22)	14.2	New Jersey (48)	9.6	Washington (47)	9.8
Indiana (25)	13.5	New Mexico (3)	21.4	West Virginia (5)	19.4
Iowa (38)	10.4	New York (16)	15.0	Wisconsin (43)	10.0
Kansas (34)	11.2	North Carolina (21)	14.4	Wyoming (38)	10.4

Source: U.S. Bureau of the Census, *Poverty in the U.S.*, 1992, Table C

Table 4.5
Change in Poverty Rate
Percent change, 1982–92

Alabama (47)	-4.5	Kentucky (2)	3.5	North Dakota (25)	-1.0
Alaska (21)	-0.6	Louisiana (8)	1.5	Ohio (19)	-0.4
Arizona (15)	0.3	Maine (17)	-0.3	Oklahoma (3)	3.0
Arkansas (50)	-6.4	Maryland (23)	-0.7	Oregon (41)	-2.6
California (5)	1.7	Massachusetts (17)	-0.3	Pennsylvania (30)	-1.8
Colorado (33)	-2.0	Michigan (42)	-2.7	Rhode Island (26)	-1.3
Connecticut (9)	1.3	Minnesota (20)	-0.5	South Carolina (38)	-2.3
Delaware (46)	-3.9	Mississippi (6)	1.6	South Dakota (33)	-2.0
D.C. (11)	1.0	Missouri (11)	1.0	Tennessee (51)	-6.6
Florida (16)	0.1	Montana (44)	-3.3	Texas (6)	1.6
Georgia (30)	-1.8	Nebraska (44)	-3.3	Utah (49)	-5.2
Hawaii (36)	-2.2	Nevada (1)	6.6	Vermont (39)	-2.5
Idaho (21)	-0.6	New Hampshire (28)	-1.7	Virginia (43)	-3.1
Illinois (4)	1.9	New Jersey (36)	-2.2	Washington (32)	-1.9
Indiana (24)	-0.9	New Mexico (27)	-1.4	West Virginia (39)	-2.5
Iowa (35)	-2.1	New York (14)	0.5	Wisconsin (9)	1.3
Kansas (13)	0.6	North Carolina (48)	-4.6	Wyoming (28)	-1.7

Source: U.S. Bureau of the Census, *Poverty in the U.S.*, 1992, Table D-1

Table 4.6
Welfare Benefits
AFDC and food stamp benefits as percent of poverty line, 1993

Alabama (50)	47.2	Kentucky (44)	54.8	North Dakota (18)	68.4
Alaska (2)	92.7	Louisiana (47)	50.5	Ohio (29)	64.2
Arizona (31)	63.6	Maine (15)	72.5	Oklahoma (35)	62.7
Arkansas (45)	51.6	Maryland (24)	66.7	Oregon (12)	75.2
California (5)	82.7	Massachusetts (9)	75.9	Pennsylvania (17)	69.2
Colorado (27)	64.4	Michigan (13)	73.0	Rhode Island (7)	79.8
Connecticut (3)	85.5	Minnesota (10)	75.5	South Carolina (46)	51.0
Delaware (33)	63.0	Mississippi (51)	43.0	South Dakota (25)	66.3
D.C. (18)	68.4	Missouri (40)	59.2	Tennessee (48)	49.9
Florida (38)	60.4	Montana (22)	67.4	Texas (49)	49.4
Georgia (41)	58.5	Nebraska (26)	64.6	Utah (22)	67.4
Hawaii (1)	98.1	Nevada (33)	63.0	Vermont (6)	82.5
Idaho (37)	61.5	New Hampshire (14)	72.8	Virginia (32)	63.2
Illinois (30)	63.8	New Jersey (18)	68.4	Washington (8)	79.3
Indiana (39)	59.4	New Mexico (28)	64.3	West Virginia (42)	57.1
Iowa (21)	68.1	New York (4)	85.1	Wisconsin (11)	75.3
Kansas (16)	70.1	North Carolina (43)	55.8	Wyoming (36)	62.0

Source: Annie E. Casey Foundation, *Kids Count Data Book*, 1994

248

Table 4.7

Life Insurance

Insurance in force, per capita, 1991

Alabama (18)	$ 40,832	Kentucky (48)	$31,054	North Dakota (17)	$40,860
Alaska (22)	39,925	Louisiana (37)	35,868	Ohio (21)	40,095
Arizona (44)	31,857	Maine (42)	32,740	Oklahoma (46)	31,652
Arkansas (50)	28,392	Maryland (9)	44,169	Oregon (43)	32,121
California (34)	36,486	Massachusetts (12)	42,939	Pennsylvania (15)	41,135
Colorado (8)	44,244	Michigan (27)	38,553	Rhode Island (24)	39,721
Connecticut (2)	62,925	Minnesota (20)	40,184	South Carolina (33)	36,796
Delaware (3)	60,803	Mississippi (47)	31,472	South Dakota (32)	36,906
D.C. (1)	115,656	Missouri (19)	40,459	Tennessee (26)	38,695
Florida (40)	33,699	Montana (41)	33,043	Texas (30)	37,332
Georgia (10)	43,922	Nebraska (13)	42,614	Utah (36)	35,872
Hawaii (5)	47,648	Nevada (49)	29,748	Vermont (28)	38,312
Idaho (38)	34,712	New Hampshire (23)	39,913	Virginia (6)	45,290
Illinois (7)	44,984	New Jersey (4)	51,237	Washington (39)	34,543
Indiana (25)	39,051	New Mexico (45)	31,791	West Virginia (51)	27,629
Iowa (16)	40,972	New York (11)	43,505	Wisconsin (35)	35,943
Kansas (14)	41,508	North Carolina (29)	37,855	Wyoming (31)	37,152

Source: American Council of Life Insurance, *1992 Life Insurance Fact Book*

Table 5.1

Racial-Ethnic Diversity

USA TODAY diversity index, 1990

Alabama (17)	40	Kentucky (41)	15	North Dakota (46)	11
Alaska (12)	43	Louisiana (8)	47	Ohio (29)	23
Arizona (9)	45	Maine (50)	4	Oklahoma (22)	33
Arkansas (24)	30	Maryland (9)	45	Oregon (36)	17
California (2)	59	Massachusetts (31)	22	Pennsylvania (31)	22
Colorado (22)	33	Michigan (24)	30	Rhode Island (34)	20
Connecticut (26)	29	Minnesota (45)	12	South Carolina (11)	44
Delaware (21)	34	Mississippi (7)	48	South Dakota (39)	16
D.C. (5)	51	Missouri (29)	23	Tennessee (26)	29
Florida (14)	42	Montana (41)	15	Texas (4)	55
Georgia (12)	43	Nebraska (44)	14	Utah (36)	17
Hawaii (3)	56	Nevada (20)	36	Vermont (50)	4
Idaho (41)	15	New Hampshire (49)	5	Virginia (19)	38
Illinois (16)	41	New Jersey (14)	42	Washington (28)	24
Indiana (35)	19	New Mexico (1)	60	West Virginia (47)	8
Iowa (47)	8	New York (6)	49	Wisconsin (39)	16
Kansas (33)	21	North Carolina (18)	39	Wyoming (36)	17

Source: Data copyright 1991, *USA TODAY*, April 11, 1991, p. A10. Reprinted with permission

Table 5.2
African American Population
Percent and number (in thousands), 1990

	PERCENT		NUMBER			PERCENT		NUMBER	
Alabama	25.3	(6)	1,021	(16)	New Jersey	13.4	(17)	1,037	(15)
Alaska	4.1	(31)	22	(42)	New Mexico	2.0	(40)	30	(40)
Arizona	3.0	(37)	111	(32)	New York	15.9	(12)	2,859	(1)
Arkansas	15.9	(12)	374	(22)	North Carolina	22.0	(8)	1,456	(7)
California	7.4	(24)	2,209	(2)	North Dakota	0.6	(45)	4	(46)
Colorado	4.0	(32)	133	(30)	Ohio	10.6	(20)	1,155	(12)
Connecticut	8.3	(22)	274	(24)	Oklahoma	7.4	(24)	234	(27)
Delaware	16.9	(10)	112	(31)	Oregon	1.6	(42)	46	(38)
D.C.	65.8	(1)	400	(21)	Pennsylvania	9.2	(21)	1,090	(13)
Florida	13.6	(16)	1,760	(4)	Rhode Island	3.9	(33)	39	(39)
Georgia	27.0	(5)	1,747	(5)	South Carolina	29.8	(4)	1,040	(14)
Hawaii	2.5	(38)	27	(41)	South Dakota	0.5	(47)	3	(48)
Idaho	0.3	(49)	3	(48)	Tennessee	16.0	(11)	778	(18)
Illinois	14.8	(14)	1,694	(6)	Texas	11.9	(18)	2,022	(3)
Indiana	7.8	(23)	432	(20)	Utah	0.7	(44)	12	(43)
Iowa	1.7	(41)	48	(37)	Vermont	0.3	(49)	2	(50)
Kansas	5.8	(28)	143	(29)	Virginia	18.8	(9)	1,163	(11)
Kentucky	7.1	(26)	263	(25)	Washington	3.1	(35)	150	(28)
Louisiana	30.8	(3)	1,299	(8)	West Virginia	3.1	(35)	56	(36)
Maine	0.4	(48)	5	(45)	Wisconsin	5.0	(29)	245	(26)
Maryland	24.9	(7)	1,190	(10)	Wyoming	0.8	(43)	4	(46)
Massachusetts	5.0	(29)	300	(23)					
Michigan	13.9	(15)	1,292	(9)					
Minnesota	2.2	(39)	95	(33)					
Mississippi	35.6	(2)	915	(17)					
Missouri	10.7	(19)	548	(19)					
Montana	0.3	(49)	2	(50)					
Nebraska	3.6	(34)	57	(35)					
Nevada	6.6	(27)	79	(34)					
New Hampshire	0.6	(45)	7	(44)					

Source: U.S. Bureau of the Census, *1990 Census Profile: Race and Hispanic Origin,* No. 2, June 1991

Table 5.3

Hispanic Population
Percent and number (in thousands), 1990

	PERCENT		NUMBER			PERCENT		NUMBER	
Alabama	0.6	(47)	25	(39)	New Jersey	9.6	(9)	740	(6)
Alaska	3.2	(22)	18	(42)	New Mexico	38.2	(1)	579	(8)
Arizona	18.8	(4)	688	(7)	New York	12.3	(6)	2,214	(3)
Arkansas	0.8	(42)	20	(41)	North Carolina	1.2	(37)	77	(28)
California	25.8	(2)	7,688	(1)	North Dakota	0.7	(44)	5	(49)
Colorado	12.9	(5)	424	(9)	Ohio	1.3	(35)	140	(16)
Connecticut	6.5	(12)	213	(13)	Oklahoma	2.7	(23)	86	(25)
Delaware	2.4	(26)	16	(43)	Oregon	4.0	(20)	113	(19)
D.C.	5.4	(14)	33	(34)	Pennsylvania	2.0	(30)	232	(11)
Florida	12.2	(7)	1,574	(4)	Rhode Island	4.6	(18)	46	(32)
Georgia	1.7	(33)	109	(20)	South Carolina	0.9	(41)	31	(37)
Hawaii	7.3	(11)	81	(27)	South Dakota	0.8	(42)	5	(49)
Idaho	5.3	(15)	53	(31)	Tennessee	0.7	(44)	33	(34)
Illinois	7.9	(10)	904	(5)	Texas	25.5	(3)	4,340	(2)
Indiana	1.8	(32)	99	(21)	Utah	4.9	(16)	85	(26)
Iowa	1.2	(37)	33	(34)	Vermont	0.7	(44)	4	(51)
Kansas	3.8	(21)	94	(22)	Virginia	2.6	(24)	160	(15)
Kentucky	0.6	(47)	22	(40)	Washington	4.4	(19)	215	(12)
Louisiana	2.2	(28)	93	(23)	West Virginia	0.5	(51)	8	(47)
Maine	0.6	(47)	7	(48)	Wisconsin	1.9	(31)	93	(23)
Maryland	2.6	(24)	125	(17)	Wyoming	5.7	(13)	26	(38)
Massachusetts	4.8	(17)	288	(10)					
Michigan	2.2	(28)	202	(14)					
Minnesota	1.2	(37)	54	(30)					
Mississippi	0.6	(47)	16	(43)					
Missouri	1.2	(36)	62	(29)					
Montana	1.5	(34)	12	(45)					
Nebraska	2.3	(27)	37	(33)					
Nevada	10.4	(8)	124	(18)					
New Hampshire	1.0	(40)	11	(46)					

Source: U.S. Bureau of the Census, *1990 Census Profile: Race and Hispanic Origin*, No. 2, June 1991

Table 5.4
Asian and Pacific Islander Population
Percent and number (in thousands), 1990

	PERCENT	NUMBER		PERCENT	NUMBER
Alabama	0.5 (43)	22 (32)	New Jersey	3.5 (6)	273 (6)
Alaska	3.6 (5)	20 (34)	New Mexico	0.9 (30)	14 (37)
Arizona	1.5 (19)	55 (19)	New York	3.9 (4)	694 (2)
Arkansas	0.5 (43)	13 (38)	North Carolina	0.8 (34)	52 (21)
California	9.6 (2)	2,846 (1)	North Dakota	0.5 (43)	3 (48)
Colorado	1.8 (15)	60 (18)	Ohio	0.8 (33)	91 (14)
Connecticut	1.5 (19)	51 (22)	Oklahoma	1.1 (26)	34 (27)
Delaware	1.4 (21)	9 (42)	Oregon	2.4 (11)	69 (17)
D.C.	1.8 (15)	11 (41)	Pennsylvania	1.2 (23)	137 (12)
Florida	1.2 (23)	154 (9)	Rhode Island	1.8 (15)	18 (35)
Georgia	1.2 (23)	76 (16)	South Carolina	0.6 (40)	22 (32)
Hawaii	61.8 (1)	685 (3)	South Dakota	0.4 (50)	3 (48)
Idaho	0.9 (30)	9 (42)	Tennessee	0.7 (38)	32 (29)
Illinois	2.5 (10)	285 (5)	Texas	1.9 (13)	319 (4)
Indiana	0.7 (38)	38 (25)	Utah	1.9 (13)	33 (28)
Iowa	0.9 (30)	25 (31)	Vermont	0.6 (40)	3 (48)
Kansas	1.3 (22)	32 (29)	Virginia	2.6 (9)	159 (8)
Kentucky	0.5 (43)	18 (35)	Washington	4.3 (3)	211 (7)
Louisiana	1.0 (29)	41 (23)	West Virginia	0.4 (50)	7 (45)
Maine	0.5 (43)	7 (45)	Wisconsin	1.1 (26)	54 (20)
Maryland	2.9 (8)	140 (11)	Wyoming	0.6 (40)	3 (48)
Massachusetts	2.4 (11)	143 (10)			
Michigan	1.1 (26)	105 (13)			
Minnesota	1.8 (15)	78 (15)			
Mississippi	0.5 (43)	13 (38)			
Missouri	0.8 (34)	41 (23)			
Montana	0.5 (43)	4 (47)			
Nebraska	0.8 (34)	12 (40)			
Nevada	3.2 (7)	38 (25)			
New Hampshire	0.8 (34)	9 (42)			

Source: U.S. Bureau of the Census, *1990 Census Profile: Race and Hispanic Origin*, No. 2, June 1991

Table 5.5

Native American Population
Percent and number (in thousands), 1990

	PERCENT		NUMBER			PERCENT		NUMBER	
Alabama	0.4	(25)	17	(26)	New Jersey	0.2	(37)	15	(27)
Alaska	15.6	(1)	86	(5)	New Mexico	8.9	(2)	134	(4)
Arizona	5.6	(6)	204	(3)	New York	0.3	(30)	63	(9)
Arkansas	0.5	(22)	13	(31)	North Carolina	1.2	(14)	80	(7)
California	0.8	(17)	242	(2)	North Dakota	4.1	(7)	26	(18)
Colorado	0.8	(17)	28	(17)	Ohio	0.2	(37)	20	(22)
Connecticut	0.2	(37)	7	(41)	Oklahoma	8.0	(3)	252	(1)
Delaware	0.3	(30)	2	(47)	Oregon	1.4	(11)	38	(15)
D.C.	0.2	(37)	1	(51)	Pennsylvania	0.1	(50)	15	(27)
Florida	0.3	(30)	36	(16)	Rhode Island	0.4	(25)	4	(46)
Georgia	0.2	(37)	13	(31)	South Carolina	0.2	(37)	8	(40)
Hawaii	0.5	(22)	5	(45)	South Dakota	7.3	(4)	51	(11)
Idaho	1.4	(11)	14	(30)	Tennessee	0.2	(37)	10	(37)
Illinois	0.2	(37)	22	(20)	Texas	0.4	(25)	66	(8)
Indiana	0.2	(37)	13	(31)	Utah	1.4	(11)	24	(19)
Iowa	0.3	(30)	7	(41)	Vermont	0.3	(30)	2	(47)
Kansas	0.9	(16)	22	(20)	Virginia	0.2	(37)	15	(27)
Kentucky	0.2	(37)	6	(43)	Washington	1.7	(9)	81	(6)
Louisiana	0.4	(25)	19	(25)	West Virginia	0.1	(50)	2	(47)
Maine	0.5	(22)	6	(43)	Wisconsin	0.8	(17)	39	(14)
Maryland	0.3	(30)	13	(31)	Wyoming	2.1	(8)	9	(38)
Massachusetts	0.2	(37)	12	(35)					
Michigan	0.6	(21)	56	(10)					
Minnesota	1.1	(15)	50	(12)					
Mississippi	0.3	(30)	9	(38)					
Missouri	0.4	(25)	20	(22)					
Montana	6.0	(5)	48	(13)					
Nebraska	0.8	(17)	12	(35)					
Nevada	1.6	(10)	20	(22)					
New Hampshire	0.2	(37)	2	(47)					

Source: U.S. Bureau of the Census, *1990 Census Profile: Race and Hispanic Origin*, No. 2, June 1991

Table 6.1

Overall Health
Northwestern National Life rankings, 1993

State	Value	State	Value	State	Value
Alabama (43)	-13	Kentucky (38)	-8	North Dakota (18)	5
Alaska (43)	-13	Louisiana (49)	-18	Ohio (16)	6
Arizona (26)	-1	Maine (14)	9	Oklahoma (29)	-2
Arkansas (43)	-13	Maryland (16)	6	Oregon (26)	-1
California (24)	1	Massachusetts (8)	14	Pennsylvania (18)	5
Colorado (9)	13	Michigan (25)	0	Rhode Island (18)	5
Connecticut (3)	19	Minnesota (1)	22	South Carolina (46)	-14
Delaware (23)	2	Mississippi (50)	-19	South Dakota (33)	-4
D.C.	no data	Missouri (29)	-2	Tennessee (40)	-9
Florida (40)	-9	Montana (26)	-1	Texas (31)	-3
Georgia (38)	-8	Nebraska (11)	12	Utah (5)	16
Hawaii (3)	19	Nevada (42)	-10	Vermont (6)	15
Idaho (31)	-3	New Hampshire (2)	21	Virginia (13)	11
Illinois (33)	-4	New Jersey (15)	7	Washington (21)	4
Indiana (22)	3	New Mexico (46)	-14	West Virginia (48)	-17
Iowa (9)	13	New York (36)	-6	Wisconsin (11)	12
Kansas (6)	15	North Carolina (37)	-7	Wyoming (35)	-5

Source: Northwestern National Life Insurance Company, used by permission

Table 6.2

Heart Disease
Death rate per 100,000 population, 1991

State	Rate	State	Rate	State	Rate
Alabama (13)	322.2	Kentucky (14)	321.6	North Dakota (27)	285.5
Alaska (51)	82.5	Louisiana (24)	292.6	Ohio (15)	319.9
Arizona (41)	234.4	Maine (21)	299.8	Oklahoma (9)	340.4
Arkansas (6)	346.0	Maryland (38)	241.5	Oregon (36)	246.4
California (45)	222.0	Massachusetts (28)	285.4	Pennsylvania (3)	363.3
Colorado (48)	181.7	Michigan (23)	294.7	Rhode Island (11)	323.4
Connecticut (25)	290.6	Minnesota (39)	241.0	South Carolina (31)	267.6
Delaware (29)	283.2	Mississippi (2)	371.6	South Dakota (10)	331.2
D.C. (17)	311.9	Missouri (8)	344.8	Tennessee (16)	312.8
Florida (5)	348.2	Montana (40)	240.5	Texas (42)	226.7
Georgia (35)	249.4	Nebraska (12)	322.4	Utah (50)	157.2
Hawaii (49)	180.4	Nevada (34)	249.8	Vermont (52)	258.7
Idaho (43)	225.0	New Hampshire (36)	246.4	Virginia (33)	250.0
Illinois (18)	309.0	New Jersey (20)	301.1	Washington (44)	223.1
Indiana (22)	299.4	New Mexico (46)	199.9	West Virginia (1)	392.8
Iowa (7)	345.7	New York (4)	353.1	Wisconsin (26)	289.5
Kansas (19)	301.3	North Carolina (30)	281.4	Wyoming (47)	197.8

Source: National Center for Health Statistics, *Monthly Vital Statistics*, Vol. 42, No. 2, 1993, Table 14

Table 6.3
Stroke
Death rate from cerebrovascular disease per 100,000 population, 1991

Alabama (5)	68.7	Kentucky (21)	63.1	North Dakota (3)	69.3
Alaska (51)	15.4	Louisiana (24)	57.2	Ohio (27)	56.2
Arizona (42)	47.7	Maine (33)	53.7	Oklahoma (16)	64.5
Arkansas (1)	89.9	Maryland (45)	45.6	Oregon (11)	66.7
California (38)	50.6	Massachusetts (32)	54.5	Pennsylvania (19)	63.9
Colorado (48)	40.4	Michigan (30)	55.3	Rhode Island (26)	56.5
Connecticut (34)	53.2	Minnesota (17)	64.4	South Carolina (9)	67.8
Delaware (36)	52.2	Mississippi (8)	68.1	South Dakota (14)	65.1
D.C. (25)	56.7	Missouri (12)	66.3	Tennessee (4)	68.8
Florida (15)	64.7	Montana (22)	62.0	Texas (41)	48.6
Georgia (27)	56.2	Nebraska (7)	68.2	Utah (49)	38.6
Hawaii (40)	49.6	Nevada (50)	37.2	Vermont (44)	46.7
Idaho (31)	54.8	New Hampshire (39)	50.4	Virginia (35)	52.6
Illinois (23)	59.5	New Jersey (37)	51.8	Washington (29)	56.0
Indiana (18)	64.2	New Mexico (47)	41.3	West Virginia (13)	65.9
Iowa (2)	74.9	New York (43)	47.5	Wisconsin (10)	66.9
Kansas (20)	63.8	North Carolina (6)	68.3	Wyoming (46)	43.9

Source: National Center for Health Statistics, *Monthly Vital Statistics*, Vol. 42, No. 2, 1993, Table 14

Table 6.4
Cancer
Death rate from malignant neoplasms per 100,000 population, 1991

Alabama (16)	215.5	Kentucky (10)	229.9	North Dakota (15)	215.6
Alaska (51)	88.2	Louisiana (26)	208.9	Ohio (14)	221.5
Arizona (36)	191.1	Maine (5)	237.8	Oklahoma (18)	214.8
Arkansas (6)	236.4	Maryland (32)	200.8	Oregon (24)	212.6
California (44)	165.1	Massachusetts (9)	230.2	Pennsylvania (4)	250.8
Colorado (46)	154.2	Michigan (29)	205.5	Rhode Island (7)	236.1
Connecticut (20)	214.0	Minnesota (39)	189.3	South Carolina (38)	190.2
Delaware (13)	223.5	Mississippi (23)	213.0	South Dakota (17)	215.2
D.C. (2)	258.7	Missouri (11)	228.8	Tennessee (21)	213.4
Florida (1)	260.4	Montana (30)	203.3	Texas (43)	167.5
Georgia (42)	175.0	Nebraska (33)	200.0	Utah (50)	111.5
Hawaii (49)	146.2	Nevada (40)	186.1	Vermont (35)	197.0
Idaho (45)	164.9	New Hampshire (31)	203.0	Virginia (37)	191.0
Illinois (25)	211.5	New Jersey (8)	234.3	Washington (41)	183.2
Indiana (19)	214.4	New Mexico (48)	151.9	West Virginia (3)	256.9
Iowa (12)	227.5	New York (22)	213.2	Wisconsin (27)	208.7
Kansas (28)	206.2	North Carolina (34)	198.4	Wyoming (47)	153.9

Source: National Center for Health Statistics, *Monthly Vital Statistics*, Vol. 42, No. 2, 1993, Table 14

Table 6.5
Breast Cancer
Age-adjusted death rate per 100,000 females, 1988–90

Alabama (33)	21.9	Kentucky (26)	22.6	North Dakota (35)	21.6
Alaska (48)	19.5	Louisiana (15)	23.6	Ohio (9)	24.8
Arizona (46)	20.2	Maine (19)	23.0	Oklahoma (42)	20.9
Arkansas (44)	20.4	Maryland (14)	23.9	Oregon (37)	21.4
California (28)	22.4	Massachusetts (9)	24.8	Pennsylvania (7)	25.2
Colorado (44)	20.4	Michigan (11)	24.2	Rhode Island (3)	26.7
Connecticut (24)	22.7	Minnesota (22)	22.8	South Carolina (21)	22.9
Delaware (2)	28.6	Mississippi (41)	21.0	South Dakota (31)	22.0
D.C. (1)	30.5	Missouri (17)	23.2	Tennessee (34)	21.7
Florida (29)	22.2	Montana (40)	21.2	Texas (47)	19.9
Georgia (35)	21.6	Nebraska (19)	23.0	Utah (50)	19.0
Hawaii (51)	15.3	Nevada (31)	22.0	Vermont (13)	24.0
Idaho (37)	21.4	New Hampshire (5)	26.2	Virginia (11)	24.2
Illinois (8)	24.9	New Jersey (4)	26.5	Washington (24)	22.7
Indiana (15)	23.6	New Mexico (49)	19.2	West Virginia (37)	21.4
Iowa (30)	22.1	New York (6)	26.0	Wisconsin (17)	23.2
Kansas (22)	22.8	North Carolina (27)	22.5	Wyoming (43)	20.7

Source: National Center for Health Statistics, *Monthly Vital Statistics*, Vol. 42, No. 8, February 11, 1994

Table 6.6
Prostate Cancer
Age-adjusted death rate per 100,000 males, 1988–90

Alabama (13)	17.7	Kentucky (38)	15.3	North Dakota (3)	20.8
Alaska (50)	11.2	Louisiana (12)	18.1	Ohio (28)	16.5
Arizona (47)	14.5	Maine (16)	17.2	Oklahoma (30)	16.0
Arkansas (26)	16.7	Maryland (7)	19.4	Oregon (29)	16.1
California (38)	15.3	Massachusetts (30)	16.0	Pennsylvania (27)	16.6
Colorado (23)	16.9	Michigan (23)	16.9	Rhode Island (41)	15.2
Connecticut (42)	15.1	Minnesota (16)	17.2	South Carolina (2)	21.1
Delaware (16)	17.2	Mississippi (7)	19.4	South Dakota (32)	15.9
D.C. (1)	29.5	Missouri (44)	15.0	Tennessee (21)	17.0
Florida (38)	15.3	Montana (10)	18.5	Texas (46)	14.8
Georgia (5)	19.9	Nebraska (35)	15.8	Utah (11)	18.2
Hawaii (51)	10.3	Nevada (44)	15.0	Vermont (4)	20.3
Idaho (23)	16.9	New Hampshire (16)	17.2	Virginia (9)	18.8
Illinois (21)	17.0	New Jersey (15)	17.4	Washington (35)	15.8
Indiana (37)	15.5	New Mexico (49)	14.4	West Virginia (47)	14.5
Iowa (32)	15.9	New York (32)	15.9	Wisconsin (16)	17.2
Kansas (42)	15.1	North Carolina (6)	19.8	Wyoming (14)	17.5

Source: National Center for Health Statistics, *Monthly Vital Statistics*, Vol. 42, No. 8, February 11, 1994

Table 6.7

AIDS Cases

Rate per 100,000 population, 1992–93

Alabama (28)	17.0	Kentucky (41)	7.9	North Dakota (51)	0.8
Alaska (47)	4.9	Louisiana (17)	26.4	Ohio (38)	10.5
Arizona (15)	29.7	Maine (45)	6.2	Oklahoma (23)	20.9
Arkansas (24)	17.9	Maryland (8)	41.7	Oregon (21)	22.1
California (4)	49.7	Massachusetts (12)	32.3	Pennsylvania (25)	17.6
Colorado (14)	31.8	Michigan (30)	16.5	Rhode Island (19)	23.7
Connecticut (7)	43.8	Minnesota (35)	13.2	South Carolina (16)	29.6
Delaware (6)	44.0	Mississippi (31)	15.3	South Dakota (50)	3.2
D.C. (1)	183.6	Missouri (13)	31.9	Tennessee (29)	16.6
Florida (3)	64.4	Montana (49)	3.4	Texas (10)	35.1
Georgia (11)	32.4	Nebraska (39)	9.5	Utah (32)	15.2
Hawaii (25)	17.6	Nevada (9)	39.6	Vermont (46)	5.1
Idaho (44)	6.4	New Hampshire (40)	8.4	Virginia (22)	21.4
Illinois (18)	24.5	New Jersey (5)	44.7	Washington (20)	22.8
Indiana (34)	13.5	New Mexico (27)	17.5	West Virginia (48)	3.9
Iowa (43)	6.8	New York (2)	77.8	Wisconsin (36)	12.5
Kansas (37)	11.9	North Carolina (33)	14.7	Wyoming (42)	7.1

Source: National Center for Infectious Diseases, *HIV/AIDS Surveillance Report*, July 1993

Table 6.8

Tuberculosis

Cases of tuberculosis per 100,000 population, 1991

Alabama (14)	10.5	Kentucky (16)	9.3	North Dakota (48)	1.4
Alaska (9)	12.3	Louisiana (19)	8.7	Ohio (37)	3.5
Arizona (20)	8.6	Maine (38)	2.7	Oklahoma (23)	6.5
Arkansas (10)	11.9	Maryland (16)	9.3	Oregon (31)	4.9
California (4)	17.4	Massachusetts (21)	7.3	Pennsylvania (23)	6.5
Colorado (39)	2.6	Michigan (33)	4.8	Rhode Island (22)	7.1
Connecticut (35)	4.5	Minnesota (44)	2.3	South Carolina (13)	11.5
Delaware (27)	5.4	Mississippi (11)	11.6	South Dakota (30)	5.0
D.C. (1)	29.3	Missouri (31)	4.9	Tennessee (11)	11.6
Florida (7)	12.8	Montana (43)	2.4	Texas (5)	14.6
Georgia (6)	13.7	Nebraska (47)	1.8	Utah (39)	2.6
Hawaii (3)	17.7	Nevada (28)	5.1	Vermont (46)	2.1
Idaho (48)	1.4	New Hampshire (51)	1.0	Virginia (26)	6.0
Illinois (15)	10.3	New Jersey (8)	12.7	Washington (25)	6.2
Indiana (34)	4.7	New Mexico (28)	5.1	West Virginia (36)	3.6
Iowa (41)	2.5	New York (2)	24.5	Wisconsin (45)	2.2
Kansas (41)	2.5	North Carolina (16)	9.3	Wyoming (50)	1.3

Source: Centers for Disease Control and Prevention, 1991, *Tuberculosis Statistics in the United States*,
        September 1993, Table 1

258

Table 6.9

Suicide
Deaths by suicide per 100,000 population, 1991

Alabama (20)	13.2	Kentucky (20)	13.2	North Dakota (37)	11.7
Alaska (24)	12.8	Louisiana (22)	13.1	Ohio (42)	11.3
Arizona (5)	17.7	Maine (12)	14.3	Oklahoma (13)	13.9
Arkansas (34)	11.9	Maryland (46)	8.8	Oregon (11)	15.5
California (30)	12.2	Massachusetts (48)	8.2	Pennsylvania (37)	11.7
Colorado (6)	16.7	Michigan (30)	12.2	Rhode Island (48)	8.2
Connecticut (44)	10.0	Minnesota (41)	11.5	South Carolina (35)	11.8
Delaware (39)	11.6	Mississippi (26)	12.5	South Dakota (16)	13.5
D.C. (51)	5.7	Missouri (14)	13.8	Tennessee (18)	13.4
Florida (10)	15.8	Montana (2)	19.9	Texas (23)	13.0
Georgia (16)	13.5	Nebraska (32)	12.0	Utah (7)	16.2
Hawaii (45)	9.4	Nevada (1)	24.8	Vermont (7)	16.2
Idaho (9)	15.9	New Hampshire (35)	11.8	Virginia (25)	12.6
Illinois (43)	10.3	New Jersey (50)	6.6	Washington (14)	13.8
Indiana (26)	12.5	New Mexico (4)	18.3	West Virginia (19)	13.3
Iowa (32)	12.0	New York (46)	8.8	Wisconsin (39)	11.6
Kansas (29)	12.4	North Carolina (26)	12.5	Wyoming (3)	18.9

Source: National Center for Health Statistics, *Monthly Vital Statistics*, Vol. 42, No. 2, 1993, Table 14

Table 7.1

Physicians
Physicians per 100,000 population, 1992

Alabama (41)	186	Kentucky (38)	196	North Dakota (33)	205
Alaska (49)	161	Louisiana (29)	217	Ohio (23)	228
Arizona (20)	235	Maine (25)	222	Oklahoma (46)	171
Arkansas (42)	182	Maryland (2)	397	Oregon (17)	245
California (11)	274	Massachusetts (3)	386	Pennsylvania (10)	278
Colorado (16)	248	Michigan (30)	212	Rhode Island (7)	299
Connecticut (5)	351	Minnesota (12)	257	South Carolina (39)	194
Delaware (21)	232	Mississippi (50)	154	South Dakota (45)	175
D.C. (1)	765	Missouri (24)	226	Tennessee (22)	229
Florida (12)	257	Montana (39)	194	Texas (36)	200
Georgia (35)	201	Nebraska (33)	205	Utah (31)	208
Hawaii (9)	283	Nevada (47)	167	Vermont (6)	307
Idaho (51)	151	New Hampshire (19)	242	Virginia (18)	243
Illinois (15)	249	New Jersey (8)	286	Washington (14)	253
Indiana (42)	182	New Mexico (26)	222	West Virginia (36)	200
Iowa (44)	178	New York (4)	363	Wisconsin (28)	218
Kansas (32)	207	North Carolina (27)	221	Wyoming (48)	163

Source: *Physician Characteristics and Distribution in the U.S.*, 1993 Edition, American Medical Association.
Used by permission

Table 7.2

Health Maintenance Organizations (HMOs)
Percent of population enrolled, 1993

Alabama (37)	6.4	Kentucky (35)	6.6	North Dakota (47)	0.5
Alaska (49)	0.0	Louisiana (31)	7.1	Ohio (20)	15.2
Arizona (4)	32.9	Maine (39)	4.3	Oklahoma (29)	7.3
Arkansas (44)	2.8	Maryland (42)	3.2	Oregon (5)	31.5
California (2)	35.0	Massachusetts (3)	34.1	Pennsylvania (13)	18.9
Colorado (9)	23.2	Michigan (15)	18.4	Rhode Island (7)	25.9
Connecticut (8)	24.5	Minnesota (6)	30.1	South Carolina (41)	3.3
Delaware (17)	17.2	Mississippi (48)	0.1	South Dakota (43)	2.9
D.C. (1)	37.6	Missouri (22)	14.3	Tennessee (38)	5.7
Florida (16)	17.6	Montana (45)	1.4	Texas (27)	9.7
Georgia (31)	7.1	Nebraska (33)	6.7	Utah (14)	18.5
Hawaii (11)	22.3	Nevada (25)	12.7	Vermont (26)	11.1
Idaho (46)	1.1	New Hampshire (23)	13.6	Virginia (30)	7.2
Illinois (18)	16.1	New Jersey (24)	13.0	Washington (20)	15.2
Indiana (33)	6.7	New Mexico (19)	15.7	West Virginia (49)	0.0
Iowa (40)	3.8	New York (12)	21.4	Wisconsin (10)	23.1
Kansas (28)	7.5	North Carolina (35)	6.6	Wyoming (49)	0.0

Source: Group Health Association of America, *Patterns in HMO Enrollment*, 1994

Table 7.3

Persons Not Covered by Health Insurance
Three year average percentage, 1990–92

Alabama (11)	17.3	Kentucky (20)	13.6	North Dakota (50)	7.4
Alaska (18)	14.9	Louisiana (4)	20.8	Ohio (40)	10.5
Arizona (14)	15.8	Maine (35)	11.1	Oklahoma (5)	19.5
Arkansas (10)	17.6	Maryland (27)	12.3	Oregon (22)	13.3
California (8)	19.0	Massachusetts (42)	10.1	Pennsylvania (46)	8.8
Colorado (26)	12.4	Michigan (43)	9.4	Rhode Island (41)	10.2
Connecticut (49)	7.5	Minnesota (45)	8.8	South Carolina (16)	15.4
Delaware (24)	12.7	Mississippi (6)	19.3	South Dakota (28)	12.2
D.C. (1)	22.0	Missouri (23)	13.1	Tennessee (20)	13.6
Florida (9)	18.7	Montana (29)	12.0	Texas (2)	21.9
Georgia (13)	16.1	Nebraska (46)	8.7	Utah (32)	11.5
Hawaii (51)	6.8	Nevada (6)	19.3	Vermont (39)	10.6
Idaho (12)	16.4	New Hampshire (37)	10.9	Virginia (15)	15.5
Illinois (31)	11.8	New Jersey (34)	11.3	Washington (38)	10.7
Indiana (32)	11.5	New Mexico (3)	21.0	West Virginia (17)	15.0
Iowa (44)	9.0	New York (25)	12.6	Wisconsin (48)	7.9
Kansas (36)	11.0	North Carolina (19)	14.2	Wyoming (30)	11.9

Source: U.S. Bureau of the Census, 1993, *Money Income of Households, Families, and Persons in the United States: 1992*, Table E

Table 7.4

Access to Primary Medical Practitioners
Percent of population underserved, 1993

Alabama (9)	16.4	Kentucky (17)	10.9	North Dakota (12)	14.6
Alaska (11)	14.7	Louisiana (4)	20.2	Ohio (34)	7.0
Arizona (36)	6.4	Maine (39)	6.1	Oklahoma (24)	9.1
Arkansas (13)	13.8	Maryland (49)	3.9	Oregon (35)	6.9
California (26)	8.0	Massachusetts (37)	6.2	Pennsylvania (43)	5.2
Colorado (44)	4.8	Michigan (25)	8.4	Rhode Island (21)	9.9
Connecticut (47)	4.2	Minnesota (45)	4.3	South Carolina (5)	19.0
Delaware (47)	4.2	Mississippi (1)	24.9	South Dakota (3)	22.0
D.C. (2)	24.6	Missouri (19)	10.3	Tennessee (20)	10.1
Florida (37)	6.2	Montana (15)	12.6	Texas (26)	8.0
Georgia (14)	13.3	Nebraska (22)	9.7	Utah (30)	7.6
Hawaii (51)	2.5	Nevada (26)	8.0	Vermont (42)	5.4
Idaho (10)	16.1	New Hampshire (49)	3.9	Virginia (40)	5.7
Illinois (32)	7.5	New Jersey (45)	4.3	Washington (33)	7.2
Indiana (30)	7.6	New Mexico (8)	17.4	West Virginia (7)	18.4
Iowa (29)	7.8	New York (17)	10.9	Wisconsin (23)	9.3
Kansas (41)	5.6	North Carolina (16)	11.3	Wyoming (6)	18.9

Source: Calculated from U.S. Census data and unpublished data from Department of Health and Human Services, Division of Shortage Designation

Table 7.5
Immunization Status of Children
Percent vaccinated for measles, mumps, and rubella, 1992–93

Alabama (23)	79.2	Kentucky (7)	86.1	North Dakota	no data
Alaska (21)	79.5	Louisiana (34)	76.0	Ohio (29)	78.0
Arizona (28)	78.4	Maine (6)	86.7	Oklahoma (24)	79.1
Arkansas (36)	74.0	Maryland	no data	Oregon	no data
California (44)	70.1	Massachusetts (2)	89.5	Pennsylvania (17)	81.4
Colorado (20)	80.7	Michigan (45)	68.8	Rhode Island (8)	85.3
Connecticut (3)	88.2	Minnesota (14)	82.5	South Carolina	no data
Delaware (15)	82.4	Mississippi (16)	81.7	South Dakota (12)	82.7
D.C. (42)	72.0	Missouri (33)	76.1	Tennessee (5)	87.8
Florida (35)	74.4	Montana (24)	79.1	Texas (41)	72.1
Georgia (36)	74.0	Nebraska	no data	Utah (38)	73.9
Hawaii (22)	79.3	Nevada (43)	70.9	Vermont (1)	91.2
Idaho (38)	73.9	New Hampshire (4)	88.0	Virginia (18)	80.8
Illinois (9)	84.0	New Jersey (40)	72.4	Washington (32)	76.5
Indiana (31)	77.0	New Mexico (18)	80.8	West Virginia (30)	77.8
Iowa (24)	79.1	New York (11)	83.7	Wisconsin (13)	82.6
Kansas (27)	78.7	North Carolina	no data	Wyoming (9)	84.0

Source: Centers for Disease Control and Prevention, National Immunization Program, unpublished statistics

Table 7.6
Hospital Expenditures
Average daily cost to community hospitals, per patient, 1991

Alabama (35)	$ 637	Kentucky (38)	$616	North Dakota (49)	$454
Alaska (1)	1,130	Louisiana (19)	764	Ohio (17)	782
Arizona (4)	955	Maine (37)	617	Oklahoma (30)	684
Arkansas (43)	571	Maryland (21)	740	Oregon (9)	896
California (3)	1,037	Massachusetts (10)	880	Pennsylvania (23)	732
Colorado (15)	801	Michigan (16)	792	Rhode Island (24)	730
Connecticut (6)	910	Minnesota (42)	582	South Carolina (30)	684
Delaware (12)	845	Mississippi (48)	479	South Dakota (51)	436
D.C. (2)	1,038	Missouri (22)	737	Tennessee (25)	716
Florida (14)	836	Montana (50)	437	Texas (11)	846
Georgia (33)	652	Nebraska (45)	546	Utah (5)	915
Hawaii (29)	686	Nevada (7)	907	Vermont (36)	621
Idaho (44)	565	New Hampshire (26)	713	Virginia (27)	701
Illinois (18)	770	New Jersey (32)	680	Washington (8)	904
Indiana (20)	745	New Mexico (13)	840	West Virginia (39)	612
Iowa (46)	538	New York (28)	694	Wisconsin (40)	611
Kansas (41)	585	North Carolina (34)	651	Wyoming (47)	489

Source: *Statistical Abstract of the U.S., 1993*

Table 7.7
Medicare Payments
Benefit payments per Medicare enrollee, 1993

Alabama (14)	$ 3,980	Kentucky (26)	$3,467	North Dakota (29)	$3,406
Alaska (35)	3,234	Louisiana (5)	4,634	Ohio (22)	3,743
Arizona (16)	3,936	Maine (45)	2,889	Oklahoma (34)	3,271
Arkansas (37)	3,186	Maryland (9)	4,270	Oregon (36)	3,191
California (3)	4,705	Massachusetts (2)	4,923	Pennsylvania (6)	4,546
Colorado (23)	3,606	Michigan (15)	3,952	Rhode Island (21)	3,810
Connecticut (10)	4,180	Minnesota (28)	3,423	South Carolina (42)	2,993
Delaware (18)	3,856	Mississippi (27)	3,459	South Dakota (44)	2,895
D.C. (1)	14,164	Missouri (20)	3,835	Tennessee (8)	4,407
Florida (4)	4,701	Montana (43)	2,955	Texas (13)	4,058
Georgia (11)	4,175	Nebraska (47)	2,816	Utah (31)	3,341
Hawaii (30)	3,350	Nevada (17)	3,912	Vermont (46)	2,873
Idaho (51)	2,402	New Hampshire (39)	3,114	Virginia (40)	3,107
Illinois (19)	3,851	New Jersey (12)	4,153	Washington (33)	3,294
Indiana (25)	3,584	New Mexico (48)	2,804	West Virginia (38)	3,159
Iowa (49)	2,783	New York (7)	4,413	Wisconsin (41)	3,095
Kansas (24)	3,586	North Carolina (32)	3,338	Wyoming (50)	2,436

Source: Health Care Financing Administration, Division of Medicare Statistics, 1993

Table 7.8
Medicaid Eligibility
Percent of population eligible for Medicaid, 1992

Alabama (19)	13.2	Kentucky (7)	17.0	North Dakota (37)	10.3
Alaska (28)	12.3	Louisiana (6)	17.1	Ohio (13)	14.7
Arizona (14)	14.4	Maine (9)	15.3	Oklahoma (23)	12.9
Arkansas (12)	15.0	Maryland (33)	10.9	Oregon (30)	11.3
California (4)	19.6	Massachusetts (25)	12.8	Pennsylvania (25)	12.8
Colorado (44)	9.5	Michigan (14)	14.4	Rhode Island (51)	0.0
Connecticut (39)	10.1	Minnesota (31)	11.2	South Carolina (19)	13.2
Delaware (41)	10.0	Mississippi (3)	20.6	South Dakota (36)	10.5
D.C. (1)	21.3	Missouri (27)	12.5	Tennessee (5)	17.6
Florida (18)	13.4	Montana (31)	11.2	Texas (21)	13.1
Georgia (16)	14.3	Nebraska (38)	10.2	Utah (43)	9.7
Hawaii (44)	9.5	Nevada (49)	7.5	Vermont (11)	15.1
Idaho (47)	9.4	New Hampshire (50)	7.1	Virginia (44)	9.5
Illinois (17)	14.1	New Jersey (39)	10.1	Washington (21)	13.1
Indiana (47)	9.4	New Mexico (10)	15.2	West Virginia (1)	21.3
Iowa (34)	10.8	New York (8)	16.2	Wisconsin (28)	12.3
Kansas (42)	9.8	North Carolina (23)	12.9	Wyoming (35)	10.6

Source: Health Care Financing Administration, Division of Medicaid Statistics, 1993

Table 7.9
Medicaid Expenditures
Average cost per recipient, 1992

Alabama (45)	$2,262	Kentucky (37)	$2,647	North Dakota (6)	$4,430
Alaska (19)	3,248	Louisiana (18)	3,530	Ohio (26)	2,987
Arizona (51)	520	Maine (11)	3,950	Oklahoma (29)	2,788
Arkansas (30)	2,758	Maryland (9)	4,276	Oregon (39)	2,532
California (49)	1,938	Massachusetts (4)	4,733	Pennsylvania (25)	3,019
Colorado (21)	3,145	Michigan (41)	2,482	Rhode Island (14)	3,628
Connecticut (2)	5,258	Minnesota (8)	4,306	South Carolina (34)	2,670
Delaware (15)	3,611	Mississippi (50)	1,809	South Dakota (17)	3,597
D.C. (5)	4,595	Missouri (42)	2,435	Tennessee (47)	2,210
Florida (44)	2,288	Montana (16)	3,599	Texas (48)	2,177
Georgia (40)	2,488	Nebraska (22)	3,103	Utah (35)	2,662
Hawaii (32)	2,706	Nevada (13)	3,635	Vermont (28)	2,863
Idaho (20)	3,159	New Hampshire (3)	4,779	Virginia (27)	2,934
Illinois (23)	3,099	New Jersey (10)	4,019	Washington (43)	2,368
Indiana (7)	4,390	New Mexico (46)	2,259	West Virginia (38)	2,580
Iowa (24)	3,065	New York (1)	5,975	Wisconsin (12)	3,811
Kansas (31)	2,730	North Carolina (36)	2,654	Wyoming (33)	2,685

Source: Health Care Financing Administration, Division of Medicaid Statistics, 1993

264

Table 8.1

Leisure-Time Physical Acitvity
Percent of population age 18 and older reporting no regular exercise or physical activity, 1991

Alabama (14)	34.2	Kentucky (3)	42.0	North Dakota (24)	28.0
Alaska (41)	22.1	Louisiana (18)	32.6	Ohio (5)	39.6
Arizona (37)	24.3	Maine (13)	34.9	Oklahoma (8)	36.6
Arkansas (11)	36.0	Maryland (26)	27.8	Oregon (46)	19.6
California (40)	23.3	Massachusetts (34)	25.1	Pennsylvania (31)	26.4
Colorado (47)	18.0	Michigan (22)	28.6	Rhode Island (25)	27.9
Connecticut (32)	25.8	Minnesota (38)	23.7	South Carolina (12)	35.4
Delaware (19)	31.4	Mississippi (1)	42.6	South Dakota (27)	27.1
D.C. (6)	39.4	Missouri (9)	36.3	Tennessee (7)	38.7
Florida (23)	28.4	Montana (48)	16.6	Texas (28)	27.0
Georgia (4)	39.9	Nebraska (34)	25.1	Utah (44)	20.8
Hawaii (39)	23.4	Nevada	no data	Vermont (30)	26.6
Idaho (42)	22.0	New Hampshire (43)	21.2	Virginia (33)	25.2
Illinois (10)	36.1	New Jersey (19)	31.4	Washington (45)	20.6
Indiana (29)	26.9	New Mexico (16)	33.7	West Virginia (2)	42.3
Iowa (21)	30.0	New York (14)	34.2	Wisconsin (36)	25.0
Kansas	no data	North Carolina (17)	33.4	Wyoming	no data

Source: Centers for Disease Control and Prevention, *MMWR*, August 27, 1993, Table 2

Table 8.2

Smokers
Percent of population 18 years and older who smoke regularly, 1991

Alabama (32)	22.0	Kentucky (1)	30.2	North Dakota (45)	19.8
Alaska (7)	25.9	Louisiana (16)	24.1	Ohio (25)	22.9
Arizona (20)	23.7	Maine (6)	26.0	Oklahoma (12)	25.0
Arkansas (4)	26.5	Maryland (35)	21.7	Oregon (43)	20.6
California (46)	19.5	Massachusetts (29)	22.5	Pennsylvania (9)	25.3
Colorado (22)	23.5	Michigan (3)	27.5	Rhode Island (13)	24.9
Connecticut (30)	22.4	Minnesota (23)	23.3	South Carolina (27)	22.8
Delaware (7)	25.9	Mississippi (16)	24.1	South Dakota (27)	22.8
D.C. (37)	21.5	Missouri (11)	25.1	Tennessee (2)	28.1
Florida (14)	24.6	Montana (41)	20.9	Texas (34)	21.8
Georgia (35)	21.7	Nebraska (32)	22.0	Utah (48)	14.3
Hawaii (44)	20.3	Nevada	no data	Vermont (37)	21.5
Idaho (40)	21.1	New Hampshire (19)	23.8	Virginia (37)	21.5
Illinois (21)	23.6	New Jersey (30)	22.4	Washington (24)	23.1
Indiana (15)	24.4	New Mexico (47)	16.4	West Virginia (10)	25.2
Iowa (41)	20.9	New York (25)	22.9	Wisconsin (5)	26.4
Kansas	no data	North Carolina (18)	23.9	Wyoming	no data

Source: Centers for Disease Control and Prevention, *MMWR*, August 27, 1993, Table 3

Table 8.3

Overweight Population

Percent of population 18 and older who are overweight, 1991

Alabama (10)	25.7	Kentucky (10)	25.7	North Dakota (21)	24.0
Alaska (15)	24.6	Louisiana (8)	26.6	Ohio (17)	24.3
Arizona (37)	20.6	Maine (25)	23.3	Oklahoma (22)	23.8
Arkansas (27)	23.1	Maryland (37)	20.6	Oregon (31)	22.1
California (31)	22.1	Massachusetts (34)	21.0	Pennsylvania (5)	27.1
Colorado (48)	17.8	Michigan (1)	28.7	Rhode Island (35)	20.9
Connecticut (37)	20.6	Minnesota (24)	23.4	South Carolina (14)	25.2
Delaware (4)	27.5	Mississippi (3)	27.8	South Dakota (18)	24.2
D.C. (7)	26.8	Missouri (22)	23.8	Tennessee (18)	24.2
Florida (33)	21.7	Montana (41)	20.5	Texas (13)	25.3
Georgia (37)	20.6	Nebraska (16)	24.4	Utah (44)	19.8
Hawaii (45)	19.6	Nevada	no data	Vermont (29)	22.6
Idaho (30)	22.5	New Hampshire (35)	20.9	Virginia (46)	18.9
Illinois (25)	23.3	New Jersey (42)	20.4	Washington (43)	20.0
Indiana (6)	26.9	New Mexico (46)	18.9	West Virginia (2)	28.0
Iowa (9)	25.9	New York (18)	24.2	Wisconsin (10)	25.7
Kansas	no data	North Carolina (28)	23.0	Wyoming	no data

Source: Centers for Disease Control and Prevention, *MMWR*, August 27, 1993, Table 1

Table 8.4

Motor Vehicle Traffic Deaths

Rate per 100,000 population, 1992

Alabama (4)	24.2	Kentucky (12)	21.8	North Dakota (33)	13.8
Alaska (22)	18.1	Louisiana (14)	20.3	Ohio (37)	13.1
Arizona (13)	21.1	Maine (24)	17.2	Oklahoma (17)	19.3
Arkansas (3)	24.5	Maryland (35)	13.5	Oregon (28)	15.6
California (42)	12.4	Massachusetts (49)	8.1	Pennsylvania (39)	12.9
Colorado (31)	15.0	Michigan (34)	13.7	Rhode Island (50)	7.9
Connecticut (48)	9.0	Minnesota (38)	13.0	South Carolina (11)	22.4
Delaware (14)	20.3	Mississippi (6)	23.1	South Dakota (10)	22.6
D.C.	no data	Missouri (18)	19.0	Tennessee (8)	23.0
Florida (20)	18.4	Montana (6)	23.1	Texas (23)	17.3
Georgia (16)	19.6	Nebraska (25)	16.8	Utah (32)	14.8
Hawaii (45)	11.0	Nevada (19)	18.9	Vermont (25)	16.8
Idaho (9)	22.8	New Hampshire (44)	11.1	Virginia (36)	13.2
Illinois (43)	11.8	New Jersey (47)	9.8	Washington (41)	12.7
Indiana (27)	15.9	New Mexico (1)	29.2	West Virginia (5)	23.2
Iowa (29)	15.5	New York (46)	9.9	Wisconsin (39)	12.9
Kansas (30)	15.3	North Carolina (20)	18.4	Wyoming (2)	25.3

Source: National Safety Council, *Accident Facts*, 1993, p. 84

Table 8.5
Seat Belt Use
Percent of population age 18 and older reporting regular seat belt use, 1991

Alabama (35)	49.2	Kentucky (41)	42.4	North Dakota (46)	29.1
Alaska (20)	60.3	Louisiana (16)	63.9	Ohio (25)	58.1
Arizona (10)	71.2	Maine (40)	42.8	Oklahoma (26)	57.2
Arkansas (34)	49.5	Maryland (8)	71.8	Oregon (2)	74.9
California (3)	74.7	Massachusetts (43)	40.0	Pennsylvania (31)	52.9
Colorado (17)	63.7	Michigan (13)	66.0	Rhode Island (44)	39.0
Connecticut (18)	62.9	Minnesota (23)	58.4	South Carolina (14)	64.6
Delaware (30)	53.0	Mississippi (45)	35.6	South Dakota (48)	22.8
D.C. (19)	62.0	Missouri (24)	58.2	Tennessee (28)	56.0
Florida (12)	68.7	Montana (37)	46.5	Texas (11)	70.8
Georgia (22)	58.7	Nebraska (47)	28.7	Utah (38)	46.4
Hawaii (1)	87.8	Nevada	no data	Vermont (33)	50.7
Idaho (36)	48.2	New Hampshire (39)	46.2	Virginia (6)	72.5
Illinois (27)	56.5	New Jersey (8)	71.8	Washington (7)	72.2
Indiana (29)	53.2	New Mexico (5)	72.7	West Virginia (42)	40.8
Iowa (21)	58.9	New York (14)	64.6	Wisconsin (32)	52.2
Kansas	no data	North Carolina (4)	73.7	Wyoming	no data

Source: Centers for Disease Control and Prevention, *MMWR*, August 27, 1993, Table 4

Table 8.6
Drug Use: Marijuana and Cocaine
Percent of population age 12 and older who have ever used marijuana or cocaine, 1992

MARIJUANA:	
National	32.8
Northeast	32.7
Midwest	29.4
South	30.0
West	41.6

COCAINE:	
National	11.0
Northeast	11.8
Midwest	8.6
South	8.4
West	17.2

Source: Department of Health and Human Services, *Substance Abuse and Mental Health*, 1992

Table 8.7

Homeless People

Homeless count at selected shelter and street locations per 100,000 population, 1990

Alabama (33)	42	Kentucky (42)	34	North Dakota (25)	49
Alaska (12)	84	Louisiana (41)	35	Ohio (40)	37
Arizona (7)	120	Maine (44)	32	Oklahoma (16)	74
Arkansas (50)	19	Maryland (20)	59	Oregon (5)	128
California (4)	158	Massachusetts (9)	110	Pennsylvania (14)	76
Colorado (12)	84	Michigan (34)	40	Rhode Island (27)	48
Connecticut (6)	127	Minnesota (23)	52	South Carolina (48)	26
Delaware (28)	47	Mississippi (51)	12	South Dakota (21)	57
D.C. (1)	761	Missouri (29)	46	Tennessee (34)	40
Florida (17)	71	Montana (22)	54	Texas (25)	49
Georgia (19)	63	Nebraska (29)	46	Utah (18)	66
Hawaii (3)	162	Nevada (9)	110	Vermont (32)	44
Idaho (37)	39	New Hampshire (45)	31	Virginia (29)	46
Illinois (14)	76	New Jersey (8)	115	Washington (11)	105
Indiana (37)	39	New Mexico (23)	52	West Virginia (49)	24
Iowa (43)	33	New York (2)	234	Wisconsin (45)	31
Kansas (39)	38	North Carolina (34)	40	Wyoming (45)	31

Source: U.S. Bureau of the Census, CPH-L-87, 1990

Table 9.1

Head Start Enrollment
Percent of preschool children enrolled, 1992

Alabama (14)	14.9	Kentucky (12)	15.1	North Dakota (29)	12.8
Alaska (32)	12.6	Louisiana (38)	11.8	Ohio (13)	15.0
Arizona (50)	7.3	Maine (3)	19.4	Oklahoma (23)	13.4
Arkansas (15)	14.8	Maryland (10)	15.2	Oregon (49)	8.5
California (45)	10.0	Massachusetts (19)	14.4	Pennsylvania (20)	13.7
Colorado (31)	12.7	Michigan (18)	14.5	Rhode Island (4)	17.8
Connecticut (7)	16.9	Minnesota (36)	12.0	South Carolina (26)	13.2
Delaware (5)	17.6	Mississippi (1)	26.8	South Dakota (41)	11.0
D.C. (2)	23.6	Missouri (22)	13.6	Tennessee (23)	13.4
Florida (44)	10.2	Montana (39)	11.6	Texas (47)	8.7
Georgia (34)	12.5	Nebraska (27)	13.0	Utah (42)	10.9
Hawaii (8)	16.1	Nevada (51)	6.7	Vermont (6)	17.1
Idaho (46)	8.9	New Hampshire (36)	12.0	Virginia (32)	12.6
Illinois (10)	15.2	New Jersey (9)	15.9	Washington (47)	8.7
Indiana (27)	13.0	New Mexico (42)	10.9	West Virginia (17)	14.6
Iowa (25)	13.3	New York (40)	11.4	Wisconsin (29)	12.8
Kansas (34)	12.5	North Carolina (20)	13.7	Wyoming (15)	14.8

Source: Congressional Quarterly, *State Fact Finder*, 1993, p. 285

Table 9.2

Fourth Grade Math and Reading Proficiency
Percent of students proficient at math and reading, 1992

MATH:	
National	18
Northeast	23
Midwest	20
South	11
West	17

READING:	
National	24
Northeast	29
Midwest	25
South	19
West	22

Source: National Center for Education Statistics, *1992 Executive Summary of NAEP*, 1993

Table 9.3
High School Dropouts
Percent of all teens (ages 16–19) not in school, 1990

Alabama (10)	12.6	Kentucky (8)	13.3	North Dakota (51)	4.6
Alaska (21)	10.9	Louisiana (11)	12.5	Ohio (37)	8.9
Arizona (2)	14.4	Maine (41)	8.3	Oklahoma (26)	10.4
Arkansas (17)	11.4	Maryland (21)	10.9	Oregon (13)	11.8
California (4)	14.2	Massachusetts (40)	8.5	Pennsylvania (35)	9.1
Colorado (32)	9.8	Michigan (29)	10.0	Rhode Island (20)	11.1
Connecticut (36)	9.0	Minnesota (50)	6.4	South Carolina (15)	11.7
Delaware (26)	10.4	Mississippi (13)	11.8	South Dakota (44)	7.7
D.C. (6)	13.9	Missouri (17)	11.4	Tennessee (7)	13.4
Florida (3)	14.3	Montana (42)	8.1	Texas (9)	12.9
Georgia (5)	14.1	Nebraska (47)	7.0	Utah (38)	8.7
Hawaii (45)	7.5	Nevada (1)	15.2	Vermont (43)	8.0
Idaho (26)	10.4	New Hampshire (34)	9.4	Virginia (29)	10.0
Illinois (24)	10.6	New Jersey (33)	9.6	Washington (24)	10.6
Indiana (17)	11.4	New Mexico (15)	11.7	West Virginia (21)	10.9
Iowa (49)	6.6	New York (31)	9.9	Wisconsin (46)	7.1
Kansas (38)	8.7	North Carolina (11)	12.5	Wyoming (48)	6.9

Source: Center for the Study of Social Policy, *The Challenge of Change*, 1992, Table 32

Table 9.4
High School Graduates
Percent of population 25 years and older who have completed high school, 1991

Alabama (50)	67.3	Kentucky (51)	67.1	North Dakota (23)	80.1
Alaska (4)	87.0	Louisiana (44)	71.1	Ohio (28)	79.4
Arizona (20)	81.0	Maine (18)	81.2	Oklahoma (35)	77.7
Arkansas (44)	71.1	Maryland (32)	78.2	Oregon (7)	86.0
California (34)	77.8	Massachusetts (15)	83.7	Pennsylvania (28)	79.4
Colorado (4)	87.0	Michigan (26)	79.8	Rhode Island (40)	76.4
Connecticut (13)	84.4	Minnesota (3)	87.3	South Carolina (46)	70.2
Delaware (30)	79.0	Mississippi (47)	68.9	South Dakota (22)	80.4
D.C. (42)	73.3	Missouri (21)	80.9	Tennessee (49)	67.4
Florida (27)	79.7	Montana (12)	84.6	Texas (38)	76.6
Georgia (41)	73.9	Nebraska (10)	85.2	Utah (1)	88.3
Hawaii (8)	85.7	Nevada (14)	83.9	Vermont (15)	83.7
Idaho (31)	78.7	New Hampshire (10)	85.2	Virginia (38)	76.6
Illinois (23)	80.1	New Jersey (18)	81.2	Washington (2)	88.1
Indiana (37)	76.9	New Mexico (36)	77.5	West Virginia (48)	68.5
Iowa (17)	81.3	New York (32)	78.2	Wisconsin (23)	80.1
Kansas (6)	86.8	North Carolina (43)	71.4	Wyoming (9)	85.3

Source: U.S. Bureau of the Census, May 1992, *Educational Attainment in the United States*, Table 13

270

Table 9.5

Projected Change in High School Graduates
Percent change, 1992–2003

Alabama (48)	1.3	Kentucky (31)	12.6	North Dakota (42)	8.5
Alaska (3)	48.0	Louisiana (49)	-4.4	Ohio (43)	6.8
Arizona (4)	47.0	Maine (47)	3.7	Oklahoma (25)	18.8
Arkansas (41)	8.6	Maryland (16)	27.5	Oregon (11)	35.2
California (8)	40.1	Massachusetts (29)	13.4	Pennsylvania (32)	12.3
Colorado (7)	41.4	Michigan (40)	8.8	Rhode Island (28)	13.8
Connecticut (34)	11.9	Minnesota (9)	38.2	South Carolina (33)	12.0
Delaware (17)	27.4	Mississippi (46)	4.9	South Dakota (13)	30.9
D.C. (50)	-10.7	Missouri (26)	18.1	Tennessee (45)	6.4
Florida (5)	45.8	Montana (6)	41.9	Texas (12)	31.2
Georgia (21)	22.4	Nebraska (22)	21.0	Utah (22)	21.0
Hawaii (36)	11.4	Nevada (1)	104.4	Vermont (24)	19.8
Idaho (10)	38.0	New Hampshire (15)	28.4	Virginia (20)	24.6
Illinois (30)	12.8	New Jersey (39)	9.2	Washington (2)	48.4
Indiana (44)	6.6	New Mexico (17)	27.4	West Virginia (51)	-13.5
Iowa (27)	17.8	New York (36)	11.4	Wisconsin (14)	29.4
Kansas (19)	27.0	North Carolina (35)	11.5	Wyoming (38)	10.8

Source: Western Interstate Commission for Higher Education, *High School Graduates: Projections by State 1992–2009*

Table 9.6

Cost per Pupil
Expenditure per pupil in public schools, 1991–92

Alabama (48)	$3,616	Kentucky (35)	$4,719	North Dakota (38)	$4,441
Alaska (4)	8,450	Louisiana (42)	4,354	Ohio (17)	5,694
Arizona (40)	4,381	Maine (19)	5,652	Oklahoma (44)	4,078
Arkansas (45)	4,031	Maryland (7)	6,679	Oregon (14)	5,913
California (34)	4,746	Massachusetts (10)	6,408	Pennsylvania (8)	6,613
Colorado (26)	5,172	Michigan (11)	6,268	Rhode Island (9)	6,546
Connecticut (5)	8,017	Minnesota (22)	5,409	South Carolina (39)	4,436
Delaware (13)	6,093	Mississippi (50)	3,245	South Dakota (43)	4,173
D.C. (1)	9,549	Missouri (33)	4,830	Tennessee (47)	3,692
Florida (25)	5,243	Montana (20)	5,423	Texas (36)	4,632
Georgia (41)	4,375	Nebraska (24)	5,263	Utah (51)	3,040
Hawaii (21)	5,420	Nevada (31)	4,926	Vermont (6)	6,944
Idaho (49)	3,556	New Hampshire (16)	5,790	Virginia (32)	4,880
Illinois (18)	5,670	New Jersey (2)	9,317	Washington (23)	5,271
Indiana (29)	5,074	New Mexico (46)	3,765	West Virginia (27)	5,109
Iowa (28)	5,096	New York (3)	8,527	Wisconsin (12)	6,139
Kansas (30)	5,007	North Carolina (37)	4,555	Wyoming (15)	5,812

Source: National Center for Education Statistics, *Digest of Education Statistics, 1993*, Table 164

Table 10.1

College Enrollment

Higher education enrollment as a percent of population, 1992

Alabama (13)	6.40	Kentucky (39)	5.02	North Dakota (14)	6.36
Alaska (34)	5.26	Louisiana (44)	4.77	Ohio (37)	5.21
Arizona (5)	7.19	Maine (47)	4.69	Oklahoma (24)	5.67
Arkansas (51)	4.06	Maryland (27)	5.57	Oregon (25)	5.62
California (12)	6.41	Massachusetts (6)	7.05	Pennsylvania (35)	5.24
Colorado (7)	7.05	Michigan (21)	5.93	Rhode Island (2)	7.88
Connecticut (38)	5.08	Minnesota (19)	6.09	South Carolina (45)	4.76
Delaware (17)	6.21	Mississippi (46)	4.73	South Dakota (32)	5.29
D.C. (1)	13.91	Missouri (23)	5.71	Tennessee (41)	4.84
Florida (48)	4.58	Montana (43)	4.81	Texas (31)	5.32
Georgia (50)	4.34	Nebraska (3)	7.63	Utah (4)	7.34
Hawaii (33)	5.27	Nevada (42)	4.81	Vermont (10)	6.56
Idaho (29)	5.42	New Hampshire (22)	5.75	Virginia (28)	5.55
Illinois (11)	6.43	New Jersey (49)	4.40	Washington (30)	5.38
Indiana (36)	5.24	New Mexico (16)	6.28	West Virginia (40)	4.98
Iowa (15)	6.32	New York (20)	5.93	Wisconsin (18)	6.15
Kansas (9)	6.72	North Carolina (26)	5.60	Wyoming (8)	6.77

Source: National Center for Education Statistics 94-104, *Trends in Enrollment*, Table 5c

Table 10.2

Two-Year College Enrollment

Two-year enrollment as a percent of undergraduate enrollment, 1991

Alabama (22)	38.8	Kentucky (34)	31.2	North Dakota (42)	22.0
Alaska (50)	1.2	Louisiana (46)	16.3	Ohio (29)	33.5
Arizona (3)	65.9	Maine (43)	16.5	Oklahoma (19)	43.3
Arkansas (40)	24.3	Maryland (9)	51.5	Oregon (8)	54.1
California (1)	71.1	Massachusetts (38)	26.5	Pennsylvania (33)	31.4
Colorado (20)	40.9	Michigan (16)	46.3	Rhode Island (39)	25.1
Connecticut (27)	34.5	Minnesota (30)	32.8	South Carolina (23)	37.7
Delaware (35)	30.9	Mississippi (12)	48.0	South Dakota (49)	1.3
D.C. (51)	0.0	Missouri (32)	31.8	Tennessee (24)	37.3
Florida (5)	60.4	Montana (47)	15.2	Texas (10)	49.9
Georgia (31)	32.0	Nebraska (26)	35.0	Utah (37)	28.5
Hawaii (15)	46.4	Nevada (7)	55.5	Vermont (43)	16.5
Idaho (36)	30.4	New Hampshire (41)	22.2	Virginia (17)	45.5
Illinois (6)	59.0	New Jersey (13)	47.9	Washington (4)	63.6
Indiana (43)	16.5	New Mexico (11)	49.8	West Virginia (48)	13.0
Iowa (25)	37.2	New York (28)	34.1	Wisconsin (21)	39.1
Kansas (18)	43.5	North Carolina (14)	47.0	Wyoming (2)	67.4

Source: National Center for Education Statistics, Integrated Postsecondary Education Data System (IPEDS),
    Fall Enrollment, 1991, Table 193

Table 10.3
Minority Enrollment
Minority Enrollment as a percent of enrollment, 1992

State	%	State	%	State	%
Alabama (14)	23.7	Kentucky (39)	8.2	North Dakota (41)	7.3
Alaska (20)	18.3	Louisiana (7)	29.7	Ohio (33)	12.1
Arizona (17)	22.1	Maine (50)	4.4	Oklahoma (21)	17.9
Arkansas (23)	16.8	Maryland (9)	27.3	Oregon (35)	10.6
California (3)	40.7	Massachusetts (28)	14.4	Pennsylvania (32)	12.5
Colorado (25)	15.8	Michigan (26)	15.3	Rhode Island (36)	10.2
Connecticut (29)	14.2	Minnesota (44)	6.8	South Carolina (14)	23.7
Delaware (24)	16.0	Mississippi (6)	29.8	South Dakota (40)	7.5
D.C. (2)	43.7	Missouri (31)	12.6	Tennessee (22)	17.1
Florida (8)	27.5	Montana (30)	12.9	Texas (5)	32.4
Georgia (11)	26.4	Nebraska (43)	7.2	Utah (46)	5.9
Hawaii (1)	69.6	Nevada (19)	18.7	Vermont (51)	4.0
Idaho (47)	5.5	New Hampshire (48)	5.4	Virginia (18)	21.3
Illinois (12)	25.6	New Jersey (13)	24.8	Washington (27)	14.8
Indiana (37)	9.8	New Mexico (4)	39.8	West Virginia (48)	5.4
Iowa (45)	6.7	New York (10)	26.8	Wisconsin (38)	8.7
Kansas (34)	10.7	North Carolina (16)	22.6	Wyoming (41)	7.3

Source: National Center for Education Statistics, *Digest of Educations Statistics*, 1993, Table 203

Table 10.4
College Graduates
Percent of persons 25 and older who have completed college, 1991

State	%	State	%	State	%
Alabama (46)	15.4	Kentucky (47)	14.8	North Dakota (21)	22.3
Alaska (12)	24.5	Louisiana (36)	18.6	Ohio (36)	18.6
Arizona (20)	22.5	Maine (31)	19.7	Oklahoma (30)	20.2
Arkansas (50)	13.7	Maryland (11)	24.9	Oregon (15)	23.8
California (13)	24.2	Massachusetts (3)	29.8	Pennsylvania (39)	18.4
Colorado (2)	32.2	Michigan (44)	17.5	Rhode Island (18)	22.8
Connecticut (4)	28.4	Minnesota (21)	22.3	South Carolina (42)	17.9
Delaware (33)	19.3	Mississippi (49)	14.5	South Dakota (35)	18.8
D.C. (1)	34.4	Missouri (34)	19.2	Tennessee (45)	15.8
Florida (32)	19.5	Montana (28)	20.5	Texas (25)	21.1
Georgia (27)	20.9	Nebraska (19)	22.7	Utah (21)	22.3
Hawaii (6)	27.0	Nevada (41)	18.3	Vermont (4)	28.4
Idaho (39)	18.4	New Hampshire (7)	26.4	Virginia (17)	23.0
Illinois (14)	24.0	New Jersey (8)	26.2	Washington (9)	26.0
Indiana (48)	14.7	New Mexico (24)	21.6	West Virginia (51)	11.9
Iowa (43)	17.6	New York (16)	23.4	Wisconsin (28)	20.5
Kansas (10)	25.0	North Carolina (38)	18.5	Wyoming (26)	21.0

Source: U.S. Bureau of the Census, *Educational Attainment in the United States, May 1992*, Table 13

Table 10.5
In-State Tuition
Average undergraduate in-state tuition at public 4-year colleges, 1992–93

Alabama (29)	$1,877	Kentucky (38)	$1,708	North Dakota (27)	$2,007
Alaska (40)	1,684	Louisiana (32)	1,840	Ohio (11)	3,108
Arizona (43)	1,554	Maine (12)	2,896	Oklahoma (44)	1,549
Arkansas (41)	1,660	Maryland (15)	2,770	Oregon (17)	2,658
California (28)	1,975	Massachusetts (3)	3,845	Pennsylvania (2)	4,022
Colorado (23)	2,216	Michigan (9)	3,189	Rhode Island (10)	3,159
Connecticut (8)	3,253	Minnesota (16)	2,660	South Carolina (18)	2,643
Delaware (4)	3,471	Mississippi (20)	2,366	South Dakota (25)	2,072
D.C. (51)	830	Missouri (21)	2,243	Tennessee (37)	1,713
Florida (39)	1,703	Montana (34)	1,834	Texas (49)	1,354
Georgia (31)	1,842	Nebraska (30)	1,859	Utah (33)	1,837
Hawaii (48)	1,399	Nevada (45)	1,536	Vermont (1)	5,321
Idaho (47)	1,416	New Hampshire (5)	3,453	Virginia (7)	3,338
Illinois (14)	2,829	New Jersey (6)	3,353	Washington (26)	2,069
Indiana (19)	2,452	New Mexico (42)	1,608	West Virginia (36)	1,759
Iowa (22)	2,228	New York (13)	2,894	Wisconsin (24)	2,173
Kansas (35)	1,803	North Carolina (50)	1,266	Wyoming (46)	1,430

Source: National Center for Education Statistics, *Digest of Education Statistics 1993*, Table 307

Table 11.1
Crime Index
Total crimes per 100,000 population, 1992

State	Value	State	Value	State	Value
Alabama (24)	5,268.1	Kentucky (47)	3,323.5	North Dakota (50)	2,903.3
Alaska (21)	5,569.5	Louisiana (6)	6,546.5	Ohio (33)	4,665.5
Arizona (4)	7,028.6	Maine (44)	3,523.6	Oklahoma (22)	5,431.6
Arkansas (31)	4,761.7	Maryland (9)	6,224.6	Oregon (16)	5,820.9
California (5)	6,679.5	Massachusetts (29)	5,002.9	Pennsylvania (46)	3,392.7
Colorado (13)	5,958.8	Michigan (20)	5,610.6	Rhode Island (36)	4,578.0
Connecticut (28)	5,052.9	Minnesota (35)	4,590.7	South Carolina (14)	5,893.1
Delaware (30)	4,848.5	Mississippi (41)	4,282.5	South Dakota (49)	2,998.9
D.C. (1)	11,407.0	Missouri (26)	5,097.1	Tennessee (25)	5,135.8
Florida (2)	8,358.2	Montana (34)	4,596.1	Texas (3)	7,057.9
Georgia (8)	6,405.4	Nebraska (38)	4,324.0	Utah (19)	5,658.5
Hawaii (12)	6,112.0	Nevada (10)	6,203.8	Vermont (45)	3,410.0
Idaho (42)	3,996.2	New Hampshire (48)	3,080.6	Virginia (40)	4,298.5
Illinois (18)	5,765.3	New Jersey (27)	5,064.4	Washington (11)	6,172.8
Indiana (32)	4,686.9	New Mexico (7)	6,434.1	West Virginia (51)	2,609.7
Iowa (43)	3,957.1	New York (15)	5,858.4	Wisconsin (39)	4,319.0
Kansas (23)	5,319.9	North Carolina (17)	5,802.2	Wyoming (37)	4,575.1

Source: Federal Bureau of Investigation, *Crime in the United States, 1992*, Table 4

Table 11.2
Police
Full-time officers per 10,000 population, 1992

State	Value	State	Value	State	Value
Alabama (24)	21	Kentucky (46)	16	North Dakota (42)	17
Alaska (37)	18	Louisiana (3)	35	Ohio (33)	19
Arizona (24)	21	Maine (37)	18	Oklahoma (30)	20
Arkansas (33)	19	Maryland (7)	26	Oregon (37)	18
California (24)	21	Massachusetts (6)	27	Pennsylvania (30)	20
Colorado (10)	25	Michigan (24)	21	Rhode Island (12)	24
Connecticut (15)	23	Minnesota (46)	16	South Carolina (20)	22
Delaware (15)	23	Mississippi (37)	18	South Dakota (46)	16
D.C. (1)	89	Missouri (20)	22	Tennessee (24)	21
Florida (12)	24	Montana (42)	17	Texas (15)	23
Georgia (10)	25	Nebraska (33)	19	Utah (46)	16
Hawaii (12)	24	Nevada (15)	23	Vermont (42)	17
Idaho (30)	20	New Hampshire (33)	19	Virginia (7)	26
Illinois (5)	31	New Jersey (4)	34	Washington (46)	16
Indiana (37)	18	New Mexico (20)	22	West Virginia (51)	14
Iowa (42)	17	New York (2)	38	Wisconsin (15)	23
Kansas (20)	22	North Carolina (24)	21	Wyoming (7)	26

Source: U.S. Department of Justice, *Statistical Abstract of the United States,* 1993, Table 325

Table 11.3

Incarceration Rate
Adult inmates per 1,000 population, 1993

Alabama (6)	4.38	Kentucky (25)	2.65	North Dakota (51)	0.68
Alaska (5)	4.40	Louisiana (12)	3.78	Ohio (18)	3.55
Arizona (7)	4.34	Maine (48)	1.25	Oklahoma (9)	3.96
Arkansas (16)	3.60	Maryland (9)	3.96	Oregon (35)	2.14
California (13)	3.70	Massachusetts (44)	1.63	Pennsylvania (36)	2.12
Colorado (33)	2.17	Michigan (8)	4.02	Rhode Island (25)	2.65
Connecticut (17)	3.59	Minnesota (50)	0.89	South Carolina (3)	4.71
Delaware (2)	6.00	Mississippi (15)	3.62	South Dakota (32)	2.18
D.C. (1)	18.75	Missouri (22)	3.16	Tennessee (34)	2.16
Florida (13)	3.70	Montana (40)	1.86	Texas (19)	3.54
Georgia (11)	3.86	Nebraska (45)	1.61	Utah (45)	1.61
Hawaii (29)	2.43	Nevada (4)	4.47	Vermont (47)	1.54
Idaho (37)	2.06	New Hampshire (42)	1.65	Virginia (21)	3.24
Illinois (24)	2.83	New Jersey (27)	2.50	Washington (42)	1.65
Indiana (30)	2.33	New Mexico (38)	1.91	West Virginia (49)	1.03
Iowa (41)	1.67	New York (20)	3.50	Wisconsin (38)	1.91
Kansas (28)	2.47	North Carolina (23)	3.06	Wyoming (31)	2.31

Source: American Correctional Association, *1994 Directory of Juvenile and Adult Correctional Departments, Institutions, Agencies and Paroling Authorities*

Table 11.4

Drunk Driving Report Card
MADD's evaluation of states, 1993

Alabama	D+	Kentucky	C+	North Dakota	D
Alaska	C	Louisiana	C-	Ohio	B+
Arizona	B+	Maine	C	Oklahoma	C-
Arkansas	C+	Maryland	B	Oregon	B
California	B	Massachusetts	C-	Pennsylvania	B
Colorado	B	Michigan	C	Rhode Island	C
Connecticut	C	Minnesota	B	South Carolina	B-
Delaware	C	Mississippi	D-	South Dakota	C+
D.C.	C	Missouri	D+	Tennessee	C-
Florida	C+	Montana	C	Texas	C
Georgia	C	Nebraska	B-	Utah	B-
Hawaii	C+	Nevada	B-	Vermont	D+
Idaho	D+	New Hampshire	C	Virginia	C
Illinois	A-	New Jersey	B	Washington	C
Indiana	C	New Mexico	B+	West Virginia	C-
Iowa	C+	New York	B-	Wisconsin	C
Kansas	B-	North Carolina	B+	Wyoming	D

Source: Mothers Against Drunk Driving, 1993

Table 11.5
Firearm and Motor Vehicle Deaths
Ratio of firearm to motor vehicle deaths, 1991

Alabama (25)	0.76	Kentucky (29)	0.74	North Dakota (50)	0.46
Alaska (10)	0.96	Louisiana (2)	1.27	Ohio (22)	0.78
Arizona (17)	0.86	Maine (38)	0.63	Oklahoma (29)	0.74
Arkansas (25)	0.76	Maryland (8)	1.00	Oregon (31)	0.73
California (7)	1.01	Massachusetts (46)	0.50	Pennsylvania (25)	0.76
Colorado (31)	0.73	Michigan (9)	0.99	Rhode Island (40)	0.59
Connecticut (17)	0.86	Minnesota (40)	0.59	South Carolina (34)	0.69
Delaware (46)	0.50	Mississippi (25)	0.76	South Dakota (45)	0.51
D.C. (1)	5.21	Missouri (13)	0.92	Tennessee (17)	0.86
Florida (13)	0.92	Montana (20)	0.80	Texas (4)	1.15
Georgia (11)	0.94	Nebraska (43)	0.56	Utah (20)	0.80
Hawaii (51)	0.41	Nevada (3)	1.22	Vermont (15)	0.90
Idaho (42)	0.58	New Hampshire (44)	0.54	Virginia (6)	1.02
Illinois (11)	0.94	New Jersey (46)	0.50	Washington (33)	0.72
Indiana (34)	0.69	New Mexico (37)	0.67	West Virginia (36)	0.68
Iowa (49)	0.48	New York (5)	1.13	Wisconsin (39)	0.60
Kansas (22)	0.78	North Carolina (15)	0.90	Wyoming (24)	0.77

Source: Centers for Disease Control and Prevention, *MMWR*, Vol. 43, No. 3, Table 1

Table 12.1
Women in Poverty
Percent of women age 18 and older living in poverty, 1990

Alabama (6)	19.4	Kentucky (7)	19.0	North Dakota (17)	14.3
Alaska (47)	8.5	Louisiana (2)	23.6	Ohio (25)	12.6
Arizona (16)	14.6	Maine (27)	12.3	Oklahoma (9)	17.1
Arkansas (3)	19.8	Maryland (46)	8.8	Oregon (23)	12.7
California (35)	11.6	Massachusetts (45)	9.3	Pennsylvania (34)	11.7
Colorado (31)	11.9	Michigan (21)	13.3	Rhode Island (40)	10.9
Connecticut (51)	7.0	Minnesota (38)	11.0	South Carolina (12)	16.4
Delaware (44)	9.6	Mississippi (1)	25.2	South Dakota (14)	16.2
D.C. (11)	16.5	Missouri (19)	13.8	Tennessee (12)	16.4
Florida (23)	12.7	Montana (10)	16.8	Texas (8)	17.4
Georgia (15)	15.1	Nebraska (31)	11.9	Utah (27)	12.3
Hawaii (48)	8.2	Nevada (42)	10.7	Vermont (40)	10.9
Idaho (20)	13.6	New Hampshire (50)	7.4	Virginia (37)	11.2
Illinois (33)	11.8	New Jersey (49)	7.8	Washington (38)	11.0
Indiana (36)	11.5	New Mexico (4)	19.7	West Virginia (5)	19.6
Iowa (29)	12.2	New York (22)	12.8	Wisconsin (42)	10.7
Kansas (30)	12.1	North Carolina (18)	14.1	Wyoming (26)	12.4

Source: Population Reference Bureau, *What the 1990 Census Tells Us About Women*, Table 22.

Table 12.2
Income Disparity in Professional Occupations
Average income of women as a percentage of men's income, 1990

Alabama (47)	52.1	Kentucky (43)	54.4	North Dakota (51)	50.1
Alaska (1)	72.1	Louisiana (48)	52.0	Ohio (27)	58.3
Arizona (28)	58.2	Maine (3)	64.9	Oklahoma (45)	53.5
Arkansas (46)	52.2	Maryland (15)	60.7	Oregon (8)	62.8
California (7)	63.2	Massachusetts (4)	64.0	Pennsylvania (23)	59.4
Colorado (14)	61.2	Michigan (13)	61.3	Rhode Island (22)	59.5
Connecticut (12)	61.7	Minnesota (11)	62.0	South Carolina (38)	55.5
Delaware (19)	60.0	Mississippi (50)	50.2	South Dakota (17)	60.4
D.C. (2)	67.1	Missouri (32)	57.0	Tennessee (34)	56.2
Florida (41)	54.7	Montana (10)	62.4	Texas (40)	55.0
Georgia (36)	55.9	Nebraska (35)	56.1	Utah (31)	57.5
Hawaii (21)	59.6	Nevada (5)	63.5	Vermont (25)	58.9
Idaho (41)	54.7	New Hampshire (16)	60.5	Virginia (20)	59.7
Illinois (26)	58.4	New Jersey (24)	59.2	Washington (9)	62.6
Indiana (29)	58.1	New Mexico (18)	60.1	West Virginia (49)	51.1
Iowa (37)	55.6	New York (5)	63.5	Wisconsin (30)	58.0
Kansas (39)	55.4	North Carolina (33)	56.9	Wyoming (44)	54.0

Source: Population Reference Bureau, *What the 1990 Census Tells Us About Women*, Table 20

Table 12.3
Women in State Legislatures
Women as a percent of legislators, 1993

Alabama (49)	5.7	Kentucky (50)	4.3	North Dakota (34)	16.3
Alaska (21)	21.7	Louisiana (48)	6.9	Ohio (22)	21.2
Arizona (2)	35.6	Maine (6)	31.2	Oklahoma (47)	9.4
Arkansas (46)	9.6	Maryland (17)	23.4	Oregon (12)	26.7
California (18)	23.3	Massachusetts (20)	23.0	Pennsylvania (45)	9.9
Colorado (3)	34.0	Michigan (25)	19.6	Rhode Island (14)	24.7
Connecticut (13)	25.1	Minnesota (9)	27.4	South Carolina (40)	12.9
Delaware (38)	14.5	Mississippi (44)	10.9	South Dakota (24)	20.0
D.C. (51)	no data	Missouri (27)	19.3	Tennessee (42)	12.1
Florida (31)	17.5	Montana (27)	19.3	Texas (36)	16.0
Georgia (32)	17.4	Nebraska (23)	20.4	Utah (39)	13.5
Hawaii (16)	23.7	Nevada (11)	27.0	Vermont (4)	33.9
Idaho (7)	30.5	New Hampshire (5)	33.5	Virginia (43)	11.4
Illinois (19)	23.2	New Jersey (41)	12.5	Washington (1)	39.5
Indiana (27)	19.3	New Mexico (25)	19.6	West Virginia (33)	16.4
Iowa (37)	14.7	New York (35)	16.1	Wisconsin (10)	27.3
Kansas (8)	28.5	North Carolina (30)	18.2	Wyoming (15)	24.4

Source: Congressional Quarterly, *State Fact Finder*, 1993, p. 293

Table 12.4
Teen Birth Rate
Births per 1,000 females age 15–19, 1991

Alabama (13)	74	Kentucky (17)	69	North Dakota (50)	36
Alaska (7)	78	Louisiana (8)	76	Ohio (21)	61
Arizona (3)	81	Maine (41)	44	Oklahoma (15)	72
Arkansas (4)	80	Maryland (30)	54	Oregon (28)	55
California (10)	75	Massachusetts (48)	38	Pennsylvania (36)	47
Colorado (26)	58	Michigan (24)	59	Rhode Island (40)	45
Connecticut (46)	40	Minnesota (29)	37	South Carolina (14)	73
Delaware (21)	61	Mississippi (2)	86	South Dakota (36)	47
D.C. (1)	114	Missouri (19)	65	Tennessee (10)	75
Florida (17)	69	Montana (36)	47	Texas (6)	79
Georgia (8)	76	Nebraska (44)	42	Utah (35)	48
Hawaii (24)	59	Nevada (10)	75	Vermont (47)	39
Idaho (30)	54	New Hampshire (51)	33	Virginia (34)	53
Illinois (19)	65	New Jersey (44)	42	Washington (30)	54
Indiana (23)	60	New Mexico (4)	80	West Virginia (26)	58
Iowa (43)	43	New York (39)	46	Wisconsin (41)	44
Kansas (28)	55	North Carolina (16)	71	Wyoming (30)	54

Source: Child Trends, Inc., *Facts at a Glance*, January 1994, Table 2

Table 12.5

Non-marital Births to Teens

Mothers under age 20: percent non-marital births, 1991

State	%	State	%	State	%
Alabama (42)	65	Kentucky (48)	53	North Dakota (15)	75
Alaska (41)	67	Louisiana (15)	75	Ohio (13)	76
Arizona (15)	75	Maine (15)	75	Oklahoma (45)	58
Arkansas (44)	60	Maryland (12)	79	Oregon (35)	69
California (37)	68	Massachusetts (2)	86	Pennsylvania (6)	83
Colorado (37)	68	Michigan (35)	69	Rhode Island (3)	85
Connecticut (4)	84	Minnesota (7)	82	South Carolina (25)	73
Delaware (8)	81	Mississippi (15)	75	South Dakota (15)	75
D.C. (1)	95	Missouri (27)	72	Tennessee (43)	64
Florida (25)	73	Montana (27)	72	Texas (51)	39
Georgia (27)	72	Nebraska (21)	74	Utah (49)	50
Hawaii (21)	74	Nevada (37)	68	Vermont (27)	72
Idaho (49)	50	New Hampshire (13)	76	Virginia (32)	71
Illinois (8)	81	New Jersey (4)	84	Washington (34)	70
Indiana (27)	72	New Mexico (21)	74	West Virginia (47)	56
Iowa (21)	74	New York (8)	81	Wisconsin (8)	81
Kansas (37)	68	North Carolina (32)	71	Wyoming (45)	58

Source: Child Trends, Inc., *Facts at a Glance*, January 1994, Table 1

Table 12.6

Abortion

Abortions per 1,000 women age 15–44, 1992

State	Rate	State	Rate	State	Rate
Alabama (27)	18.2	Kentucky (44)	11.4	North Dakota (46)	10.7
Alaska (30)	16.5	Louisiana (39)	13.4	Ohio (25)	19.5
Arizona (16)	24.1	Maine (34)	14.7	Oklahoma (40)	12.5
Arkansas (38)	13.5	Maryland (12)	26.4	Oregon (18)	23.9
California (5)	42.1	Massachusetts (10)	28.4	Pennsylvania (26)	18.6
Colorado (19)	23.6	Michigan (15)	25.2	Rhode Island (8)	30.0
Connecticut (13)	26.2	Minnesota (33)	15.6	South Carolina (36)	14.2
Delaware (6)	35.2	Mississippi (41)	12.4	South Dakota (50)	6.8
D.C. (1)	138.4	Missouri (43)	11.6	Tennessee (31)	16.2
Florida (8)	30.0	Montana (27)	18.2	Texas (20)	23.1
Georgia (17)	24.0	Nebraska (32)	15.7	Utah (47)	9.3
Hawaii (3)	46.0	Nevada (4)	44.2	Vermont (24)	21.2
Idaho (49)	7.2	New Hampshire (35)	14.6	Virginia (21)	22.7
Illinois (14)	25.4	New Jersey (7)	31.0	Washington (11)	27.7
Indiana (42)	12.0	New Mexico (29)	17.7	West Virginia (48)	7.7
Iowa (44)	11.4	New York (2)	46.2	Wisconsin (37)	13.6
Kansas (22)	22.4	North Carolina (22)	22.4	Wyoming (51)	4.3

Source: Reproduced with the permission of The Alan Guttmacher Institute from Stanley K. Henshaw and Jennifer Van Vort, "Abortion Services in the United States, 1991 and 1992," *Family Planning Perspectives*, Vol. 26, No. 3, May/June 1994

Table 13.1

Children
Percent of population under age 18, 1992

Alabama (26)	26.0	Kentucky (31)	25.7	North Dakota (14)	27.0
Alaska (2)	31.6	Louisiana (6)	28.8	Ohio (32)	25.6
Arizona (10)	27.4	Maine (39)	24.8	Oklahoma (17)	26.7
Arkansas (22)	26.2	Maryland (37)	25.0	Oregon (30)	25.8
California (12)	27.3	Massachusetts (49)	23.0	Pennsylvania (46)	23.7
Colorado (22)	26.2	Michigan (19)	26.6	Rhode Island (48)	23.2
Connecticut (47)	23.5	Minnesota (15)	26.9	South Carolina (22)	26.2
Delaware (37)	25.0	Mississippi (7)	28.7	South Dakota (7)	28.7
D.C. (51)	19.8	Missouri (26)	26.0	Tennessee (39)	24.8
Florida (49)	23.0	Montana (10)	27.4	Texas (7)	28.7
Georgia (17)	26.7	Nebraska (12)	27.3	Utah (1)	36.0
Hawaii (34)	25.3	Nevada (33)	25.4	Vermont (35)	25.2
Idaho (3)	30.4	New Hampshire (35)	25.2	Virginia (41)	24.5
Illinois (26)	26.0	New Jersey (45)	24.0	Washington (21)	26.4
Indiana (29)	25.9	New Mexico (4)	29.6	West Virginia (44)	24.2
Iowa (25)	26.1	New York (42)	24.4	Wisconsin (19)	26.6
Kansas (15)	26.9	North Carolina (43)	24.3	Wyoming (5)	29.5

Source: U.S. Bureau of the Census, *State Population Estimates, by Age and Sex: 1980 to 1992*, 1993, Table 10

Table 13.2

The Changing Child Population
Change in percent of population under age 18, 1980–90

Alabama (38)	-8.8	Kentucky (48)	-11.7	North Dakota (36)	-8.0
Alaska (2)	31.3	Louisiana (35)	-7.6	Ohio (43)	-9.4
Arizona (3)	23.7	Maine (27)	-3.8	Oklahoma (21)	-2.1
Arkansas (34)	-7.5	Maryland (19)	-0.5	Oregon (17)	0.2
California (5)	21.1	Massachusetts (42)	-9.3	Pennsylvania (46)	-10.4
Colorado (11)	6.3	Michigan (47)	-10.5	Rhode Island (32)	-6.9
Connecticut (39)	-8.9	Minnesota (18)	-0.3	South Carolina (21)	-2.1
Delaware (23)	-2.2	Mississippi (37)	-8.2	South Dakota (25)	-3.2
D.C. (50)	-18.7	Missouri (26)	-3.5	Tennessee (31)	-6.4
Florida (4)	21.4	Montana (28)	-3.9	Texas (7)	12.3
Georgia (12)	5.1	Nebraska (29)	-4.0	Utah (6)	16.3
Hawaii (15)	1.7	Nevada (1)	36.6	Vermont (20)	-1.2
Idaho (16)	0.4	New Hampshire (9)	8.2	Virginia (13)	2.0
Illinois (40)	-9.1	New Jersey (44)	-9.7	Washington (8)	10.5
Indiana (45)	-9.9	New Mexico (10)	6.8	West Virginia (51)	-20.6
Iowa (49)	-12.9	New York (41)	-9.2	Wisconsin (30)	-4.9
Kansas (13)	2.0	North Carolina (24)	-3.0	Wyoming (33)	-7.2

Source: Center for Study of Social Policy, *The Challenge of Change*, 1992, Table 2

Table 13.3
Hungry Children
Percent of children who are hungry, 1991

Alabama (8)	24.6	Kentucky (7)	25.1	North Dakota (23)	17.3
Alaska (48)	11.2	Louisiana (2)	31.9	Ohio (21)	18.0
Arizona (10)	22.2	Maine (38)	13.5	Oklahoma (11)	21.9
Arkansas (5)	25.6	Maryland (48)	11.2	Oregon (28)	15.6
California (20)	18.2	Massachusetts (40)	13.2	Pennsylvania (27)	15.8
Colorado (29)	15.4	Michigan (19)	18.6	Rhode Island (36)	13.8
Connecticut (50)	10.6	Minnesota (42)	12.7	South Carolina (12)	21.3
Delaware (44)	12.0	Mississippi (1)	34.3	South Dakota (14)	20.6
D.C. (5)	25.6	Missouri (22)	17.8	Tennessee (13)	21.2
Florida (18)	18.7	Montana (15)	20.4	Texas (8)	24.6
Georgia (16)	20.3	Nebraska (36)	13.8	Utah (43)	12.5
Hawaii (46)	11.4	Nevada (41)	13.1	Vermont (45)	11.8
Idaho (26)	16.2	New Hampshire (51)	7.2	Virginia (39)	13.3
Illinois (25)	17.2	New Jersey (47)	11.3	Washington (32)	14.3
Indiana (34)	14.2	New Mexico (3)	28.2	West Virginia (4)	26.5
Iowa (32)	14.3	New York (17)	19.2	Wisconsin (30)	14.9
Kansas (34)	14.2	North Carolina (23)	17.3	Wyoming (31)	14.4

Source: Tufts University Center on Hunger, Poverty, and Nutrition Policy, 1993

Table 13.4
Children in Mother-Headed Households
Percent of children living with their mothers, 1990

Alabama (8)	18.4	Kentucky (26)	15.3	North Dakota (48)	11.5
Alaska (41)	13.0	Louisiana (3)	21.8	Ohio (15)	16.9
Arizona (19)	16.0	Maine (36)	14.4	Oklahoma (24)	15.6
Arkansas (18)	16.5	Maryland (15)	16.9	Oregon (35)	14.7
California (28)	15.2	Massachusetts (10)	17.7	Pennsylvania (33)	14.8
Colorado (23)	15.8	Michigan (6)	19.0	Rhode Island (10)	17.7
Connecticut (17)	16.7	Minnesota (43)	12.8	South Carolina (7)	18.5
Delaware (25)	15.5	Mississippi (2)	22.2	South Dakota (45)	12.5
D.C. (1)	33.8	Missouri (19)	16.0	Tennessee (12)	17.6
Florida (9)	17.9	Montana (38)	13.9	Texas (26)	15.3
Georgia (5)	19.2	Nebraska (41)	13.0	Utah (51)	10.1
Hawaii (50)	10.8	Nevada (19)	16.0	Vermont (37)	14.1
Idaho (49)	10.9	New Hampshire (47)	11.6	Virginia (33)	14.8
Illinois (14)	17.0	New Jersey (29)	15.1	Washington (30)	15.0
Indiana (32)	14.9	New Mexico (22)	15.9	West Virginia (39)	13.6
Iowa (45)	12.5	New York (4)	19.4	Wisconsin (30)	15.0
Kansas (40)	13.5	North Carolina (13)	17.3	Wyoming (44)	12.7

Source: Center for the Study of Social Policy, *The Challenge of Change*, 1992, Table 11

Table 13.5

Children Who Do Not Speak English at Home

Percent of children age 5–17 who do not speak English, 1990

Alabama (46)	3.0	Kentucky (49)	2.8	North Dakota (50)	2.7
Alaska (15)	9.5	Louisiana (24)	5.5	Ohio (30)	5.0
Arizona (5)	22.8	Maine (35)	4.4	Oklahoma (33)	4.6
Arkansas (46)	3.0	Maryland (17)	8.4	Oregon (19)	7.0
California (1)	35.0	Massachusetts (9)	15.3	Pennsylvania (21)	6.8
Colorado (17)	8.4	Michigan (27)	5.4	Rhode Island (8)	16.3
Connecticut (10)	14.9	Minnesota (29)	5.1	South Carolina (43)	3.5
Delaware (22)	6.5	Mississippi (46)	3.0	South Dakota (37)	4.1
D.C. (13)	11.8	Missouri (41)	3.6	Tennessee (44)	3.2
Florida (7)	17.8	Montana (38)	3.9	Texas (3)	28.2
Georgia (34)	4.5	Nebraska (41)	3.6	Utah (24)	5.5
Hawaii (10)	14.9	Nevada (13)	11.8	Vermont (45)	3.1
Idaho (23)	5.8	New Hampshire (35)	4.4	Virginia (19)	7.0
Illinois (12)	14.4	New Jersey (6)	19.4	Washington (16)	8.8
Indiana (31)	4.9	New Mexico (2)	29.5	West Virginia (50)	2.7
Iowa (38)	3.9	New York (4)	23.3	Wisconsin (24)	5.5
Kansas (28)	5.3	North Carolina (32)	4.7	Wyoming (38)	3.9

Source: Center for the Study of Social Policy, *The Challenge of Change*, 1992, Table 34

Table 13.6

Child Well-Being

Casey Foundation rank, 1994

Alabama	45	Kentucky	36	North Dakota	2
Alaska	22	Louisiana	49	Ohio	25
Arizona	37	Maine	9	Oklahoma	35
Arkansas	42	Maryland	32	Oregon	16
California	33	Massachusetts	10	Pennsylvania	23
Colorado	26	Michigan	38	Rhode Island	13
				South Carolina	44
Connecticut	8	Minnesota	4		
Delaware	29	Mississippi	50	South Dakota	19
D.C.	51	Missouri	34	Tennessee	43
Florida	48	Montana	17	Texas	28
Georgia	47	Nebraska	5	Utah	7
Hawaii	18	Nevada	30	Vermont	3
Idaho	15	New Hampshire	1	Virginia	24
Illinois	39	New Jersey	21	Washington	14
Indiana	31	New Mexico	46	West Virginia	27
Iowa	6	New York	41	Wisconsin	11
Kansas	20	North Carolina	40	Wyoming	12

Source: Annie E. Casey Foundation, *Kids Count Data Book*, 1994

Table 14.1
Senior Citizens
Percent of population 65 and older, 1990

Alabama (23)	12.9	Kentucky (25)	12.7	North Dakota (8)	14.3
Alaska (51)	4.1	Louisiana (40)	11.1	Ohio (22)	13.0
Arizona (20)	13.1	Maine (17)	13.3	Oklahoma (15)	13.5
Arkansas (6)	14.9	Maryland (41)	10.8	Oregon (11)	13.8
California (45)	10.5	Massachusetts (13)	13.6	Pennsylvania (2)	15.4
Colorado (49)	10.0	Michigan (34)	11.9	Rhode Island (4)	15.0
Connecticut (13)	13.6	Minnesota (29)	12.5	South Carolina (37)	11.4
Delaware (31)	12.1	Mississippi (29)	12.5	South Dakota (7)	14.7
D.C. (24)	12.8	Missouri (10)	14.0	Tennessee (25)	12.7
Florida (1)	18.3	Montana (17)	13.3	Texas (47)	10.1
Georgia (47)	10.1	Nebraska (9)	14.1	Utah (50)	8.7
Hawaii (38)	11.3	Nevada (44)	10.6	Vermont (35)	11.8
Idaho (33)	12.0	New Hampshire (38)	11.3	Virginia (43)	10.7
Illinois (27)	12.6	New Jersey (16)	13.4	Washington (35)	11.8
Indiana (27)	12.6	New Mexico (41)	10.8	West Virginia (4)	15.0
Iowa (3)	15.3	New York (20)	13.1	Wisconsin (17)	13.3
Kansas (11)	13.8	North Carolina (31)	12.1	Wyoming (46)	10.4

Source: U.S. Bureau of the Census, *Sixty-Five Plus in America*, 1993, Table 5-2

Table 14.2
Projected Growth in Elderly Population
Percent change in population 65 and older, 1990–2010

Alabama (18)	23.4	Kentucky (30)	12.6	North Dakota (49)	-10.0
Alaska (1)	80.5	Louisiana (29)	14.5	Ohio (37)	7.5
Arizona (3)	75.4	Maine (26)	17.0	Oklahoma (42)	5.2
Arkansas (24)	20.4	Maryland (12)	46.3	Oregon (41)	5.4
California (8)	49.3	Massachusetts (35)	9.1	Pennsylvania (46)	0.9
Colorado (17)	31.4	Michigan (38)	6.8	Rhode Island (44)	3.9
Connecticut (28)	14.7	Minnesota (25)	17.6	South Carolina (13)	41.7
Delaware (11)	47.6	Mississippi (20)	23.2	South Dakota (45)	1.7
D.C. (31)	11.1	Missouri (27)	16.9	Tennessee (16)	33.9
Florida (4)	65.3	Montana (47)	-3.2	Texas (15)	37.0
Georgia (5)	61.1	Nebraska (43)	4.2	Utah (23)	21.1
Hawaii (2)	79.7	Nevada (8)	49.3	Vermont (22)	21.9
Idaho (36)	8.6	New Hampshire (6)	51.2	Virginia (10)	48.2
Illinois (39)	6.6	New Jersey (21)	22.0	Washington (18)	23.4
Indiana (33)	9.8	New Mexico (14)	40.0	West Virginia (50)	-10.5
Iowa (48)	-8.2	New York (34)	9.3	Wisconsin (40)	6.0
Kansas (31)	11.1	North Carolina (7)	50.4	Wyoming (51)	-17.4

Source: U.S. Bureau of the Census, *Sixty-Five Plus in America*, 1993, Table 5-4

Table 14.3
AARP Membership
Membership as a percent of population 50 and older, 1993

Alabama (51)	35.65	Kentucky (48)	41.09	North Dakota (46)	41.73
Alaska (11)	55.86	Louisiana (38)	46.11	Ohio (17)	53.45
Arizona (13)	54.58	Maine (20)	53.04	Oklahoma (37)	46.71
Arkansas (41)	45.90	Maryland (9)	56.67	Oregon (15)	54.20
California (44)	43.21	Massachusetts (12)	54.70	Pennsylvania (21)	52.61
Colorado (8)	57.56	Michigan (5)	60.51	Rhode Island (40)	45.91
Connecticut (4)	62.18	Minnesota (31)	49.29	South Carolina (39)	45.96
Delaware (2)	66.44	Mississippi (49)	40.78	South Dakota (47)	41.60
D.C. (10)	56.58	Missouri (16)	53.64	Tennessee (45)	42.10
Florida (23)	52.53	Montana (26)	51.82	Texas (28)	50.41
Georgia (34)	47.43	Nebraska (43)	45.00	Utah (42)	45.05
Hawaii (50)	35.85	Nevada (19)	53.29	Vermont (3)	64.91
Idaho (29)	50.06	New Hampshire (1)	67.28	Virginia (26)	51.82
Illinois (18)	53.40	New Jersey (7)	58.33	Washington (25)	52.27
Indiana (30)	49.88	New Mexico (33)	48.02	West Virginia (32)	48.76
Iowa (36)	46.87	New York (24)	52.39	Wisconsin (21)	52.61
Kansas (14)	54.35	North Carolina (35)	47.01	Wyoming (6)	60.40

Source: ©1993 American Association of Retired Persons, reprinted with permission

Table 14.4
Retirement Facilities
Number of facilities, 1993

Alabama (31)	188	Kentucky (25)	242	North Dakota (19)	311
Alaska (50)	35	Louisiana (41)	114	Ohio (9)	560
Arizona (5)	786	Maine (14)	419	Oklahoma (26)	221*
Arkansas (45)	102	Maryland (38)	133	Oregon (7)	765
California (1)	4,387	Massachusetts (16)	388	Pennsylvania (2)	2,342
Colorado (23)	248	Michigan (13)	479	Rhode Island (22)	258
Connecticut (24)	244	Minnesota (8) 622		South Carolina (28)	212
Delaware (47)	62	Mississippi (42)	112	South Dakota (34)	168
D.C. (49)	43	Missouri (6)	782	Tennessee (18)	350
Florida (3)	1,365	Montana (48)	51	Texas (17)	377
Georgia (12)	481	Nebraska (36)	138	Utah (44)	106
Hawaii (43)	109	Nevada (32)	176	Vermont (33)	175
Idaho (40)	116	New Hampshire (39)	126	Virginia (10)	517
Illinois (15)	404	New Jersey (11)	507	Washington (20)	298
Indiana (30)	200	New Mexico (36)	138	West Virginia (51)	31
Iowa (21)	285	New York (4)	1,079	Wisconsin (29)	203
Kansas (34)	168	North Carolina (27)	216	Wyoming (46)	88

Source: *Directory of Retirement Facilities, 1994*, HCIA, Inc., 1993
*1992 data

Table 14.5

Nursing Home Residents
Percent of population, 1990

Alabama (31)	0.6	Kentucky (20)	0.8	North Dakota (1)	1.3
Alaska (51)	0.2	Louisiana (20)	0.8	Ohio (12)	0.9
Arizona (46)	0.4	Maine (20)	0.8	Oklahoma (12)	0.9
Arkansas (12)	0.9	Maryland (31)	0.6	Oregon (31)	0.6
California (44)	0.5	Massachusetts (12)	0.9	Pennsylvania (12)	0.9
Colorado (31)	0.6	Michigan (31)	0.6	Rhode Island (8)	1.0
Connecticut (12)	0.9	Minnesota (6)	1.1	South Carolina (44)	0.5
Delaware (24)	0.7	Mississippi (31)	0.6	South Dakota (1)	1.3
D.C. (4)	1.2	Missouri (8)	1.0	Tennessee (24)	0.7
Florida (31)	0.6	Montana (8)	1.0	Texas (31)	0.6
Georgia (31)	0.6	Nebraska (4)	1.2	Utah (46)	0.4
Hawaii (49)	0.3	Nevada (49)	0.3	Vermont (12)	0.9
Idaho (31)	0.6	New Hampshire (24)	0.7	Virginia (31)	0.6
Illinois (20)	0.8	New Jersey (31)	0.6	Washington (24)	0.7
Indiana (12)	0.9	New Mexico (46)	0.4	West Virginia (24)	0.7
Iowa (1)	1.3	New York (24)	0.7	Wisconsin (8)	1.0
Kansas (6)	1.1	North Carolina (24)	0.7	Wyoming (31)	0.6

Source: U.S. Bureau of the Census, *Sixty-Five Plus in America*, 1993, Table 6-6

Table 15.1
Leading Religious Denominations, 1990

(No table: generalized from *Major Denominational Families by Counties of the United States: 1990*, published by Glenmary Research Center, Atlanta, Georgia)

Table 15.2
Population with No Religious Identification
Percent of population, 1990

Alabama (44)	3.9	Kentucky (25)	6.5	North Dakota (49)	1.6
Alaska	no data	Louisiana (46)	2.9	Ohio (17)	7.4
Arizona (6)	12.2	Maine (11)	10.0	Oklahoma (25)	6.5
Arkansas (35)	5.8	Maryland (20)	7.2	Oregon (1)	17.2
California (5)	13.0	Massachusetts (19)	7.3	Pennsylvania (40)	4.9
Colorado (8)	11.4	Michigan (13)	8.7	Rhode Island (32)	6.0
Connecticut (35)	5.8	Minnesota (38)	5.6	South Carolina (45)	3.2
Delaware (20)	7.2	Mississippi (47)	2.8	South Dakota (48)	2.5
D.C. (30)	6.3	Missouri (25)	6.5	Tennessee (32)	6.0
Florida (20)	7.2	Montana (10)	10.2	Texas (40)	4.9
Georgia (43)	4.6	Nebraska (23)	7.0	Utah (16)	7.8
Hawaii	no data	Nevada (4)	13.2	Vermont (8)	11.4
Idaho (7)	11.9	New Hampshire (14)	8.1	Virginia (28)	6.4
Illinois (23)	7.0	New Jersey (39)	5.5	Washington (2)	14.0
Indiana (17)	7.4	New Mexico (11)	10.0	West Virginia (15)	8.0
Iowa (34)	5.9	New York (28)	6.4	Wisconsin (31)	6.1
Kansas (37)	5.7	North Carolina (42)	4.8	Wyoming (3)	13.5

Source: *The National Survey of Religious Identification, 1989–90*, March 1991

287

Table 15.3
Political Affiliation
Party voting in presidential elections, 1960–92

	ELECTORAL VOTES 1992	1960	1964	1968	1972	1976	1980	1984	1988	1992
AL	9	O	R	O	R	D	R	R	R	R
AK	3	R	D	R	R	R	R	R	R	R
AZ	8	R	R	R	R	R	R	R	R	R
AR	6	D	D	D	R	D	R	R	R	D
CA	54	R	D	R	R	R	R	R	R	D
CO	8	R	D	R	R	R	R	R	R	D
CT	8	D	D	D	R	R	R	R	R	D
DE	3	D	D	R	R	D	R	R	R	D
DC	3	N	D	D	D	D	D	D	D	D
FL	25	R	D	R	R	D	R	R	R	R
GA	13	D	R	O	R	D	D	R	R	D
HI	4	D	D	D	R	D	D	R	D	D
ID	4	R	D	R	R	R	R	R	R	R
IL	22	D	D	R	R	R	R	R	R	D
IN	12	R	D	R	R	R	R	R	R	R
IA	7	R	D	R	R	R	R	R	D	D
KS	6	R	D	R	R	R	R	R	R	R
KY	8	R	D	R	R	D	R	R	R	D
LA	9	D	R	O	R	D	R	R	R	D
ME	4	R	D	D	R	R	R	R	R	D
MD	10	D	D	D	R	D	D	R	R	D
MA	12	D	D	D	D	D	R	R	D	D
MI	18	D	R	D	R	R	R	R	R	D
MN	10	D	D	D	R	D	D	D	D	D
MS	7	O	D	O	R	D	R	R	R	R
MO	11	D	D	R	R	D	R	R	R	D
MT	3	R	D	R	R	R	R	R	R	D
NE	5	R	D	R	R	R	R	R	R	R
NV	4	D	D	R	R	R	R	R	R	D
NH	4	R	D	R	R	R	R	R	R	D
NJ	15	D	D	R	R	R	R	R	R	D
NM	5	D	D	R	R	R	R	R	R	D
NY	33	D	D	D	R	D	R	R	D	D
NC	14	D	D	R	R	D	R	R	R	R
ND	3	R	D	R	R	R	R	R	R	R
OH	21	R	D	R	R	D	R	R	R	D
OK	8	R	D	R	R	R	R	R	R	R
OR	7	R	D	R	R	R	R	R	D	D
PA	23	D	D	D	R	D	R	R	R	D
RI	4	D	D	D	R	D	D	R	D	D
SC	8	D	R	R	R	D	R	R	R	R
SD	3	R	D	R	R	R	R	R	R	R
TN	11	R	D	R	R	D	R	R	R	D
TX	32	D	D	D	R	D	R	R	R	R
UT	5	R	D	R	R	R	R	R	R	R
VT	3	R	D	R	R	R	R	R	R	D
VA	13	R	D	R	R	R	R	R	R	R
WA	11	R	D	D	R	R	R	R	D	D
WV	5	D	D	D	R	D	D	R	D	D
WI	11	R	D	R	R	D	R	R	D	D
WY	3	R	D	R	R	R	R	R	R	R

D - voted Democrat
O - Majority of electoral vote awarded to minority party candidates
N - D.C. residents did not vote in federal elections in 1960.
R - voted Republican

Source: Congressional Quarterly, *America Votes 20*, 1993

Table 15.4
Voter Turnout: 1992 Presidential Election
Percent of voting age population who voted

Alabama (29)	55.2	Kentucky (35)	53.7	North Dakota (6)	67.3
Alaska (9)	65.4	Louisiana (24)	59.8	Ohio (21)	60.6
Arizona (33)	54.1	Maine (1)	72.0	Oklahoma (25)	59.7
Arkansas (34)	53.8	Maryland (36)	53.4	Oregon (8)	65.7
California (47)	49.1	Massachusetts (22)	60.2	Pennsylvania (32)	54.3
Colorado (17)	62.7	Michigan (20)	61.7	Rhode Island (27)	58.4
Connecticut (13)	63.8	Minnesota (2)	71.6	South Carolina (50)	45.0
Delaware (29)	55.2	Mississippi (37)	52.8	South Dakota (7)	67.0
D.C. (46)	49.6	Missouri (19)	62.0	Tennessee (39)	52.4
Florida (43)	50.2	Montana (3)	70.1	Texas (47)	49.1
Georgia (49)	46.9	Nebraska (14)	63.2	Utah (12)	65.1
Hawaii (51)	41.9	Nevada (45)	50.0	Vermont (5)	67.5
Idaho (11)	65.2	New Hampshire (15)	63.1	Virginia (37)	52.8
Illinois (26)	58.9	New Jersey (28)	56.3	Washington (23)	59.9
Indiana (29)	55.2	New Mexico (40)	51.6	West Virginia (42)	50.6
Iowa (10)	65.3	New York (41)	50.9	Wisconsin (4)	69.0
Kansas (16)	63.0	North Carolina (44)	50.1	Wyoming (18)	62.3

Source: Congressional Quarterly, *America Votes 20*, 1993

Table 16.1
Composite Ranking
Rankings of states on 17 indicators of social well-being

	MAP 2.3	2.5	4.1	4.2	4.4	6.9
Alabama (49)	49	43	45	41	45	31
Alaska (26)	24	40	2	45	16	28
Arizona (35)	24	44	25	22	32	47
Arkansas (45)	42	48	49	22	44	18
California (30)	10	16	9	50	37	21
Colorado (13)	13	33	15	12	21	46
Connecticut (2)	15	2	1	22	3	8
Delaware (28)	41	22	11	13	1	12
D.C. (43)	51	19	28	49	48	1
Florida (47)	34	38	37	32	35	42
Georgia (43)	46	37	34	18	40	35
Hawaii (1)	5	16	3	5	6	7
Idaho (22)	20	40	39	21	33	43
Illinois (29)	43	10	13	38	30	9
Indiana (31)	38		36	13	26	24
Iowa (11)	17	12	31	4	13	19
Kansas (9)	22	26	24	9	17	23
Kentucky (40)	29	42	47	22	46	31
Louisiana (51)	40		46	38	50	30
Maine (18)	2	21	30	48	26	40
Maryland (16)	32	6	6	22	12	5
Massachusetts (11)	8	1	8	31	15	3
Michigan (32)	47	15	17	32	28	21
Minnesota (4)	11	6	21	11	24	11
Mississippi (50)	50	33	51	27	51	24
Missouri (37)	33	22	35	28	33	37
Montana (24)	23	26	44	19	37	50
Nebraska (3)	7	13	29	1	7	19
Nevada (36)	5	49	12	36	22	51
New Hampshire (5)	1	25	5	30	2	16
New Jersey (15)	27	4	4	38	4	2
New Mexico (42)	21	38	41	41	49	48
New York (32)	24	2	16	46	35	5
North Carolina (38)	45	29	38	8	31	24
North Dakota (7)	17	6	40	6	25	14
Ohio (23)	29	22	23	29	23	10
Oklahoma (39)	36	47	43	19	41	39
Oregon (21)	14	29	22	36	19	41
Pennsylvania (27)	27	4	26	32	17	14
Rhode Island (19)	19	6	18	46	7	3
South Carolina (48)	47	18	33	41	43	16
South Dakota (25)	43	13	42	2	28	35
Tennessee (46)	38	45	48	17	39	34
Texas (34)	16	33	32	32	42	29
Utah (10)	3	29	20	3	10	44
Vermont (6)	8	26	19	15	19	44
Virginia (19)	37	20	7	9	10	27
Washington (13)	3	36	10	41	5	37
West Virginia (41)	34	32	50	51	47	33
Wisconsin (8)	12	10	14	7	7	12
Wyoming (17)	31	46	27	15	13	49

290

	MAP 7.3	7.4	8.2	9.3	10.4	10.5
Alabama (49)	41	43	16	42	46	23
Alaska (26)	34	41	41	29	12	12
Arizona (35)	38	16	29	50	20	9
Arkansas (45)	42	39	45	33	50	11
California (30)	44	24	3	48	13	24
Colorado (13)	26	8	27	20	2	29
Connecticut (2)	3	4	18	16	4	44
Delaware (28)	28	4	41	24	33	48
D.C. (43)	51	50	10	46	1	1
Florida (47)	43	14	35	49	32	13
Georgia (43)	39	38	13	47	27	21
Hawaii (1)	1	1	5	7	6	4
Idaho (22)	40	42	9	24	39	5
Illinois (29)	21	20	28	27	14	38
Indiana (31)	19	21	34	33	48	33
Iowa (11)	8	23	7	3	43	30
Kansas (9)	16	11		13	10	17
Kentucky (40)	31	34	48	44	47	14
Louisiana (51)	48	48	32	40	36	20
Maine (18)	17	13	43	11	31	40
Maryland (16)	25	2	13	29	11	37
Massachusetts (11)	10	14	20	12	3	49
Michigan (32)	9	27	46	22	44	43
Minnesota (4)	6	6	26	2	21	36
Mississippi (50)	45	51	32	38	49	32
Missouri (37)	29	33	38	33	34	31
Montana (24)	23	37	7	10	28	18
Nebraska (3)	5	30	16	5	19	22
Nevada (36)	45	24		51	41	7
New Hampshire (5)	15	2	30	18	7	47
New Jersey (15)	18	6	18	19	8	46
New Mexico (42)	49	44	2	36	24	10
New York (32)	27	34	23	21	16	39
North Carolina (38)	33	36	31	40	38	2
North Dakota (7)	2	40	4	1	21	25
Ohio (23)	12	18	23	15	36	41
Oklahoma (39)	47	28	37	24	30	8
Oregon (21)	30	17	6	38	15	35
Pennsylvania (27)	6	9	40	17	39	50
Rhode Island (19)	11	31	36	32	18	42
South Carolina (48)	36	47	21	36	42	34
South Dakota (25)	24	49	21	8	35	27
Tennessee (46)	31	32	47	45	45	15
Texas (34)	50	24	15	43	25	3
Utah (10)	19	21	1	13	21	19
Vermont (6)	13	10	10	9	4	51
Virginia (19)	37	12	10	22	17	45
Washington (13)	14	19	25	27	9	26
West Virginia (41)	35	45	39	29	51	16
Wisconsin (8)	4	29	44	6	28	28
Wyoming (17)	22	46		4	26	6

Table 16.1 (cont.)

	MAP 11.1	12.3	12.5	13.6	15.4	TOTAL	AVERAGE
Alabama (49)	28	49	10	45	29	626	36.8
Alaska (26)	31	21	11	22	9	418	24.6
Arizona (35)	48	2	32	37	33	508	29.9
Arkansas (45)	21	46	8	42	34	594	34.9
California (30)	47	18	11	33	47	455	26.8
Colorado (13)	39	3	11	26	17	348	20.5
Connecticut (2)	24	13	47	8	13	245	14.4
Delaware (28)	22	38	41	29	29	437	25.7
D.C. (43)	51		51	51	46	554	34.6
Florida (47)	50	31	26	48	43	602	35.4
Georgia (43)	44	32	21	47	49	588	34.6
Hawaii (1)	40	16	28	18	51	219	12.9
Idaho (22)	10	7	2	15	11	400	23.5
Illinois (29)	34	19	41	39	26	450	26.5
Indiana (31)	20	27	21	31	29	453	28.3
Iowa (11)	9	37	28	6	10	300	17.6
Kansas (9)	29	8	11	20	16	272	17.0
Kentucky (40)	5	50	4	36	35	565	33.2
Louisiana (51)	46	48	32	49	24	627	39.2
Maine (18)	8	6	32	9	1	378	22.2
Maryland (16)	43	17	40	32	36	368	21.6
Massachusetts (11)	23	20	50	10	22	299	17.6
Michigan (32)	32	25	16	38	20	482	28.4
Minnesota (4)	17	9	45	4	2	258	15.2
Mississippi (50)	11	44	32	50	37	657	38.6
Missouri (37)	26	27	21	34	19	513	30.2
Montana (24)	18	27	21	17	3	408	24.0
Nebraska (3)	14	23	28	5	14	257	15.1
Nevada (36)	42	11	11	30	45	482	30.1
New Hampshire (5)	4	5	38	1	15	261	15.4
New Jersey (15)	25	41	47	21	28	356	20.9
New Mexico (42)	45	25	28	46	40	587	34.5
New York (32)	37	35	41	41	41	483	28.4
North Carolina (38)	35	30	19	40	44	523	30.8
North Dakota (7)	2	34	32	2	6	277	16.3
Ohio (23)	19	22	38	25	21	406	23.9
Oklahoma (39)	30	47	6	35	25	542	31.9
Oregon (21)	36	12	16	16	8	390	22.9
Pennsylvania (27)	6	45	46	23	32	433	25.5
Rhode Island (19)	16	14	49	13	27	388	22.8
South Carolina (48)	38	40	26	44	50	612	36.0
South Dakota (25)	3	24	32	19	7	412	24.2
Tennessee (46)	27	42	9	43	39	596	35.1
Texas (34)	49	36	1	28	47	505	29.7
Utah (10)	33	39	2	7	12	296	17.4
Vermont (6)	7	4	21	3	5	268	15.8
Virginia (19)	12	43	19	24	37	388	22.8
Washington (13)	41	1	18	14	23	349	20.5
West Virginia (41)	1	33	5	27	42	570	33.5
Wisconsin (8)	13	10	41	11	4	280	16.5
Wyoming (17)	15	15	6	12	18	351	21.9

Table 16.2 (Data compiled from Tables 1.1 and 16.1)

Sources

Advisory Commisssion on Intergovernmental Relations. 1992. *Significant Features of Fiscal Federalism, Revenues and Expenditures, 1992*. Washington, DC: ACIR.

American Association of Retired Persons. 1993. *Membership in AARP as a Proportion of Population Aged 50 and Over, 1993. AARP/NRTA Membership Report, 1993.* Washington, DC: AARP.

American Correctional Association. 1993. *Directory of Juvenile and Adult Correctional Departments, Institutions, Agencies, and Paroling Authorities.* Laurel, MD: American Correctional Association.

American Council of Life Insurance. 1993. *1992 Life Insurance Fact Book*. Washington, DC: ACLI.

American Heart Association. *1993 Heart and Stroke Facts Statistics.* American Heart Association. Dallas, TX: 1993.

American Hospital Association. 1993. *Hospital Statistics, 1993–94 Edition.* Chicago, IL: American Hospital Association.

American Medical Association. 1993. *Physician Characteristics and Distribution in the U.S.* Chicago, IL: Survey and Data Resources, AMA.

———. 1993. Factors Contributing to the Health Care Cost Problem (March).

Annie E. Casey Foundation. 1994. *Kids Count Data Book: State Profiles of Child Well-Being.* Baltimore, MD: Annie E. Casey Foundation.

Bradley, Martin B. et al. 1992. *Churches and Church Membership in the United States 1990.* Atlanta, GA: Glenmary Research Center.

Brown, David. NIH Backs Operation for Strokes. *Washington Post*, 10 January 1994, p. A1.

Byerly, Edwin R. 1993. *State Population Estimates by Age And Sex: 1980 to 1992*. U.S. Bureau of the Census, Current Population Reports, P-25-1106. Washington, DC: U.S. Government Printing Office.

Center for the Study of Social Policy. 1992. *The Challenge of Change: What the 1990 Census Tells Us About Children.* Washington, DC: Population Reference Bureau for the Center for the Study of Social Policy.

Centers for Disease Control and Prevention. 1994. Deaths from Breast Cancer—United States, 1991. *Morbidity and Mortality Weekly Report (MMWR)* 43, no. 15 (April 22): 273–81.

———. 1994. Deaths Resulting from Firearm and Motor Vehicle-Related Injuries—United States, 1968–91. *Morbidity and Mortality Weekly Report (MMWR)* 42, no. 3 (January 28): 37–42.)

———. 1993. CDC Surveillance Summaries—Special Focus: Surveillance for Reproductive Health. *Morbidity and Mortality Weekly Report (MMWR)* 42, no. SS-6 (December 17).

———. 1993. U.S. AIDS cases reported through June 1993. *HIV/AIDS Surveillance Report* 5, no. 2 (July).

———. 1993. CDC Surveillance Summaries—Special Focus: Behavioral Risk Factor Surveillance—United States 1991. *Morbidity And Mortality Weekly Report (MMWR)* 42, no. SS-4 (August 27).

———. 1992. Abortion Surveillance—United States, 1989. Influenza Surveillance—United States, 1991–92. *Morbidity and Mortality Weekly Report (MMWR)* 41, no. SS-5 (September 4).

Centers for Disease Control and Prevention/National Center for Health Statistics. 1993. *Monthly Vital Statistics Report* 41, no. 13 (September 28).

———. 1993. *Monthly Vital Statistics Report* 42, no. 2(S) (August 31).

Centers for Disease Control and Prevention, National Center for Infectious Diseases, 1993. *1991 Tuberculosis Statistics in the United States.* Atlanta, GA: CDC.

Cherlin, Andrew J. 1992. *Marriage, Divorce, Remarriage.* Cambridge, MA: Harvard University Press.

Child Trends, Inc. 1994. *Facts at a Glance.* Washington, DC.

———. 1991. *A State-By-State Look at Teenage Childbearing in the United States.* Washington, DC.

Children's Defense Fund. 1991. *The State of America's Children 1991.* Children's Defense Fund.

Congressional Quarterly. 1992. *America Votes 20.* Washington, DC: 1993.

Dacquel, Laarni T. and Dahmann, Donald C. 1993. *Residents of Farms and Rural Areas: 1991.* U.S. Department of Agriculture and Bureau of the Census, Current Population Reports, P-20-472. Washington, DC: U.S. Government Printing Office.

Frey, William H. 1993. *Interstate Migration and Immigration for Whites and Minorities, 1985–90: The Emergence of Multi-ethnic States.* Research Reports. University of Michigan: Population Studies Center, no. 93–297 (October).

———. 1993. *Race, Class and Poverty Polarization across Metro Area and States: Population Shifts and Migration Dynamics.* Research Reports. University of Michigan: Population Studies Center. no. 93–293 (September).

Gober, Patricia. 1994. Why Abortion Rates Vary: A Geographical Examination of the Supply and Demand for Abortion Services in the United States. *Annals of the Association of American Geographers* 84, no. 2 (June): 230–250.

———. 1993. Americans on the Move. *Population Bulletin* 48, no. 3 (November): 2–40.

Group Health Association of America, Inc. 1993. *Patterns in HMO Enrollment.* Third Edition. Group Health Association of America, Inc. (June).

HCIA Inc. 1993. *The Directory of Retirement Facilities, 1994.* Baltimore, MD: HCIA Inc.

Henshaw, Stanley K. and Van Vort, Jennifer. 1994. Abortion Services in the United States, 1991 and 1992. *Family Planning Perspectives* 26 (May/June): 100–112.

Interagency Council on the Homeless. 1994. *Priority: Home! The Federal Plan to Break the Cycle of Homelessness.* Washington, DC: U.S. Department of Housing and Urban Development (HUD-1454-CAD).

Kosmin, Barry A. and Lachman, Seymour P. 1993. *One Nation Under God: Religion in Contemporary American Society.* New York, NY: Harmony Books.

_____. March 1991. Research Report: The National Survey of Religious Identification. New York: Graduate School and University Center of the City University of New York.

Lexicon Medical Encyclopedia and Guide to Family Health, 8th ed. 1988. New York: Lexicon Publications, Inc.

McAdoo, Harriette Pipes, ed. 1993. *Family Ethnicity: Strength in Diversity.* Newbury Park, CA: Sage Publications.

Miringoff, Marc L. 1990. Monitoring the Social Well-Being of the Nation. *Public Welfare* 48 (Fall): 34–38.

Morrill, Richard L. 1990. Regional Demographic Structure of the United States. *Professional Geographer* 42, no. 1 (February): 38–53.

National Center for Education Statistics. 1993. *Digest of Education Statistics, 1993.* Washington, DC.

_____. 1993. *Executive Summary of the NAEP 1992 Reading Report Card for the Nation and the States.* Educational Testing Service. no. 23-ST08 (September).

_____. 1993. *Mini-Digest of Education Statistics, 1993.* Washington, DC.

_____. 1993. *Projections of Education Statistics to 2004.* Washington, DC.

_____. 1993. *Executive Summary of the NAEP 1992 Mathematics Report Card for the Nation and the States.* Educational Testing Service. no. 23-ST03 (April).

National Center on Child Abuse and Neglect. 1993. *National Child Abuse and Neglect Data System.* Working Paper 2. 1991 Summary Data Component (May).

National Center on Child Abuse Prevention. 1993. *Current Trends in Child Abuse Reporting and Fatalities: The Results of the 1992 Annual Fifty State Survey.* Research Working Paper Number 808 (April).

National Center on Homelessness and Mental Illness. 1992. *Research Findings on Severe Mental Illness among Homeless Populations.* National Center on Homelessness and Mental Illness (October).

National Safety Council. 1993. *Accident Facts, 1993 Edition.* Itasca, IL: National Safety Council.

National Women's Political Caucus. 1993. *Fact Sheet on Women's Political Progress.* Washington, DC: National Women's Political Caucus and American Council of Life Insurance.

Northwestern National Life Insurance Company. 1993. *The NWNL State Health Ranking: Results, Methodology, and Discussion 1993 Edition.* Chicago, IL: Northwestern National Life Insurance Company.

Peters, Gary L. and Larkin, Robert P. 1993. *Population Geography.* Dubuque, IA: Kendall/Hunt Publishing Co.

Population Reference Bureau. 1993. *U.S. Metro Data Sheet.* Second Edition. Washington, DC: Population Reference Bureau.

Population Reference Bureau (with the support of the Ford Foundation). 1993. *What the 1990 Census Tells Us About Women: A State Factbook.* Washington, DC: Population Reference Bureau.

Population Today, Coastal Living, July/August 1993.

Raspberry, William. Out of Wedlock, Out of Luck. *Washington Post*, February 24, 1994. Editorial Section.

Russell, Christine, AIDS Is Leading Killer of Blacks 25 to 44. *Washington Post*, June 28, 1994, Health Section.

Scammon, Richard M.and McGillivray, Alice V. 1993. *America Votes 20: A Handbook of Contemporary American Election Statistics.* Washington, DC: Elections Research Center. Congressional Quarterly.

Smith, David M. 1973. *The Geography of Social Well-Being in the United States.* McGraw Hill.

Tufts University. Center on Hunger, Poverty, and Nutrition Policy. 1993. *States Sorted by Percentage of Hungry Children* (press release).

U.S. Bureau of the Census. 1994. Service Annual Survey: 1992. *Current Business Reports* BS/92. Washington, DC: U.S. Government Printing Office.

_____. 1993. *Statistical Abstract of the United States, 1993.* Washington, DC: U.S. Government Printing Office.

_____. 1993. We the American Blacks (WE-1), We the American Hispanics (WE-2), We the American Asians (WE-3), We the American Pacific Islanders (WE-4), We the First Americans (WE-5), We the American Women (WE-8), We the American Elderly (WE-9). *We Series* (September).

_____. 1992. *1990 Census of Population and Housing. Summary Social, Economic, and Housing Characteristics—United States.* CPH-5-1. Washington, DC: U.S. Government Printing Office.

_____. 1992. Money Income of Households, Families, and Persons in the United States: 1992. *Current Population Reports.* Consumer Income Series P60-184. Washington, DC: U.S. Government Printing Office.

_____. 1992. Educational attainment in the U.S. March 1991 and March 1990. *Current Population Reports* Series P20-462. Washington, DC: U.S. Government Printing Office.

_____. 1992. *Fact Sheet for 1990 Decennial Census Counts of Persons in Selected Locations Where Homeless Persons Are Found.* CPH-L-87.

_____. 1992. Poverty in the United States: 1992. *Current Population Reports.* Consumer Income Series P60-185. Washington, DC: U.S. Government Printing Office.

_____. Geographical Mobility: March 1990 to March 1991. *Current Population Reports.* Population Characteristics P20-463. Washington, DC: U.S. Government Reporting Office.

_____. 1991. Race and Hispanic Origin. 1990 Census Profile, no.2 (June).

U.S. Department of Commerce News. 1993. Nursing Home Population Increases In Every State. *Census Bureau Reports.* (June 28).

U.S. Department of Health and Human Services. 1993. *Medicaid Statistics—Program and Financial Statistics, Fiscal Year 1992. HCFA* no. 10129 (October).

_____. Division of Shortage Designation. 1993. *Selected Statistics on Health Professional Shortage Areas.*

_____. Medicaid Bureau. 1992. *Medicaid Expenditures: Fiscal Years 1980 to 1991.* Washington, DC.

_____. Social Security Administration. 1993. *OASDI Beneficiaries by State and County,* December 1991. *SSA* no.13-11954 (June).

_____. Substance Abuse and Mental Health Services Administration. 1993. *National Household Survey on Drug Abuse: Population Estimates 1992.*

U.S. Department of Justice, Federal Bureau of Investigation. 1993. *Uniform Crime Reports for the United States 1992.* Washington, DC: U.S. Department of Justice.

U.S. Department of Justice. 1993. *Source Book of Criminal Justice Statistics-1992.* Washington, DC: Bureau of Justice Statistics.

_____. 1993. *Census of State and Local Law Enforcement Agencies, 1992.* Washington, DC: Bureau of Justice Statistics.

_____. 1992. *Drugs, Crime, and the Justice System.* Washington, DC: Bureau of Justice Statistics.

U.S. Department of Labor. 1994. *Annual Average Unemployment Rates, 1993.* Washington, DC: Bureau of Labor Statistics.

U.S. Health Care Financing Administration, Medicaid Bureau. 1993. *Medicaid Expenditures: Fiscal Years 1980 to 1991.* Washington, DC.

_____. 1992. *Health Care Financing Review* (Winter).

U.S. Immigration and Naturalization Service. 1994. *Persons Naturalized by Region and Selected Country of Former Allegiance,* 1993. Washington, DC.

_____. 1994. *Persons Naturalized by State of Residence.* Washington, DC.

Western Interstate Commission for Higher Education. 1993. *High School Graduates: Projections by State, 1992–2009.* Boulder, CO: Western Interstate Commission for Higher Education.

Index